CONVERSATIONAL

Spanish for Hospitality Managers and Supervisors

BASIC LANGUAGE SKILLS FOR DAILY OPERATIONS

Matt A. Casado
School of Hotel and Restaurant Management
Northern Arizona University

JOHN WILEY & SONS, INC.
New York • Chichester • Brisbane • Toronto • Singapore

Library of Congress Cataloging-in-Publication Data:

Casado, Matt A., 1937-
   Conversational Spanish for hotel and restaurant operators / Matt
A. Casado.
       p.   cm.
   Includes bibliographical references.
   ISBN 0-471-05959-5 (pbk. : alk. paper)
   1. Spanish language—Conversation and phrase books (for restaurant
and hotel personnel)   2. Hotel management—Terminology.
3. Restaurant management—Terminology.   I. Title.
PC4120.R4C37   1995
C647'.94'03—dc20   94-37418

CONVERSATIONAL

Spanish for Hospitality Managers and Supervisors

Contents

Preface

The number of hourly employees of Hispanic descent working in the hospitality industry is very high; in some states, Spanish-speaking people employed in hotels, restaurants, hospitals, and catering institutions are the majority. Effective communication with Hispanics is becoming increasingly necessary in this industry. The primary purpose of this book is to provide hospitality managers and supervisors with basic Spanish skills that can be applied to their daily operations. The secondary intention is to prepare future hospitality managers who are taking management courses with a basic framework of the Spanish language prior to their graduation. An elementary knowledge of this language will provide future hospitality operators with communication skills sought by recruiters who manage establishments in urban areas with large concentrations of Hispanic workers. *Spanish for Hospitality Managers and Supervisors* offers material for conversation that can be put into practice immediately, even without a formal knowledge of the Spanish language.

The book also offers specialized vocabulary, standard operating procedures, job descriptions, and a sample employee handbook that covers topics common to hospitality operations. Its purpose is to help managers and supervisors who don't speak Spanish communicate with Spanish-speaking employees in the personnel, housekeeping, engineering, and food and beverage departments.

While this book is not intended to be a grammar text, essential structures and pronunciation rules have been incorporated. Because of the usually formal boss-worker relationship, the informal pronouns *tú* and *vosotros* (**you**, singular and plural) will not be used. Instead, the formal *usted* and *ustedes* (**you**) forms are presented.

Matt A. Casado, Ed.D., C.H.A.
School of Hotel and Restaurant Management
Northern Arizona University
Flagstaff, Arizona

Introduction

Hospitality managers need communicative competence to understand the language and cultural differences of working personnel and visitors from other countries. The cultural differences between Hispanic and Anglo-American civilizations stem from a long series of historical circumstances. While English culture was basically insular, meaning geographically and ideologically integrated, the Spanish culture was a mixture of European, Arabic, Mediterranean, and Middle Eastern influences.

These differences were the driving forces in the colonization of the New World: the English kept a marked distance between themselves and the natives, both physically and culturally; the Spanish continued their tradition of interracial interaction.

Although gregarious with others, Hispanic people are deeply individualistic. This characteristic, which *hispanos* see as a measure of resistance to standardization, clashes with the Anglo-American inclination to follow clearly defined, established rules of behavior. This can be seen in the tendency of Spanish people to avoid lines, to speak all at the same time, and to distrust collective political, working, and educational gatherings.

As Anglo-Americans believe that time is gold and rush forward in a frenzied search for the future, *hispanos* cultivate the present, reasoning that the future has not yet arrived. The Anglo-American culture has been built around a strong work ethic, with emphasis on the search for efficiency and aiming at constantly improving the current mechanical and technological frontiers. Hispanic-Americans are culturally bound, obsessed with concepts like individualism, family, and leisure. In spite of these differences, in the United States, particularly in the hospitality industry, these two cultures are destined to work side by side.

The vehicle that best promotes understanding, of each other's idiosyncrasies is, without any doubt, language. Spanish-speaking managers will be able to bridge the gap between the two cultures if they are able to communicate with the people they supervise day after day. For these two cultures to understand each other is to understand two different meanings of time, culture, and thought.

CONVERSATIONAL

Spanish for Hospitality Managers and Supervisors

PART I

Pronunciation

The Alphabet Sounds in Spanish

a	(ah)	like the **a** in father: *nada, casa*
b	(beh)	like **b** in **boy**: *bar, botón*
c	(seh)	like **c** in **car** before a,o,u: *cama, copa, cuna.*
		like **s** in **cent** before e,i: *cena, cien*
ch	(cheh)	like **ch** in **child**: *chile, chocolate*
d	(deh)	like **d** in **done**: *dedo, duro*
e	(eh)	like **e** in **bet**: *enero, escoba*
f	(eh-feh)	like **f** in **far**: *favor, fuego*
g	(heh)	like **g** in **gate** before a,o,u: *gana, gota, gustar*
		like **h** in **ham** before e,i: *gente, ginebra*
		(When followed by *ue* or *ui*, the *u* is silent and the *g* will sound like the *g* in **gate**: *guinda*.)
h	(ah-cheh)	always silent, unless preceded by *c*
i	(ee)	like **ee** in **feet**: *vino, vaso*
j	(hoh-tah)	like **h** in **ham**: *jamón, jerez*
k	(kah)	like **k** in **kilo**: *kilo, kiwi*
l	(eh-leh)	like **l** in **let**: *libro, litro*
ll	(eh-yeh)	like **y** in **yet**: *lluvia, llave*
m	(eh-meh)	like **m** in **man**: *mano, menú*
n	(eh-neh)	like **n** in **no**: *noche, nieve*
ñ	(eh-nyeh)	like **ny** in **canyon**: *baño, piña*
o	(oh)	like **o** in **organ**: *ocho, once*
p	(peh)	like **p** in **put**: *pan, pera*
q	(koo)	like **k** in **kilo**: *queso, quince*
		(*Q* is always followed by *ue* or *ui*, but the *u* is silent.)
r	(eh-reh)	like **r** in **rat**: *rueda, rato*
rr	(eh-rreh)	like **r** in **rat** but strongly rolled: *carro, perro*
s	(eh-seh)	like **s** in **see**: *siete, seta*

3

t	(teh)	like **t** in **top**: *teléfono, tenedor*
u	(oo)	like **oo** in **boot**: *jugo, cubo*
v	(oo-beh)	like **b** in **boy**: *vino, vaso*
x	(eh-kees)	like **s** in **sit** before a consonant: *expreso, excusa*
		like x in **examine** before a vowel: *éxito, exacto*
y	(ee)	like **ee** in **feet** when alone or at the end of a word: *y, doy*
		like **y** in **yet** as a consonant: *yema, yarda*
z	(seh-tah)	like **s** in **see**: *zapato, zumo*

Stress in Spanish Words

Words with an accent mark (*é* for example) always receive the stress on the syllable that carries the accent mark: *jabón* (hah-**bóhn**), difícil (dee-**fée**-seel).

Words without accent marks are governed by the following two rules:

1. In words that end in a vowel, *n* or *s*, the stress falls on the next to the last syllable: *mesero* (meh-**séh**-roh), *lavan* (**láh**-bahn), carros (**cáh**-rrohs).
2. In words that end in consonants (except *n* or *s*), the stress falls on the last syllable: *hotel* (oh-**téhl**), *usted* (oos-**téhd**), *favor* (fah-**bóhr**).

PART II

Essential Grammar

Parts of Speech

In Spanish, as in English, there are nine parts of speech: articles, nouns, pronouns, verbs, adjectives, adverbs, prepositions, conjunctions, and interjections.

Articles

The English definite article **the** has four different forms in Spanish:

el   (ehl)   is used before a masculine singular noun: *el hotel* (ehl oh-téhl), the hotel.

la   (lah)   is used before a feminine singular noun: *la cocina* (lah coh-sée-nah), the kitchen.

los   (lohs)   is used before a masculine plural noun: *los platos* (lohs pláh-tohs), the plates.

las   (lahs)   is used before a feminine plural noun: *las bandejas* (lahs bahn-déh-hahs), the trays.

The English indefinite article **a** also has four forms:

un   (oon)   is used before a masculine singular noun: *un cuchillo* (oon coo-chée-yoh), a knife.

una   (oo-nah)   is used before a feminine singular noun: *una cuchara* (óo-nah coo-cháh-rah), a spoon.

unos   (oo-nohs)   is used before a masculine plural noun: *unos clientes* (óo-nohs clee-éhn-tehs), some customers.

unas   (oo-nahs)   is used before a feminine plural noun: *unas toallas* (oó-nahs toh-áh-yahs), some towels.

9

Nouns

All nouns in Spanish are either masculine or feminine. Most nouns ending in *o* are masculine, while those ending in *a*, *d*, or *ción* are usually feminine. There are a few exceptions like *la mano* (lah máh-noh), the hand, which is feminine, and *el día* (ehl dée-ah), the day, that is masculine.

The plural of nouns is formed by adding *s* to words ending with a vowel and *es* to words ending with a consonant: *vino* (bée-noh), wine, and *vinos* (bée-nohs), wines; *director* (dee-rehc-tóhr), manager, and *directores* (dee-rehc-tóh-rehs), managers.

Pronouns

Subject pronouns

yo	(yoh)	I
usted	(oos-téhd)	you (singular)
él	(ehl)	he
ella	(éh-yah)	she
nosotros	(noh-sóh-trohs)	we (masculine)
nosotras	(noh-sóh-trahs)	we (feminine)
ustedes	(oos-téh-dehs)	you (plural)
ellos	(éh-yohs)	they (masculine)
ellas	(éh-yahs)	they (feminine)

Object pronouns

As in English, object pronouns are either direct or indirect.

Direct			Indirect		
me	(meh)	me	*me*	(meh)	(to) me
lo	(loh)	him, you, it (masc.)	*le*	(leh)	(to) you, him, her
la	(lah)	her, you, it (fem.)			
nos	(nohs)	us	*nos*	(nohs)	(to) us
los	(lohs)	you (masc. pl.) them	*les*	(lehs)	(to) you, them
las	(lahs)	you (fem. pl.) them	*les*	(lehs)	(to) you, them

Their position is before the verb, except with the infinitive, with the gerund, or with affirmative commands. In these three cases, they are affixed to the end of the verb. Here are some examples.

Yo lo sirvo.	=	I serve it.
Yo le sirvo.	=	I serve you, him, her.

Yo deseo verle.	=	I wish to see you, him, her.
Yo estoy asándolo.	=	I am roasting it.
¡Áselo!	=	roast it!
Ellos nos lo preparan.	=	They prepare it for us.
Yo se lo doy.	=	I give it to you, him, her.
Ella se los envía.	=	she sends them to you, him, her, theirs.

When there are two subject pronouns in the sentence, the indirect object is placed before the direct object. If both subject pronouns, however, are third person, the indirect pronoun becomes *se* instead of *le* or *les*. **Examples**:

Personal Pronoun Chart

Subject	Indirect Object	Direct Object
yo	*me*	*me*
usted	*le*	*lo, la*
él	*le*	*lo*
ella	*le*	*la*
nosotros (nosotras)	*nos*	*nos*
ustedes	*les*	*los, las*
ellos	*les*	*los*
ellas	*les*	*las*

Verbs

Most verbs in Spanish are regular, meaning that they have similar, predictable endings when they are conjugated. However, there are some irregular verbs which are very commonly used. Irregular verbs are those that don't follow the conjugation pattern of regular verbs. Knowing the present tense of high-frequency regular and irregular verbs will be sufficient to help you get by in most situations. Because of the conciseness of this book past, future, conditional, and compound tenses, as well as the subjunctive mood, have been omitted[1].

ar Verbs

The present tense of all regular verbs whose infinitive ends in *ar* is formed by dropping the *ar* and adding *o*, *a*, *amos*, and *an*. **Example**:

---

[1] The subject pronouns *yo, él, ella, usted, nosotros (as), ellos, and ellas*, are often omitted, unless their presence in the sentence is necessary for understanding.

hablar	(ah-bláhr)	to speak
hablo	(áh-bloh)	I speak[2]
habla	(áh-blah)	you, he, she speak(s)
hablamos	(áh-bláh-mohs)	we speak
hablan	(áh-blahn)	they speak

er Verbs

The present tense of all regular verbs whose infinitive ends in *er* is formed by dropping *er* and adding *o, e, emos,* and *en.* **Example:**

barrer	(bah-rréhr)	to sweep
barro	(báh-rroh)	I sweep
barre	(báh-rreh)	you, he, she sweep(s)
barremos	(bah-rréh-mohs)	we sweep
barren	(báh-rrehn)	they sweep

ir Verbs

The present tense of all regular verbs whose infinitive ends in *ir* is formed by dropping *ir* and adding *o, e, imos,* and *en.* Example:

subir	(soo-béer)	to go up
subo	(sóo-boh)	I go up
sube	(sóo-beh)	you, he, she go(es) up
subimos	(soo-bée-mohs)	we go up
suben	(sóo-behn)	they go up

Irregular Verbs

The following irregular verbs are very frequently used in everyday situations. Their endings don't follow the pattern of regular verbs. Fortunately, the list of essential irregular verbs in Spanish is not very long. Here are the most important Spanish irregular verbs.

dar	(dahr)	to give
	doy, da, damos, dan	
decir	(deh-séer)	to say, to tell
	digo, dice, decimos, dicen	

---

[2] Notice that in Spanish, the verb alone shows the subject. Subject pronouns are typically used only when necessary to clarify the subject.

estar	(ehs-táhr)	to be
	estoy, está, estamos, están	
hacer	(ah-séhr)	to do, to make
	hago, hace, hacemos, hacen	
ir	(eer)	to go
	voy, va, vamos, van	
oir	(oh-éer)	to hear
	oigo, oye, oímos, oyen	
poder	(poh déhr)	to be able to, can
	puedo, puede, podemos, pueden	
poner	(poh-néhr)	to put
	pongo, pone, ponemos, ponen	
querer	(keh-réhr)	to want
	quiero, quiere, queremos, quieren	
saber	(sah-béhr)	to know
	sé, sabe, sabemos, saben	
salir	(sah-léer)	to go out
	salgo, sale, salimos, salen	
ser	(sehr)	to be
	soy, es, somos, son	
tener	(teh-néhr)	to have
	tengo, tiene, tenemos, tienen	
traer	(trah-éhr)	to bring
	traigo, trae, traemos, traen	
venir	(beh-néer)	to come
	vengo, viene, venimos, vienen	
ver	(behr)	to see
	veo, ve, vemos, ven	

Ser and estar

Although *ser* and *estar* translate in English as **to be**, they are not inter-
changeable in Spanish. There are as many exceptions as there are rules for
the use of these verbs. But, in general, *ser* is used to express a relatively permanent quality, as in *Antonio es alto* (Antonio is tall); to indicate origin, as in
Antonio es de México (Antonio is from Mexico); to tell time, as in *Son las seis*
(It is six o'clock); and to express a profession, as in *Antonio es cajero* (Antonio is a cashier). Generally, *ser* answers the questions what?, of what?, for
what?, for whom?, and whose?

Estar expresses a number of more relational or temporary conditions, such as location, as in *Antonio está en Mexico* (Antonio is in Mexico); health, as in *Antonio está enfermo* (Antonio is sick); temporary emotional conditions, as in *Antonio está contento* (Antonio is happy); and in progressive tenses, as in *Antonio está comiendo* (Antonio is eating).

Stem-changing Verbs

Some verbs show a change in the stem vowel (the part of the verb that is left after you remove the *ar*, *er*, or *ir* ending):

- the *e* of the last syllable of the stem changes to *ie* or *i* ,
- the *o* of the last syllable changes to *ue*.

These changes occur in all persons of the present tense except the first person plural (*nosotros, nosotras*). Here are the most common stem-changing verbs.

almorzar (*ue*)	(ahl-mohr-sáhr)	to have lunch
	almuerzo, almuerza, almorzamos, almuerzan	
cerrar (*ie*)	(seh-rráhr)	to close, shut
	cierro, cierra, cerramos, cierran	
comenzar (*ie*)	(coh-mehn-sáhr)	to begin, start
	comienzo, comienza, comenzamos, comienzan	
contar (*ue*)	(cohn-táhr)	to count
	cuento, cuenta, contamos, cuentan	
costar (*ue*)	(cohs-táhr)	to cost
	cuesto, cuesta, costamos, cuestan	
devolver (*ue*)	(deh-bohl-béhr)	to give back, return
	devuelvo, devuelve, devolvemos, devuelven	
dormir (*ue*)	(dohr-méer)	to sleep
	duermo, duerme, dormimos, duermen	
empezar (*ie*)	(ehm-peh-sáhr)	to begin, start
	empiezo, empieza, empezamos, empiezan	
encender (*ie*)	(ehn-sehn-déhr)	to light, turn on
	enciendo, enciende, encendemos, encienden	
encontrar (*ue*)	(ehn-cohn-tráhr)	to find
	encuentro, encuentra, encontramos, encuentran	
entender (*ie*)	(ehn-tehn-déhr)	to understand
	entiendo, entiende, entendemos, entienden	

mover (*ue*)	(moh-béhr)	to move
	muevo, mueve, movemos, mueven	
pedir (*i*)	(peh-déer)	to ask for
	pido, pide, pedimos, piden	
perder (*ie*)	(pehr-déhr)	to lose
	pierdo, pierde, perdemos, pierden	
preferir (*ie*)	(preh-feh-réer)	to prefer
	prefiero, prefiere, preferimos, prefieren	
probar (*ue*)	(proh-báhr)	to prove, taste, try
	pruebo, prueba, probamos, prueban	
querer (*ie*)	(keh-réhr)	to want, wish, love
	quiero, quiere, queremos, quieren	
recordar (*ue*)	(reh-cohr-dáhr)	to remember
	recuerdo, recuerda, recordamos, recuerdan	
reír (*i*)	(reh-éer)	to laugh
	río, ríe, reímos, ríen	
rogar (*ue*)	(roh-gáhr)	to beg, ask
	ruego, ruega, rogamos, ruegan	
sentar (*ie*)	(sehn-táhr)	to seat
	siento, sienta, sentamos, sientan	
sentir (*ie*)	(sehn-téer)	to feel
	siento, siente, sentimos, sienten	
servir (*i*)	(sehr-béer)	to serve
	sirvo, sirve, servimos, sirven	
vestir (*i*)	(behs-téer)	to dress
	visto, viste, vestimos, visten	
volver (*ue*)	(bohl-béhr)	to come back
	vuelvo, vuelve, volvemos, vuelven	

Reflexive Verbs

Spanish verbs that have the pronoun *se* attached to their infinitive forms are called reflexive verbs. These verbs are preceded by the following reflexive pronouns:

me	(meh)	myself
se	(seh)	yourself, himself, herself, itself
nos	(nohs)	ourselves
se	(seh)	yourselves, themselves

Reflexive verbs show that the action of the verb is directed toward the person referred to by the reflexive pronouns. *Me visto,* for example, means **I dress myself**. A typical reflexive verb in Spanish is *vestirse.* The present form is:

me visto	(meh bées-toh)	I dress myself (I get dressed)
se viste	(seh bées-teh)	you, he, she dress(es) yourself, himself, herself (you, he, she get(s) dressed)
nos vestimos	(nohs behs-tée-mohs)	we dress ourselves (we get dressed)
se visten	(seh bées-tehn)	you, they dress themselves (you, they get dressed)

Here are some important reflexive verbs in Spanish. (Letters in parenthesis show changes in the stem.)

acordarse (*ue*)	(ah-cohr-dáhr-seh)	to remember
acostarse (*ue*)	(ah-cohs-táhr-seh)	to go to bed
alegrarse	(ah-leh-gráhr-seh)	to be glad
asustarse	(ah-soos-táhr-seh)	to be frightened
bajarse	(bah-háhr-seh)	to get down
caerse	(cah-éhr-seh)	to fall down
calmarse	(cahl-máhr-seh)	to calm down
callarse	(cah-yáhr-seh)	to stop talking
cambiarse	(cahm-bee-áhr-seh)	to change (clothes)
cansarse	(cahn-sáhr-seh)	to get tired
casarse	(cah-sáhr-seh)	to get married
cortarse	(cohr-táhr-seh)	to cut oneself
desmayarse	(dehs-mah-yáhr-seh)	to faint
despedirse (i)	(dehs-peh-déer-seh)	to say goodbye
despertarse (ie)	(dehs-pehr-táhr-seh)	to wake up
divertirse (ie)	(dee-behr-téer-seh)	to have a good time
dormirse (ue)	(dohr-méer-seh)	to fall sleep
ducharse	(doo-cháhr-seh)	to take a shower
enfadarse	(ehn-fah-dáhr-seh)	to be angry
equivocarse	(eh-kee-boh-cáhr-seh)	to be mistaken, make a mistake
esconderse	(ehs-cohn-déhr-seh)	to hide
irse	(éer-seh)	to go away
lastimarse	(lahs-tee-máhr-seh)	to get hurt
lavarse	(lah-báhr-seh)	to wash oneself
levantarse	(leh-bahn-táhr-seh)	to get up
limpiarse	(leem-pee-áhr-seh)	to clean oneself
marcharse	(mahr-cháhr-seh)	to go away

mejorarse	(meh-hoh-ráhr-seh)	to get well
pararse	(pah-ráhr-seh)	to stop
peinarse	(peh-ee-náhr-seh)	to comb one's hair
ponerse	(poh-néhr-seh)	to put on (clothing)
preocuparse	(preh-oh-coo-páhr-seh)	to worry
quedarse	(keh-dáhr-seh)	to remain
quejarse	(keh-háhr-seh)	to complain
quemarse	(keh-máhr-seh)	to burn oneself
quitarse	(kee-táhr-seh)	to take off (clothing)
reirse	(reh-éer-seh)	to laugh
romperse	(rohm-péhr-seh)	to break
sentarse (*ie*)	(sehn-táhr-seh)	to sit down
sentirse (*ie*)	(sehn-téer-seh)	to feel
torcerse (*ue*)	(tohr-séhr-seh)	to twist
vestirse (*i*)	(vehs-téer-seh)	to get dressed

The Command Form of Verbs

Most verbs form the command form from the first person singular (*yo*). The *o* is dropped and the following endings are added:

- *ar* verbs add *e*:
- *er* verbs add *a*:
- *ir* verbs add *a*:

- *hablar* (to speak)
- *comer* (to eat)
- *subir* (to go up)

- *hable* (háh-bleh) speak
- *coma* (cóh-mah) eat
- *suba* (sóo-bah) go up

In all cases, plural commands are formed by adding *n* to the singular form: *hablen, coman, suban*. Negative commands are formed by placing *no* before the command form: *no hablen, no coman, no suban*.

Object pronouns and reflexive pronouns are **attached** to affirmative commands.

Dígame.	(Dée-gah-meh.)	Tell me.
Siéntense.	(See-éhn-tehn-seh.)	Sit down (plural).

Object pronouns and reflexive pronouns are placed **before** negative commands.

No me diga.	(Nohmehdée-gah.)	Don't tell me.
No se sienten.	(Nohsehsee-éhn-tehn.)	Don't sit down.

Generally, commands should be followed by **please**, *por favor* (pohr fah-bóhr).

Two important irregular verbs form their command as follows:

dar (dahr) to give
dé (deh), *den* (dehn)

ir	(eer)	to go

vaya (báh-yah), *vayan* (báh-yahn)

Adjectives

In English, adjectives don't have to agree with the nouns or pronouns they accompany, but in Spanish adjectives must agree with the word they qualify. Adjectives ending in *o* form the feminine by changing *o* to *a*:

blanco	(bláhn-coh)	white (masc. sing.)
blanca	(bláhn-cah)	white (fem. sing.)

As with nouns, the plural of adjectives is formed by adding *s* to adjectives ending in *o* or *a*.

blancos	(bláhn-cohs)	white (masc. plural)
blancas	(bláhn-cahs)	white (fem. plural)

Unlike English, Spanish descriptive adjectives usually follow the noun they qualify:

vino blanco	(bée-noh bláhn-coh)	white wine
carne tierna	(cáhr-neh tee-éhr-nah)	tender meat

Possessive Adjectives

Singular Object

mi	(mee)	my
su	(soo)	your, his, her, its
nuestro(m)	(noo-éhs-troh)	our
nuestra(f)	(noo-éhs-trah)	our

Plural Object

mis	(mees)	my
sus	(soos)	their, your
nuestros	(noo-éhs-trohs)	our (masc.)
nuestras	(noo-éhs-trahs)	our (fem.)

Possessive adjectives must agree in number and gender with the nouns they modify.

nuestro carro	our car
nuestros carros	our cars
nuestra casa	our house
nuestras casas	our houses

Possession in Spanish can also be expressed with *de* (of).

Example: Pedro's car = the car of Pedro: *el carro de Pedro* (ehl cáh-rroh deh Péh-droh)

Apostrophes are never used to express possession in Spanish.

Demonstrative Adjectives

Demonstrative adjectives are used to single out and express the location of the nouns they modify.

Singular

este (masc.)	(éhs-teh)	this
esta (fem.)	(éhs-tah)	this
ese (masc.)	(éh-seh)	that
esa (fem.)	(éh-sah)	that
aquel (masc.)	(ah-kéhl)	that (far away)
aquella (fem.)	(ah-kéh-yah)	that (far away)

Plural

estos (masc.)	(éhs-tohs)	these
estas (fem.)	(éhs-tahs)	these
esos (masc.)	(éh-sohs)	those
esas (fem.)	(éh-sahs)	those
aquellos(masc.)	(ah-kéh-yohs)	those (far away)
aquellas (fem.)	(áh-kéh-yahs)	those (far away)

Adverbs

Adverbs in English are often formed by adding the suffix **ly** to an adjective. In Spanish, many adverbs are formed by adding *mente* to the feminine form of adjectives.

Example: *rápido* (*ráh-pee-doh*) quick, *rapidamente* (rah-pee-dah-méhn-teh) quickly

Here are some important adverbs of time.

anoche	(ah-nóh-cheh)	last night
antes	(áhn-tehs)	before
ayer	(ah-yéhr)	yesterday
después	(dehs-poo-éhs)	later
en seguida	(ehn-seh-guée-dah)	at once

hoy	(óh-ee)	today
mañana	(mah-nyáh-nah)	tomorrow
nunca	(nóon-cah)	never
siempre	(see-éhm-preh)	always
tarde	(táhr-deh)	late
temprano	(tehm-práh-noh)	early
todavía	(toh-dah-bée-ah)	still

Here are some common adverbs of manner.

así	(ah-sée)	thus, in this way
bajo	(báh-hoh)	low
bien	(bee-éhn)	well
despacio	(dehs-páh-see-oh)	slowly
mal	(mahl)	badly
mejor	(meh-hóhr)	better
peor	(peh-óhr)	worse

Some adverbs of place are:

abajo	(ah-báh-hoh)	down, downstairs
adentro	(ah-déhn-troh)	inside
afuera	(ah-foo-éh-rah)	outside
ahí	(ah-ée)	there (closer)
allá	(ah-yáh)	there (further)
aquí	(ah-kée)	here
arriba	(ah-rrée-bah)	up
cerca	(séhr-cah)	near
enfrente	(ehn-fréhn-teh)	opposite, in front of
lejos	(léh-hohs)	far

Here are some adverbs of intensity.

bastante	(bahs-táhn-teh)	enough
casi	(cáh-see)	almost
demasiado	(deh-mah-see-áh-doh)	too much
más	(mahs)	more
menos	(méh-nohs)	less
mucho	(móo-choh)	much, a lot
poco	(póh-coh)	little
suficiente	(soo-fee-see-éhn-teh)	enough

Prepositions

The use of prepositions in Spanish is difficult to master as very few of them correspond exactly with English prepositions. Here are some high-frequency prepositions.

bajo	(báh-hoh)	under
con	(cohn)	with
contra	(cóhn-trah)	against
de	(deh)	of
desde	(déhs-deh)	from
durante	(doo-ráhn-teh)	during
en	(ehn)	in
entre	(éhn-treh)	between
hasta	(áhs-tah)	until
para	(páh-rah)	for
por	(pohr)	by, through, along
sin	(seen)	without
sobre	(sóh-breh)	on

Conjunctions

Here are the most common Spanish conjunctions.

aunque	(ah-óon-keh)	although
cuando	(coo-áhn-doh)	when
donde	(dóhn-deh)	where
pero	(péh-roh)	but
porque	(póhr-keh)	because
que	(keh)	that
si	(see)	if
y	(ee)	and

Interjections

Here are some common words that express sudden feelings in Spanish.

¡qué lástima!	(Keh láhs-tee-mah!)	What a pity!
¡caramba!	(Cah-ráhm-bah!)	Good gracious!
¡qué pena!	(Keh péh-nah!)	What a disgrace!
¡qué alegría!	(Keh ah-leh-grée-ah!)	What joy!

Questions

Usually, a question in Spanish is formed by placing the verb before the subject.
Example:

> *¿Trabaja Pedro aquí?*
>
> (Trah-báh-hah Péh-droh ah-kée?)
>
> Does Pedro work here?

An affirmative statement may be turned into a question by adding *¿no?* (noh?) or *¿verdad?* (behr-dáhd?).
Examples:

> *Antonio habla inglés, ¿no?*
>
> (Ahn-tóh-nee-oh áh-blah een-gléhs, noh?)
>
> Antonio speaks English, doesn't he?
>
> *Antonio habla inglés, ¿verdad?*
>
> (Ahn-tóh-nee-oh áh-blah een-gléhs, behr-dáhd?)
>
> Antonio speaks English, doesn't he?

Important interrogative words are:

¿Qué?	(Keh?)	What?
¿Cómo?	(Cóh-moh?)	How?
¿Cuándo?	(Coo-áhn-doh?)	When?
¿Dónde?	(Dóhn-deh?)	Where?
¿Cuál?	(Coo-áhl?)	Which?
¿Cuánto?	(Coo-áhn-toh?)	How much?
¿Cuántos?	(Coo-áhn-tohs?)	How many?
¿Por qué?	(Pohr keh?)	Why?
¿Quién?	(Kee-éhn?)	Who?
¿De quién?	(Deh kee-éhn?)	Whose?

Negations

A sentence can be made negative by placing *no* (noh) immediately before the verb.
Example:

> *Antonio no habla inglés.*
>
> (Ahn-tóh-nee-oh noh áh-blah-een-gléhs.)
>
> Antonio does not speak English.

Double negation is correct in Spanish, although it is not in English. When using two words for negation the first word, *no*, usually precedes the verb while the second negative follows it.

Antonio no toma nunca vino.

(Ahn-tóh-nee-oh noh tóh-mah nóon-cah bée-noh.)

Antonio never drinks wine.

Here are the most common words expressing negation.

nada	(náh-dah)	nothing
nadie	(náh-dee-eh)	nobody, no one
ni. . .ni	(nee. . .nee)	neither. . .nor
ninguno	(neen-góo-noh)	no one
no	(noh)	no, not
nunca	(nóon-cah)	never
tampoco	(tahm-póh-coh)	neither
todavía	(toh-dah-bée-ah)	yet

PART III

Common Expressions

Everyday Conversation

All languages have a number of expressions that are used very often in everyday life. Anyone attempting to speak and understand Spanish needs to be familiar with simple expressions ranging from greetings and introductions to telling time. The following is a list of idiomatic expressions classified into different categories.

Greetings

> *Buenos días.*
> (Boo-éh-nohs dée-ahs.)
> Good morning.

> *Buenas tardes.*
> (Boo-éh-nahs táhr-dehs.)
> Good afternoon.

> *Buenas noches.*
> (Boo-éh-nahs nóh-chehs.)
> Good evening.

> *¡Hola!*
> (Óh-lah!)
> Hi!

> *¿Qué tal?*
> (Keh tahl?)
> How is it going?

Introductions

Me llamo...
(Meh yáh-moh...)
My name is...

Soy...
(Sóh-ee...)
I am...

¿cómo se llama usted?
(cóh-moh seh yáh-mah oos-téhd?)
What is your name?

Me alegro de conocerle.
(Meh ah-léh-groh deh coh-noh-séhr leh.)
I am glad to meet you.

Me alegro de verle.
(Meh ah-léh-groh deh béhr-leh.)
I am glad to see you.

Tanto qusto.
(Táhn-toh góos-toh.)
Glad to meet you.

Encantado/Encantada. *
(Ehn-cahn-táh-doh/Ehn-cahn-táh-dah.)
Pleased to meet you.

El gusto es mío.
(Ehl góos-toh ehs mée-oh.)
The pleasure is mine.

¿Como está usted?
(Cóh-moh ehs-táh oos-téhd?)
How are you?

Bien, gracias, ¿y usted?
(Bee-éhn, gráh-see-ahs, ee oos-téhd?)
Very well, thank you, and you?

Communication and Courtesy

¿Sabe usted inglés?
(Sáh-beh oos-téhd een-gléhs?)
Do you know English?

*Men use *Encantado*. Women use *Encantada*.

¿Habla usted inglés?
(Áh-blah oos-téhd een-gléhs?)
Do you speak English?

Gracias.
(Gráh-see-ahs.)
Thank you.

Muchas gracias.
(Móo-chahs gráh-see-ahs.)
Thank you very much.

De nada.
(Deh náh-da.)
You're welcome.

Por favor.
(Pohr fah-bóhr.)
Please.

¿Comprende?
(Cohm-préhn-deh?)
Do you understand?

¿Sabe usted escribir?
(Sáh-beh oos-téhd ehs-cree-béer?)
Do you know how to write?

¿Como se dice... en español?
(cóh-moh seh dée-seh...ehn ehs-pah-nyóhl?)
How do you say...in Spanish?

Repita, por favor.
(Reh-pée-tah, pohr fah-bóhr.)
Please repeat.

Hable más despacio.
(Áh-bleh mahs dehs-páh-see-oh.)
Speak more slowly.

No hable tan de prisa.
(Noh áh-bleh tahn deh prée-sah.)
Don't speak so fast.

Hable más alto.
(Áh-bleh mahs áhl-toh.)
Speak louder.

No comprendo bien el español.
(Noh cohm-préhn-doh bee-éhn ehl ehs-pah-nyóhl.)
I don't understand Spanish well.

No entiendo lo que dice.
(Noh ehn-tee-éhn-doh loh keh dée-seh.)
I don't understand what you are saying.

¿Que pasa?
(Keh páh-sah?)
What is the matter? or, what's new?

¿Cómo se escribe...?
(Cóh-moh seh ehs-crée-beh...?)
How do you write...?

Con permiso. *
(Cohn pehr-mée-soh.)
Excuse me.

Perdón. **
(Pehr-dóhn.)
Pardon me.

Lo siento.
(Loh see-éhn-toh.)
I am sorry.

Farewell

Adiós.
(Ah-dee-óhs.)
Good bye.

Hasta luego.
(Áhs-tah loo-éh-goh.)
See you later.

Hasta mañana.
(Áhs-tah mah-nyáh-nah.)
See you tomorrow.

Hasta la vista.
(Áhs-tah lah vées-tah.)
See you again. (later).

Nos vemos.
(Nohs véh-mohs.)
See you.

*It's also used to move through a crowd!
**It's also used when you don't understand what somebody talking to you is saying!

Que lo pase bien.
(Keh loh páh-seh bee-éhn.)
Have a good time.

Basic Vocabulary

Numbers

0	*cero*	(séh-roh)
1	*uno, una*	(óo-noh, óo-nah)
2	*dos*	(dohs)
3	*tres*	(trehs)
4	*cuatro*	(coo-áh-troh)
5	*cinco*	(séen-coh)
6	*seis*	(séh-ees)
7	*siete*	(see-éh-teh)
8	*ocho*	(óh-choh)
9	*nueve*	(noo-éh-beh)
10	*diez*	(dee-éhs)
11	*once*	(óhn-seh)
12	*doce*	(dóh-seh)
13	*trece*	(tréh-seh)
14	*catorce*	(cah-tóhr-seh)
15	*quince*	(kéen-seh)
16	*dieciséis*	(dee-éhs-ee-séh-ees)
17	*diecisiete*	(dee-éhs-ee-see-éh-teh)
18	*dieciocho*	(dee-éhs-ee-óh-choh)
19	*diecinueve*	(dee-éhs-ee-noo-éh-beh)
20	*veinte*	(véh-een-teh)
21	*veinte y uno*	(véh-een-teh ee óo-noh)
30	*treinta*	(tréh-een-ta)
31	*treinta y uno*	(tréh-een-tah ee óo-noh)
40	*cuarenta*	(coo-ah-réhn-tah)
41	*cuarenta y uno*	(coo-ah-réhn-tah ee óo-noh)

32

50	*cincuenta*	(seen-coo-éhn-tah)
51	*cincuenta y uno*	(seen-coo-éhn-tah ee óo-noh)
60	*sesenta*	(seh-séhn-tah)
61	*sesenta y uno*	(seh-séhn-tah ee óo-noh)
70	*setenta*	(seh-téhn-tah)
71	*setenta y uno*	(seh-téhn-tah ee óo-noh)
80	*ochenta*	(oh-chéhn-tah)
81	*ochenta y uno*	(oh-chéhn-tah ee óo-noh)
90	*noventa*	(noh-béhn-tah)
91	*noventa y uno*	(noh-béhn-tah ee óo-noh)
100	*cien*	(see-éhn)
101	*ciento uno*	(see-éhn-toh óo-noh)
200	*doscientos*	(dohs-see-éhn-tohs)
300	*trescientos*	(trehs-see-éhn-tohs)
400	*cuatrocientos*	(coo-ah-troh-see-éhn-tohs)
500	*quinientos*	(kee-nee-éhn-tohs)
600	*seiscientos*	(seh-ees-see-éhn-tohs)
700	*setecientos*	(seh-teh-see-éhn-tohs)
800	*ochocientos*	(oh-choh-see-éhn-tohs)
900	*novecientos*	(noh-beh-see-éhn-tohs)
1000	*mil*	(meel)
1001	*mil uno*	(meel óo-noh)
1101	*mil ciento uno*	(meel see-éhn-toh óo-noh)
2000	*dos mil*	(dohs meel)

primero	(pree-méh-roh)	first
segundo	(seh-góon-doh)	second
tercero	(tehr-séh-roh)	third
cuarto	(coo-áhr-toh)	fourth
quinto	(kéen-toh)	fifth
sexto	(séhs-toh)	sixth
séptimo	(séhp-tee-moh)	seventh
octavo	(ohc-táh-boh)	eighth
noveno	(noh-béh-noh)	ninth
décimo	(déh-see-moh)	tenth

Time

The expression **o'clock** is not translated when telling time in Spanish. Instead, Spanish expresses this idea by saying **It is one, It is two-thirty,** etc. The forms of the verb *ser* (*es* and *son*) are always used with the articles *la* or *las*; *es* and *la* for one o'clock and *son* and *las* for the rest of the hours.

The day is divided into four parts: *mañana* (mah-nyáh-nah) from sunrise to noon, *tarde* (táhr-deh) from noon to sunset, *noche* (nóh-cheh) from sunset to midnight, and *madrugada* (mah-droo-gáh-dah) from midnight to sunrise.

To express time before and after the hour, *media* (méh-dee-ah) translates for **half** and *cuarto* (coo-áhr-toh) for **quarter**. To express time from the hour to the half hour, minutes are added to the hour with *y* (ee). To tell time from the half hour to the hour, minutes are subtracted from the next hour using the word *menos* (méh-nohs).

¿Qué hora es?
(Keh óh-rah ehs?)
What time is it?

Es la una.
(Ehs lah óo-nah.)
It's one o'clock.

Son las dos.
(Sohn lahs dohs.)
It's two o'clock.

Son las tres.
(Sohn lahs trehs.)
It's three o'clock.

Son las cuatro.
(Sohn lahs coo-áh-troh.)
It's four o'clock.

Son las cinco.
(Sohn lahs séen-coh.)
It's five o'clock.

Son las seis.
(Sohn lahs séh-ees.)
It's six o'clock.

Son las siete.
(Sohn lahs see-éh-teh.)
It's seven o'clock.

Son las ocho.
(Sohn lahs óh-choh.)
It's eight o'clock.

Son las nueve.
(Sohn lahs noo-éh-beh.
It's nine o'clock.

Son las diez.
(Sohn lahs dee-éhs.)
It's ten o'clock.

Son las once.
(Sohn lahs óhn-seh.)
It's eleven o'clock.

Son las doce.
(Sohn lahs dóh-seh.)
It's twelve o'clock.

Es la una y media.
(Ehs lah óo-nah ee méh-dee-ah.)
It's 1:30.

Son las dos y media.
(Sohn lahs dohs ee méh-dee-ah.)
It's 2:30.

Es la una y cuarto.
(Ehs lah óo-nah ee coo-áhr-toh.)
It's 1:15.

Son las dos y cuarto.
(Sohn lahs dohs ee coo-áhr-toh.)
It's 2:15.

Es la una menos cuarto.
(Ehs lah óo-nah méh-nohs coo-áhr-toh.)
It's 12:45.

Son las dos menos cuarto.
(Sohn lahs dohs méh-nohs coo-áhr-toh.)
It's 1:45.

Es la una y cinco.
(Ehs lah óo-nah ee séen-coh.)
It's 1:05.

Son las dos y cinco.
(Sohn lahs dohs ee séen-coh.)
It's 2:05.

Es la una menos diez.
(Ehs lah óo-nah méh-nohs dee-éhs.)
It's 12:50.

Son las dos menos diez.
(Sohn lahs dohs méh-nohs dee-éhs.)
It's 1:50.

A la una.
(Ah lah óo-nah.)
At one o'clock.

A las dos.
(Ah lahs dohs.)
At two o'clock.

A las dos y cuarto.
(Ah lahs dohs ee coo-áhr-toh.)
At 2:15.

A las nueve de la mañana.
(Ah lahs noo-éh-beh deh lah mah-nyáh-nah.)
At nine o'clock in the morning. (A.M.)

A las tres de la tarde.
(Ah lahs trehs deh lah táhr-deh.)
At three o'clock in the afternoon (P.M.)

A la una de la madrugada.
(Ah lah óo-nah deh lah mah-droo-gáh-dah.)
At one o'clock in the morning. (A.M.)

The Calendar

¿Cuál es la fecha?
(Coo-áhl ehs lah féh-chah?)
What day is today?

¿A cómo estamos?
(Ah cóh-moh ehs-táh-mohs?)
What day is today?

¿Que día es hoy?
(Keh dée-ah ehs óh-ee?)
What day of the week is today?

Hoy es lunes.
(Óh-ee ehs lóo-nehs.)
Today is Monday.

Estamos a cinco de mayo de mil novecientos noventa y cinco.
(Ehs-táh-mohs ah séen-coh deh máh-yoh deh meel noh-beh-see-éhn-tohs noh-béhn-tah ee séen-coh.)
Today is May 5th, 1995.

los meses del año	(lohs méh-sehs dehl áh-nyoh)	the months of the year
enero	(eh-néh-roh)	January
febrero	(feh-bréh-roh)	February
marzo	(máhr-soh)	March
abril	(ah-bréel)	April
mayo	(máh-yoh)	Mayo
junio	(hóo-nee-oh)	June
julio	(hóo-lee-oh)	July
agosto	(ah-góhs-toh)	August
septiembre	(sehp-tee-éhm-breh)	September
octubre	(ohc-tóo-breh)	October
noviembre	(noh-bee-éhm-breh)	November
diciembre	(dee-see-éhm-breh)	December
días de la semana	(dée-ahs deh lah seh-máh-nah)	days of the week
lunes	(lóo-nehs)	Monday
martes	(máhr-tehs)	Tuesday
miércoles	(mee-éhr-coh-lehs)	Wednesday
jueves	(hoo-éh-behs)	Thursday
viernes	(bee-éhr-nehs)	Friday
sábado	(sáh-bah-doh)	Saturday
domingo	(doh-méen-goh)	Sunday
estaciones del año	(ehs-tah-see-óh-nehs dehl áh-nyoh)	seasons of the year
primavera	(pree-mah-béh-rah)	spring
verano	(beh-ráh-noh)	summer
otoño	(oh-tóh-nyoh)	autumn
invierno	(een-bee-éhr-noh)	winter

Colors

amarillo	(ah-mah-rée-yoh)	yellow
anaranjado	(ah-nah-rahn-háh-doh)	orange
azul	(ah-sóol)	blue
blanco	(bláhn-coh)	white
castaño	(cahs-táh-nyoh)	chestnut
claro	(cláh-roh)	clear
dorado	(doh-ráh-doh)	golden
gris	(grees)	gray
marrón	(mah-rróhn)	brown
morado	(moh-ráh-doh)	purple
moreno	(moh-réh-noh)	brown

naranja	(nah-ráhn-hah)	orange
negro	(néh-groh)	black
oscuro	(ohs-cóo-roh)	dark
pálido	(páh-lee-doh)	pale
pardo	(páhr-doh)	brown
plateado	(plah-teh-áh-doh)	silver
rojo	(róh-hoh)	red
rosado	(roh-sáh-doh)	pink
rubio	(róo-bee-oh)	blonde
verde	(béhr-deh)	green
violeta	(bee-oh-léh-tah)	violet

The Housekeeping Department

Technical Vocabulary

absenteeism
ausencia (excesiva)
(ah-oo-séhn-see-ah ehx-seh-sée-bah)

address
domicilio/dirección
(doh-mee-sée-lee-oh)/(dee-rehc-see-óhn)

alcoholic beverages
bebidas alcohólicas
(beh-bée-dahs ahl-coh-óh-lee-cahs)

application form
solicitud de ingreso
(soh-lee-see-tóod deh een-gréh-soh)

appointment
cita
(sée-tah)

appraisal
evaluación
(eh-bah-loo-ah-see-óhn)

apprenticeship
aprendizaje
(ah-prehn-dee-sáh-heh)

aptitude test
test de aptitud
(tehst deh ahp-tee-tóod)

attitude
actitud
(ahc-tee-tóod)

birthday
cumpleaños
(coom-pleh-áh-nyohs)

break
descanso
(dehs-cáhn-soh)

(to) call
llamar
(yah-máhr)

change of address
cambio de dirección
(cáhm-bee-oh deh dee-rehc-see-óhn)

citizen
ciudadano, ciudadana
(see-oo-dah-dáh-noh) (see-oo-dah-dáh-nah)

city
ciudad
(see-oo-dáhd)

(to) clock in
marcar antes del turno
(mahr-cáhr áhn-tehs dehl tóor-noh)

(to) clock out
marcar después del turno
(mahr-cáhr dehs-poo-éhs dehl tóor-noh)

(to) coach
entrenar
(ehn-treh-náhr)

company
empresa
(ehm-préh-sah)

competent
competente
(cohm-peh-téhn-teh)

county
condado
(cohn-dáh-doh)

date
fecha
(féh-chah)

(to) date
fechar
(feh-cháhr)

dental insurance
seguro dental
(seh-góo-roh dehn-táhl)

department head
jefe de departamento
(héh-feh deh deh-pahr-tah-méhn-toh)

disciplinary action
acción disciplinaria
(ahc-see-óhn dees-see-plee-náh-ree-ah)

driver's license
licencia para manejar
(lee-séhn-see-ah páh-rah mah-neh-háhr)

drugs
drogas
(dróh-gahs)

education
escolaridad
(ehs-coh-lah-ree-dáhd)

employee
empleado /empleada
(ehm-pleh-áh-doh) (ehm-pleh-áh-dah)

employee appraisal
evaluación de empleados
(eh-bah-loo-ah-see-óhn deh ehm-pleh-áh-dohs)

employee cafeteria
cafetería de empleados
(cah-feh-teh-rée-ah deh ehm-pleh-áh-dohs)

employee entrance
entrada de empleados
(ehn-tráh-dah deh ehm-pleh-áh-dohs)

employee exit
salida de empleados
(sah-lée-dah de ehm-pleh-áh-dohs)

employee handbook
manual de empleados
(mah-noo-áhl deh ehm-pleh-áh-dohs)

employee lounge
salón de descanso
(sah-lóhn deh dehs-cáhn-soh)

employer
patrón / patrona
(pah-tróhn) (pah-tróhn-ah)

equal-opportunity employer
empresa de igual oportunidad
(ehm-préh-sah deh ee-goo-áhl oh-pohr-too-nee-dáhd)

experience
experiencia
(ehs-peh-ree-éhn-see-ah)

felony
delito mayor
(deh-lée-toh mah-yóhr)

(to) fill out
rellenar
(reh-yeh-náhr)

first interview
entrevista previa
(ehn-treh-bées-tah préh-bee-ah)

first name
nombre
(nóhm-breh)

free meal
comida gratis
(coh-mée-dah gráh-tees)

full-time job
empleo de tiempo completo
(ehm-pléh-oh deh tee-éhm-poh cohm-pléh-toh)

green card
tarjeta verde
(tahr-héh-tah béhr-deh)

grooming
apariencia personal
(ah-pah-ree-éhn-see-ah pehr-soh-náhl)

high school diploma
diploma de educación secundaria
(dee-plóh-mah deh eh-doo-cah-see-óhn seh-coon-dá-ree-ah)

(to) hire
contratar
(cohn-trah-táhr)

hiring
contratación
(cohn-trah-tah-see-óhn)

holiday
día festivo
(dée-ah fehs-tée-boh)

honesty
honradez
(ohn-rah-déhs)

human resources
recursos humanos
(reh-cóor-sohs oo-máh-nohs)

hygiene
higiene
(ee-hee-éh-neh)

identification card
tarjeta de identificación
(tahr-héh-tah deh ee-dehn-tee-fee-cah-see-óhn)

insubordination
insubordinación
(een-soo-bohr-dee-nah-see-óhn)

interview
entrevista
(ehn-treh-bées-tah)

job
trabajo
(trah-báh-hoh)

job applicant
solicitante de empleo
(soh-lee-see-táhn-teh deh ehm-pléh-oh)

job application
solicitud de empleo
(soh-lee-see-tóod deh ehm-pléh-oh)

job description
descripción del puesto
(dehs-creep-see-óhn dehl poo-éhs-toh)

job experience
experiencia en esta clase de trabajo
(ehs-peh-ree-éhn-see-ah ehn éhs-tah cláh-seh deh trah-báh-hoh)

job opening
vacante
(bah-cáhn-teh)

last name
apellido
(ah-peh-yée-doh)

legal immigrant
inmigrante legal
(een-mee-gráhn-teh leh-gáhl

legal resident
residente legal
(reh-see-déhn-teh leh-gáhl)

letter
carta
(cáhr-tah)

life insurance
seguro de vida
(seh-góo-roh deh bée-dah)

lunch break
descanso para el almuerzo
(dehs-cáhn-soh páh-rah ehl ahl-moo-éhr-soh)

mailing address
dirección postal
(dee-rehc-see-óhn pohs-táhl)

manager
gerente
(heh-réhn-teh)

medical insurance
seguro de enfermedad
(seh-góo-roh deh ehn-fehr-meh-dáhd)

message
mensaje
(mehn-sáh-heh)

minimum wage
salario mínimo
(sah-láh-ree-oh mée-nee-moh)

name
nombre
(nóhm-breh)

name tag
etiqueta con su nombre
(eh-tee-kéh-tah cohn soo nóhm-breh)

nickname
apodo
(ah-póh-doh)

(to) notify
notificar
(noh-tee-fee-cáhr)

no smoking
no fumar
(noh foo-máhr)

opening
vacante
(bah-cáhn-teh)

overtime
horas extra
(óh-rahs éhs-trah)

parking
aparcamiento
(ah-pahr-cah-mee-éhn-toh)

part-time job
empleo de tiempo parcial
(ehm-pléh-oh deh tee-éhm-poh pahr-see-áhl)

pay check
cheque salarial
(chéh-keh sah-lah-ree-áhl)

pay day
día de pago
(dée-ah deh páh-goh)

pay raise
aumento salarial
(ah-oo-méhn-toh sah-lah-ree-áhl)

permanent job
empleo permanente
(ehm-pléh-oh pehr-mah-néhn-teh)

personal hygiene
higiene personal
(ee-hee-éh-neh (pehr-soh-náhl)

personal information
datos personales
(dáh-tohs pehr-soh-náh-lehs)

personnel department
departamento de personal
(deh-pahr-tah-méhn-toh deh pehr-soh-náhl)

phone
teléfono
(teh-léh-foh-noh)

physical examination
examen médico
(ehc-sáh-mehn meh-dee-coh)

position
puesto
(poo-éhs-toh)

probationary period
período de prueba
(peh-rée-oh-doh deh proo-éh-bah)

professional test
test profesional
(tehst proh-feh-see-oh-náhl)

punctual
puntual
(poon-too-áhl)

punctuality
puntualidad
(poon-too-ah-lee-dáhd)

recruiting
reclutamiento
(reh-cloo-tah-mee-éhn-toh)

references
recomendación
(reh-coh-mehn-dah-see-óhn)

reliable
seguro
(seh-góo-roh)

responsibility
responsabilidad
(rehs-pohn-sah-bee-lee-dáhd)

resume
currículum vitae
(coo-rrée-coo-loom bée-tah)

retirement plan
plan de retiro
(plahn deh reh-tée-roh)

rise
aumento
(ah-oo-méhn-toh)

rules and regulations
ordenanzas
(ohr-deh-náhn-sahs)

salary
salario
(sah-láh-ree-oh)

screening
selección
(seh-lehc-see-óhn)

seasonal work
trabajo temporal
(trah-báh-hoh tehm-poh-ráhl)

selection process
proceso selectivo
(proh-séh-soh seh-lehc-tée-boh)

sex
sexo
(séhc-soh)

sexual harassment
acoso sexual
(ah-cóh-soh sehc-soo-áhl)

shift
turno
(tóor-noh)

(to) sign
firmar
(feer-máhr)

signature
firma
(féer-mah)

skill
experiencia
(ehs-peh-ree-éhn-see-ah)

(to) smoke
fumar
(foo-máhr)

Social Security
Seguridad Social
(seh-goo-ree-dáhd soh-see-áhl)

Social Security number
número de la Seguridad Social
(nóo-meh-roh deh lah Seh-goo-ree-dáhd Soh-see-áhl)

state
estado
(ehs-táh-doh)

street
calle
(cáh-yeh)

substance abuse
abuso de sustancias
(ah-bóo-soh deh soos-táhn-see-ahs

suggestion box
buzón de sugerencias
(boo-sóhn deh soo-heh-réhn-see-ahs)

supervisor
supervisor, (*supervisora*)
(soo-pehr-bee-sóhr) (soo-pehr-bee-sóh-rah)

tardiness
llegar tarde
(yeh-gáhr táhr-deh)

telephone
teléfono
(teh-léh-foh-noh)

temporary job
empleo temporal
(ehm-pléh-oh tehm-poh-ráhl)

termination
despido
(dehs-pée-doh)

test
test
(tehst)

theft
robo
(róh-boh)

time clock
reloj registrador
(reh-lohh reh-hees-trah-dóhr)

time card
tarjeta registradora
(tahr-héh-tah reh-hees-trah-dóh-rah)

(to) train
entrenar
(ehn-treh-náhr)

training
entrenamiento
(ehn-treh-nah-mee-éhn-toh)

transportation
medio de locomoción
(méh-dee-oh deh loh-coh-moh-see-óhn)

(to) type
escribir a máquina
(ehs-cree-béer ah máh-kee-nah)

uniform
uniforme
(oo-nee-fóhr-meh)

vacations
vacaciones
(bah-cah-see-óh-nehs)

(to) verify
verificar
(beh-ree-fee-cáhr)

wage
salario por horas
(sah-láh-ree-oh pohr óh-rahs)

waiting list
lista de espera
(lées-tah deh ehs-péh-rah)

weapons
armas
(áhr-mahs)

weekend
fin de semana
(feen deh seh-máh-nah)

work
trabajo
(trah-báh-hoh)

(to) work
trabajar
(trah-bah-háhr)

work contract
contrato de trabajo
(cohn-tráh-toh deh trah-báh-hoh)

workday
jornada de trabajo
(hohr-náh-dah deh trah-báh-hoh)

work hours
horario de trabajo
(oh-ráh-ree-oh deh trah-báh-hoh)

working days
días laborables
(dée-ahs lah-boh-ráh-blehs)

zip code
código postal
(cóh-dee-goh pohs-táhl)

Professional Interaction

Before the Interview

1. Do you speak English?
   ¿Habla usted inglés?
2. Please fill out this job application.
   Por favor, rellene este formulario de empleo.
3. How did you find out about this opening?
   ¿Cómo se enteró usted de esta vacante?
4. Do you have any experience in this type of work?
   ¿Tiene usted experiencia en este tipo de trabajo?
5. Do you live in the city?
   ¿Vive usted en la ciudad?
6. Where have you worked before?
   ¿Dónde ha trabajado usted anteriormente?
7. Are you a legal resident in the U.S.?
   ¿Es usted residente legal en los Estados Unidos?
8. This is a part-time job.
   La vacante es para empleo de tiempo parcial.
9. The job is to work twenty hours a week.
   La vacante es para trabajar veinte horas a la semana.
10. This is a full-time job.
    Es un empleo de tiempo completo.
11. This job pays minimum salary.
    Este trabajo paga el salario mínimo.

12. This job pays five dollars per hour.
    Este trabajo paga cinco dólares por hora.

13. Can you work all shifts?
    ¿Puede usted trabajar todos los turnos?

14. Can you work weekends?
    ¿Puede usted trabajar los fines de semana?

15. Can you work the graveyard shift?
    ¿Puede usted trabajar el turno de madrugada?

16. Are you willing to work evenings?
    ¿Podrá usted trabajar el turno de noche?

17. Have you been employed here before?
    ¿Ha trabajado usted aquí anteriormente?

18. Are you over twenty-one years of age?
    ¿Es usted mayor de veintiún años?

19. I am sorry, but the position has been filled.
    Lo siento, pero la vacante ha sido cubierta.

20. We will let you know within two days.
    Le daremos contestación dentro de dos días.

21. What is your telephone number?
    ¿Cuál es su número de teléfono?

22. What is your Social Security number?
    ¿Cuál es su número de la Seguridad Social?

23. What is your address?
    ¿Cuál es su dirección?

24. Your interview is Monday at three o'clock P.M.
    Su entrevista es el lunes a las tres de la tarde.

25. Are you interested in an apprenticeship job?
    ¿Le interesa un trabajo como aprendiz?

26. Do you mind taking an aptitude test?
    ¿Le importa tomar un test de aptitud profesional?

27. We will call you later about the job.
    Le llamaremos después para darle una contestación.

28. Are you an American citizen?
    ¿Es usted ciudadano (a) norteamericano (a)*?

29. Sorry, we don't have any job openings.
    Lo siento, no tenemos vacantes de trabajo.

*Be sure to use the *a* endings when addressing women.

30. Write your mailing address here.
    Escriba su dirección postal aquí.

31. Do you feel qualified for this job?
    ¿Se considera usted competente para desempeñar este trabajo?

32. Would you mind taking a physical examination?
    ¿Le importaría tomar un examen médico?

33. We only have a busperson position.
    Sólo tenemos un puesto de ayudante de mesero.

34. You must take a professional test.
    Debe tomar un test profesional.

35. Write your personal data here.
    Escriba sus datos personales aquí.

36. Do you have a resume?
    ¿Tiene usted un currículum vitae?

37. Sign and date the form here.
    Firme y feche la solicitud aquí.

38. Do you have the right skills for this job?
    ¿Tiene usted la experiencia necesaria para este trabajo?

39. Do you have a driver's license?
    ¿Tiene usted permiso para manejar?

40. Do you have legal documents to work in this country?
    ¿Tiene usted documentos legales para trabajar en este país?

41. Do you have a high school diploma?
    ¿Tiene usted diploma de estudios secundarios?

42. Do you have any experience as a cook?
    ¿Tiene usted experiencia como cocinero (a)?

43. Do you have a green card?
    ¿Tiene usted tarjeta verde?

44. Come back to the personnel department tomorrow.
    Venga al departamento de personal mañana.

45. Do you have any personal references?
    ¿Tiene usted cartas de recomendación?

46. Write your first and last names here.
    Escriba su nombre y apellido aquí.

47. Are you a legal immigrant?
    ¿Es usted un(a) inmigrante legal?

48. Please, show me your ID card.
    Por favor, muéstreme su tarjeta de identidad.

49. We are hiring for seasonal work only.
    Sólo estamos contratando para trabajo temporal.

50. Are you a member of a union?
    ¿Esta usted afiliado(a) a un sindicato?

51. Do you have your own transportation?
    ¿Tiene usted medio de locomoción propio?

52. Can you type?
    ¿Sabe usted escribir a máguina?

53. We can put you on our waiting list.
    Podemos ponerlo (la) en nuestra lista de espera.

54. We are going to verify your personal data.
    Vamos a verificar sus datos personales.

55. You have an appointment with your department head tomorrow at nine o'clock A.M.
    Tiene usted una cita con su jefe de departamento mañana a las nueve de la mañana.

56. Why do you like being a dishwasher?
    ¿Por qué le gusta a usted ser lavaplatos?

57. We don't have any full-time jobs at this time.
    No tenemos puestos de tiempo completo en este momento.

58. When can you come back for your first interview?
    ¿Cuándo puede usted volver para su primera entrevista?

59. Why should we hire you for this position?
    ¿Por qué deberíamos contratarle para este puesto?

60. Where can we contact you?
    ¿Dónde podemos ponernos en contacto con usted?

61. Where can we leave a message for you?
    ¿Dónde podemos dejar un mensaje para usted?

62. Do you smoke?
    ¿Fuma usted?

63. We will notify you of our decision by mail.
    Le notificaremos nuestra decisión por correo.

64. We are looking for reliable help.
    Deseamos contratar trabajadores que cumplan bien su trabajo.

65. In this hotel, we don't allow tardiness.
    En este hotel no permitimos llegar tarde al trabajo.

66. Which is your Zip Code?
    ¿Cuál es su código postal?

67. In this job the work hours often change.
   En este empleo el horario de trabajo cambia frecuentemente.

68. Would you be willing to sign a work contract?
   ¿Le importaría firmar un contrato de trabajo?

69. Thank you for applying to us.
   Gracias por haber solicitado trabajo en esta empresa.

During the Interview

1. Can you read English well?
   ¿Sabe usted leer inglés bien?

2. Did you fill in this application by yourself?
   ¿Rellenó usted mismo(a) esta solicitud?

3. Our company does not permit the use of drugs, alcohol, and tobacco. How do you feel about this?
   Nuestra empresa no permite el uso de drogas, bebidas alcohólicas o tabaco. ¿Qué opina usted de esto?

4. Why did you leave your last job?
   ¿Por qué dejó usted su último trabajo?

5. Are you currently employed?
   ¿Está usted empleado(a) ahora?

6. What appeals to you most about this type of business?
   ¿Qué le atrae más en este tipo de trabajo?

7. Should you be offered a job, when could you start work?
   ¿Si decidimos emplearlo (la), cuando podría usted empezar a trabajar?

8. Why do you want to work as a housekeeper?
   ¿Por qué quiere usted trabajar como camarista?

9. Do you consider yourself a competent worker?
   ¿Se considera usted un(a)trabajador (a) competente?

10. Do you mind signing a work contract for six months?
   ¿Le importaría firmar un contrato de trabajo por seis meses?

11. As a worker, what do you have to offer this company?
   ¿Como trabajador(a), qué puede usted ofrecer a esta empresa?

12. Do you think you could do a good job as a busperson?
   ¿Crée usted que puede ser un(a) buen(a) ayudante de mesero?

13. Can you work holidays and weekends?
   ¿Puede usted trabajar los días festivos y fines de semana?

14. Do you have a phone where we can call you?
    ¿Tiene usted teléfono donde podemos llamarle?
15. How soon can you start working?
    ¿Cuando podría empezar a trabajar?
16. Would you work overtime if necessary?
    ¿Trabajaría usted horas extras si fuera necesario?
17. Would you work less than forty hours from time to time?
    ¿Trabajaría usted menos de cuarenta horas de vez en cuando?
18. This company requires a 90-day probationary period.
    Esta empresa requiere un período de prueba de noventa días.
19. Can you arrive to work on time?
    ¿Puede usted llegar a tiempo a trabajar?
20. Do you have any questions?
    ¿Quiere usted preguntarme algo sobre este trabajo?
21. What do you need to know about the job?
    ¿Qué desea saber sobre el trabajo que ofrecemos?
22. Do you want to know about the company's benefits?
    ¿Quiere saber los beneficios que ofrece la empresa?
23. We still have to interview other candidates.
    Todavía tenemos que entrevistar a otros candidatos.
24. This is just a screening process.
    Estamos en el proceso de selección.
25. Thank you for interviewing with us.
    Gracias por venir a entrevistarse con nosotros.

After the Interview

1. We're sorry, we cannot hire you at this time.
   Sentimos no poder contratarlo (la) en esta ocasión.
2. We would like you to start Monday.
   Quisiéramos que empezara a trabajar el lunes.
3. Your first evaluation will be after the probationary period.
   Su primera evaluación será después del período de prueba.
4. If your work is satisfactory, we'll offer you fixed employment.
   Si su trabajo es satisfactorio, le ofreceremos un puesto permanente.

5. You must report to work five minutes before your shift starts.
   Debe presentarse al trabajo cinco minutos antes del comienzo de su turno.

6. Once you are in uniform, you must clock in using your time card.
   Cuando se ponga el uniforme, marque su tarjeta en el reloj registrador.

7. You must clock out at the end of your shift.
   Debe marcar su tarjeta en el reloj registrador al terminar su turno.

8. The use or possession of drugs or alcoholic beverages will be cause for dismissal from your job.
   El uso o posesión de drogas o bebidas alcohólicas es causa de despido en esta empresa.

9. Excessive tardiness will result in termination.
   Llegar tarde al trabajo repetidamente será causa de despido.

10. Overtime must be authorized by your supervisor.
    Las horas extras deberán ser autorizadas por su supervisor(a).

11. Overtime is paid at time and a half.
    Las horas extras son pagadas con un cincuenta por ciento de bonificación.

12. We don't tolerate work absenteeism.
    No toleramos excesivas ausencias del trabajo.

13. We provide you with a work uniform.
    La empresa le proporciona uniforme de trabajo.

14. You must buy your own uniform.
    Debe comprarse su uniforme de trabajo.

15. We clean our employees' uniforms.
    La empresa se encarga del mantenimiento de su uniforme.

16. You must clean your own uniform.
    La limpieza de su uniforme es a cargo suyo.

17. The company provides one free meal per full shift.
    La empresa concede una comida gratis por cada turno completo.

18. You can purchase your meals at discounted prices.
    Ofrecemos comidas para los empleados a precio reducido.

19. If you are unable to show up for work you must notify your supervisor at least two hours before your shift begins.
    Si no puede presentarse al trabajo, debe notificarlo a su supervisor(a) dos horas antes del comienzo de su turno.

20. Your personal appearance must be very good during work hours.
    Su apariencia personal debe ser excelente durante las horas de trabajo.

21. We don't allow sneakers.
    No se permite llevar zapatos tenis.

22. You must return your uniform before receiving your final pay check.
    Para poder recibir su paga final, deberá entregar su uniforme a su supervisor (a).

23. You will be trained before you can work on your own.
    Tendrá un período de entrenamiento antes de desempeñar su trabajo usted solo (a).

24. We promote from within before we hire outsiders.
    En los ascensos, damos prioridad a los empleados de la empresa.

25. Employees addicted to substances are required to seek professional help.
    Los empleados adictos a cualquier tipo de substancia deberán obtener ayuda profesional.

26. Your performance will be appraised every thirty days by your supervisor.
    Su trabajo será evaluado cada treinta días por su supervisor (a).

27. You are allowed a fifteen-minute break during your shift.
    Se le permite un descanso de quince minutos durante su turno.

28. You will follow a trainer for the first two days.
    Un(a) entrenador(a) le mostrará su trabajo durante los dos primeros días.

29. Please notify us if you change address or telephone number.
    Por favor, notifíquenos si cambia de dirección o de número de teléfono.

30. Your immediate supervisor is the department head of your department.
    Su supervisor(a) inmediato(a) es el (la) jefe (a) de su departamento.

31. We need your driver's license number.
    Necesitamos el número de su licencia de manejar.

32. We need your Social Security number.
    Necesitamos el número de su Seguridad Social.

33. You must use the employee entrance when entering or exiting the restaurant.
    Debe usar la puerta de servicio cuando entre o salga del restaurante.

34. All meals must be taken in the employee lounge.
    Todas las comidas deben consumirse en el salón de descanso.

35. Your personal grooming is very important.
    Su apariencia personal es de suma importancia.

36. This is your job description in Spanish.
    Aquí tiene la descripción de su trabajo en español.

37. Your supervisor will tell you your job duties.
    Su supervisor (a) le explicará las responsabilidades de su puesto.

38. Lunch break is between twelve o'clock and twelve thirty.
    El descanso para almorzar es entre las doce y las doce y media.

39. The company provides medical and dental insurance.
    La empresa provee seguro de enfermedad y dental.

40. Smoking is not allowed while working.
    No se permite fumar durante el trabajo.

41. You are allowed to smoke in the employee lounge.
    Se permite fumar en el salón de descanso.

42. You must wear your name tag at all times.
    Debe llevar la etiqueta con su nombre en todo momento.

43. The employee parking lot is located at the back of the restaurant.
    El aparcamiento de empleados está detrás del restaurante.

44. Payday is Friday.
    El día de pago es el viernes.

45. The rules and regulations of the company are listed in the employee handbook.
    Las ordenanzas de la empresa están en el manual de empleados.

46. Your supervisor is Mr. Pérez.
    El señor Pérez es su supervisor.

    Your supervisor is Mrs. Robinson.
    La señora Robinson es su supervisora.

47. There is a suggestion box in the employee cafeteria.
    Hay un buzón de sugerencias en la cafetería de empleados.

48. You must keep good personal hygiene.
    Debe mantener una buena higiene personal.

49. Before beginning work you must attend an orientation seminar.
    Antes de comenzar su trabajo debe asistir a una sesión de orientación.

50. I wish you luck in your new job.
    Buena suerte en su nuevo trabajo.

The Housekeeping Department

Technical Vocabulary

air-conditioned
aire acondicionado
(áh-ee-reh ah-cohn-dee-see-oh-náh-doh)

air vent
rejilla
(reh-hée-yah)

A.M. report
reporte de mañana
(reh-póhr-teh deh mah-nyáh-nah)

(to) announce
anunciar
(ah-noon-see-áhr)

armchair
sillón
(see-yóhn)

ashes
cenizas
(seh-née-sahs)

ashtray
cenicero
(seh-nee-séh-roh)

assistant
asistente
(ah-sees-téhn-teh)

65

babysitter
niñera
(nee-nyéh-rah)

balcony
terraza
(teh-rráh-sah)

bath mat
tapete de baño
(tah-péh-teh deh báh-nyoh)

bathroom
baño
(báh-nyoh)

bath soap
jabón de baño
(hah-bóhn deh báh-nyoh)

bath towel
toalla de baño
(toh-áh-yah deh báh-nyoh)

bathtub
bañera
(bah-nyéh-rah)

bed
cama
(cáh-mah)

bed cover
cobertor
(coh-behr-tóhr)

bed linen
blancos
(bláhn-cohs)

bedspread
cobertor
(coh-behr-tóhr)

blackboard
pizarrón
(pee-sah-rróhn)

blanket
manta
(máhn-tah)

blocked
bloqueado
(bloh-keh-áh-doh)

bottle opener
destapador
(dehs-tah-pah-dóhr)

bottom sheet
sábana bajera
(sáh-bah-nah bah-héh-rah)

broom
escoba
(ehs-cóh-bah)

brush
cepillo
(seh-pée-yoh)

bucket
balde
(báhl-deh)

button
botón
(boh-tóhn)

candle
vela
(béh-lah)

carpet
alfombra
(ahl-fóhm-brah)

cart
carro de servicio
(cáh-rroh deh sehr-bée-see-oh)

ceiling
techo
(téh-choh)

chair
silla
(sée-yah)

(to) check
comprobar
(cohm-proh-báhr)

checkout
salida
(sah-lée-dah)

cigarette butt
colilla
(koh-lée-yah)

(to) clean
limpiar
(leem-pee-áhr)

clean linen
ropa limpia
(róh-pah léem-pee-ah)

cleaning equipment
equipo de limpieza
(eh-kée-poh deh leem-pee-éh-sah)

cleaning powder
polvo limpiador
(póhl-boh leem-pee-ah-dóhr)

cleaning supplies
suministros de limpieza
(soo-mee-nées-trohs deh leem-pee-éh-sah)

(to) close
cerrar
(seh-rráhr)

closet
clóset
(clóh-seht)

cold
frío
(frée-oh)

comment card
tarjeta de comentarios
(tahr-héh-tah deh coh-mehn-táh-ree-ohs)

courteous
cortés
(cohr-téhs)

cot
cama portátil
(cáh-mah pohr-táh-teel)

couch
sofá
(soh-fáh)

counter
mostrador
(mohs-trah-dóhr)

crib
cuna
(cóo-nah)

curtain
cortina
(cohr-tée-nah)

cushion
cojín
(coh-héen)

(to) deep clean
limpiar a fondo
(leem-pee-áhr ah fóhn-doh)

deodorant
desodorante
(dehs-oh-doh-ráhn-teh)

department
departamento
(deh-pahr-tah-méhn-toh)

department meeting
junta de departamento
(hóon-tah deh deh-pahr-tah-méhn-toh)

departure room
cuarto de salida
(coo-áhr-toh deh sah-lée-dah)

de-stain
desmanchar
(dehs-mahn-cháhr)

desk
escritorio
(ehs-cree-tóh-ree-oh)

detergent
detergente
(deh-tehr-héhn-teh)

dirt
mugre
(móo-greh)

dirty
sucio
(sóo-see-oh)

disinfectant
desinfectante
(dehs-een-fehc-táhn-teh)

dishwasher
lavaplatos
(lah-bah pláh-tohs)

do not disturb sign
tarjeta de no molestar
(tahr-héh-tah deh noh moh-lehs-táhr)

door
puerta
(poo-éhr-tah)

door stopper
tope de puerta
(tóh-peh deh poo-éhr-tah)

downstairs
abajo
(ah-báh-hoh)

drain
desagüe
(deh-sáh-goo-eh)

(to) draw the curtain
correr la cortina
(coh-rréhr lah cohr-tée-nah)

drawer
cajón
(cah-hóhn)

dresser
tocador
(toh-cah-dóhr)

drycleaning
lavado a seco
(lah-báh-doh ah séh-coh)

dryer
secadora
(seh-cah-dóh-rah)

dust
polvo
(póhl-boh)

(to) dust
sacudir
(sah-coo-déer)

dustpan
recogedor
(reh-coh-heh-dóhr)

elevator
elevador
(eh-leh-bah-dóhr)

elevator
ascensor
(ahs-sehn-sóhr)

entrance
entrada
(ehn-tráh-dah)

envelope
sobre
(sóh-breh)

empty
vacío
(bah-sée-oh)

(to) empty
vaciar
(bah-see-áhr)

executive housekeeper
ama de llaves
(áh-mah deh yáh-behs)

facial tissue
pañuelos desechables
(pah-nyoo-éh-lohs dehs-eh-cháh-blehs)

fan
ventilador
(behn-tee-lah-dóhr)

faucet
grifo
(grée-foh)

fire
fuego
(foo-éh-goh)

floor
suelo
(soo-éh-loh)

floor (story)
piso
(pée-soh)

floor closet
estación de servicio
(ehs-tah-see-óhn deh sehr-bée-see-oh)

floor lamp
lámpara de pie
(láhm-pah-rah deh pee-éh)

floor mop
trapeador
(trah-peh-ah-dóhr)

(to) fold
doblar
(doh-bláhr)

folder
doblador
(doh-blah-dóhr)

freezer
congelador
(cohn-heh-lah-dóhr)

frock
bata
(báh-tah)

front desk
recepción
(reh-sehp-see-óhn)

front of the house
áreas públicas
(áh-reh-ahs póo-blee-cahs)

fruit basket
canasta de frutas
(cah-náhs-tah deh fróo-tahs)

fungi
hongos
(óhn-gohs)

furniture
muebles
(moo-éh-blehs)

garbage
basura
(bah-sóo-rah)

general manager
gerente general
(heh-réhn-teh heh-neh-ráhl)

germicidal
germicida
(hehr-mee-sée-dah)

glass
vidrio
(bée-dree-oh)

glasses
vasos
(báh-sohs)

gloves
guantes
(goo-áhn-tehs)

guest
huésped
(oo-éhs-pehd)

guest supplies
suministros de clientes
(soo-mee-nées-trohs deh clee-éhn-tehs)

hand brush
cepillo de mano
(seh-pée-yoh deh máh-noh)

hand soap
jabón de tocador
(hah-bóhn deh toh-cah-dóhr)

hand towel
toalla de mano
(toh-áh-yah deh máh-noh)

hallway
pasillo
(pah-sée-yoh)

(to) hang
colgar
(cohl-gáhr)

hangers
ganchos
(gáhn-chohs)

heating
calefacción
(cah-leh-fahc-see-óhn)

hot
caliente
(cah-lee-éhn-teh)

housekeeper
camarista
(cah-mah-rées-tah)

housekeeper report
reporte de camarista
(reh-póhr-teh deh cah-mah-rées-tah)

housekeeper room table tent
tarjeta de presentación
(tahr-héh-tah deh preh-sehn-tah-see-óhn)

housekeeping department
departamento de ama de llaves
(deh-pahr-tah-méhn-toh deh áh-mah deh yáh-behs)

housekeeping supervisor
supervisor (supervisora) de cuartos
(soo-pehr-bee-sóhr deh coo-áhr-tohs) (soo-pehr-bee-sóh-rah deh coo-áhr-tohs)

houseperson
mozo (moza) de pisos
(móh-soh deh pée-sohs) (móh-sah deh pée-sohs)

ice
hielo
(ee-éh-loh)

ice bucket
cubeta para hielo
(coo-béh-tah páh-rah ee-éh-loh)

ice machine
máquina de hielo
(máh-kee-nah deh ee-éh-loh)

(to) inspect
inspeccionar
(eens-pehc-see-oh-náhr)

inspection
inspección
(eens-pehc-see-óhn)

inventory
inventario
(een-behn-táh-ree-oh)

iron
plancha
(pláhn-chah)

(to) iron
planchar
(plahn-cháhr)

ironers
planchadores
(plahn-chah-dóh-rehs)

ironing board
tabla de planchar
(táh-blah deh plahn-cháhr)

janitor
mozo (moza) de limpieza
(móh-soh deh leem-pee-éh-sah) (móh-sah deh leem-pee-éh-sah)

johnny mop
escobilla
(ehs-coh-bée-yah)

key
llave
(yáh-beh)

kitchen
cocina
(coh-sée-nah)

(to) knock at the door
tocar a la puerta
(toh-cáhr ah lah poo-éhr-tah)

laundry bag
bolsa de lavandería
(bóhl-sah deh lah-bahnd-deh-rée-ah)

laundry list
lista de lavandería
(lées-tah deh lah-bahn-deh-rée-ah)

laundry products
productos de lavandería
(proh-dóoc-tohs deh lah-bahn-deh-rée-ah)

laundry room
lavandería
(lah-bahn-deh-rée-ah)

letterheads
papel de escribir timbrado
(pah-péhl deh ehs-cree-béer teem-bráh-doh)

light bulbs
focos
(fóh-cohs)

light switch
apagador
(ah-pah-gah-dóhr)

linen
lencería
(lehn-seh-rée-ah)

linen control
control de ropa
(cohn-tróhl deh róh-pah)

linen folder
doblador
(doh-blah-dóhr)

liquid soap
jabón líquido
(hah-bóhn leé-kee-doh)

living room
sala
(sáh-lah)

lobby
lobby
(lóh-bee)

lock
cerradura
(seh-rrah-dóo-rah)

(to) lock
cerrar con llave
(seh-rráhr cohn yáh-beh)

locker room
vestidor de empleados
(behs-tee-dóhr deh ehm-pleh-áh-dohs)

log book
bitácora
(bee-táh-coh-rah)

lost and found
objetos extraviados
(ohb-héh-tohs ehs-trah-bee-áh-dohs)

luggage
equipaje
(eh-kee-páh-heh)

luggage rack
portamaletas
(pohr-tah-mah-léh-tahs)

main entrance
entrada principal
(ehn-tráh-dah preen-see-páhl)

maintenance
mantenimiento
(mahn-teh-nee-mee-éhn-toh)

(to) make the bed
tender la cama
(tehn-déhr lah cáh-mah)

mangle
mangle
(máhn-gleh)

master key
llave maestra
(yáh-beh mah-éhs-trah)

matches
cerillos
(seh-rée-yohs)

material
material
(mah-teh-ree-áhl)

mattress
colchón
(cohl-chóhn)

mattress pad
protector de colchón
(proh-tehc-tóhr deh cohl-chóhn)

mattress rotation
volteo de colchón
(bohl-téh-oh deh cohl-chóhn)

mirror
espejo
(ehs-péh-hoh)

(to) miter
hacer ingletes
(ah-séhr een-gléh-tehs)

mop
trapeador
(trah-peh-ah-dóhr)

(to) mop
trapear
(trah-peh-áhr)

napkins
servilletas
(sehr-bee-yéh-tahs)

needle
aguja
(ah-góo-hah)

newspaper
periódico
(peh-ree-óh-dee-coh)

night stand
mesa de noche
(méh-sah deh nóh-cheh)

no baggage
sin equipaje
(seen eh-kee-páh-heh)

note pad
bloc de notas
(blohc deh nóh-tahs)

occupancy report
reporte de ocupación
(reh-póhr-teh deh oh-coo-pah-see-óhn)

occupied
ocupado
(oh-coo-páh-doh)

office
oficina
(oh-fee-sée-nah)

out of order
fuera de servicio
(foo-éh-rah deh sehr-bée-see-oh)

oven
horno
(óhr-noh)

paper napkin
servilleta de papel
(sehr-bee-yéh-tah deh pah-péhl)

paper towel
toalla de papel
(toh-áh-yah deh pah-péhl)

paperwork
papelería
(pah-peh-leh-rée-ah)

pass key
llave de paso
(yáh-beh deh páh-soh)

pen
pluma
(plóo-mah)

pencil
lápiz
(láh-pees)

pick-up room
cuarto de repaso
(coo-áhr-toh deh reh-páh-soh)

picture
cuadro
(coo-áh-droh)

pillow
almohada
(ahl-moh-áh-dah)

pillowcase
funda de almohada
(fóon-dah deh ahl-moh-áh-dah)

plastic glass
vaso de plástico
(báh-soh deh pláhs-tee-coh)

P.M. report
reporte de tarde
(reh-póhr-teh deh táhr-deh)

poison
veneno
(beh-néh-noh)

(to) polish
pulir
(poo-léer)

postcard
tarjeta postal
(tahr-héh-tah pohs-táhl)

public areas
áreas públicas
(áh-reh-ahs poó-blee-cahs)

public bathroom
baño público
(báh-nyoh póo-blee-coh)

queen-sized bed
cama matrimonial
(cáh-mah mah-tree-moh-nee-áhl)

quilt
colcha
(cóhl-chah)

radio
radio
(ráh-dee-oh)

rag
trapo
(tráh-poh)

ready room
cuarto listo
(coo-áhr-toh lées-toh)

ready to rent
listo para alquilar
(lées-toh páh-rah ahl-kee-láhr)

refrigerator
refrigerador
(reh-free-heh-rah-dóhr)

report
reporte
(reh-póhr-teh)

requisition
requisición
(reh-kee-see-see-óhn)

restroom
baño
(báh-nyoh)

(to) rinse
enjuagar
(ehn-hoo-ah-gáhr)

room
cuarto/habitación
(coo-áhr-toh) / (ah-bee-tah-see-óhn)

room attendant
camarista
(cah-mah-rées-tah)

room division
división cuartos
(dee-bee-see-óhn coo-áhr-tohs)

room section
sección de cuartos
(sehc-see-óhn deh coo-áhr-tohs)

room service
room service
(róom séhr-bees)

(to) rotate
rotar
(roh-táhr)

rug
alfombra
(ahl-fóhm-brah)

rug shampooer
máquina para lavar alfombras
(máh-kee-nah páh-rah lah-báhr ahl-fóhm-brahs)

sanitary bag
bolsa sanitaria
(bóhl-sah sah nee-táh-ree-ah)

(to) scrape
rascar
(rahs-cáhr)

screen
pantalla
(pahn-táh-yah)

(to) scrub
restregar
(rehs-treh-gáhr)

section housekeeper
camarista
(cah-mah-rées-tah)

security
seguridad
(seh-goo-ree-dáhd)

service
servicio
(sehr-bée-see-oh)

service directory
directorio de servicios
(dee-rehc-tóh-ree-oh deh sehr-bée-see-ohs)

service stairs
escalera de servicio
(ehs-cah-léh-rah deh sehr-bée-see-oh)

(to) sew
coser
(coh-séhr)

shampoo
champú
(chahm-póo)

sheers
visillos
(bee-sée-yohs)

sheet
sábana
(sáh-bah-nah)

shelf
repisa
(reh-pée-sah)

shower
ducha
(dóo-chah)

shower cap
gorra de baño
(góh-rrah deh báh-nyoh)

shower curtain
cortina de ducha
(cohr-tée-nah deh dóo-chah)

shower head
regadera
(reh-gah-déh-rah)

shift
turno
(tóor-noh)

shift turnover
cambio de turno
(cáhm-bee-oh deh tóor-noh)

sink
lavabo
(lah-báh-boh)

shoes
zapatos
(sah-páh-tohs)

(to) soak
empapar
(ehm-pah-páhr)

soap
jabón
(hah-bóhn)

soap dish
jabonera
(hah-boh-néh-rah)

sofa
sofá
(soh-fáh)

soiled linen
ropa sucia
(róh-pah sóo-see-ah)

sponge
esponja
(ehs-póhn-hah)

stain
mancha
(máhn-chah)

starch
almidón
(ahl-mee-dóhn)

(to) starch
almidonar
(ahl-mee-doh-náhr)

stationery
papelería
(pah-peh-leh-rée-ah)

stock
stock
(ehs-tóhc)

storeroom
almacén
(ahl-mah-séhn)

suitcase
maleta
(mah-léh-tah)

supervisor
supervisor (supervisora)
(soo-pehr-bee-sóhr) (soo-pehr-bee-sóhr-ah)

supplies
suministros
(soo-mee-nées-trohs)

(to) sweep
barrer
(bah-rréhr)

swing team
equipo de relevo
(eh-kée-poh deh reh-léh-boh)

swimming pool
alberca
(ahl-béhr-cah)

swimming pool
piscina
(pees-sée-nah)

table
mesa
(méh-sah)

tablecloth
mantel
(mahn-téhl)

telephone
teléfono
(teh-léh-foh-noh)

telephone book
directorio telefónico
(dee-rehc-tóh-ree-oh teh-leh-fóh-nee-coh)

television
televisión
(teh-leh-bee-see-óhn)

team
equipo
(eh-kée-poh)

terry cloth
felpa
(féhl-pah)

thermostat
termostato
(tehr-mohs-táh-toh)

tile
azulejo
(ah-soo-léh-hoh)

toilet
inodoro
(ee-noh-dóh-roh)

toilet paper
papel higiénico
(pah-péhl ee-hee-éh-nee-coh)

towel
toalla
(toh-áh-yah)

towel rack
toallero
(toh-ah-yéh-roh)

trash
basura
(bah-sóo-rah)

trash bag
bolsa de basura
(bóhl-sah deh bah-sóo-rah)

tray
charola
(chah-róh-lah)

turndown service
cortesía
(cohr-teh-sée-ah)

(to) turn off
apagar
(ah-pah-gáhr)

(to) turn on
encender
(ehn-sehn-déhr)

T.V. set
televisor
(teh-leh-bee-sóhr)

T.V. guide
guía de tele
(guí-ah deh téh-leh)

uniform
uniforme
(oo-nee-fóhr-meh)

unoccupied
desocupado
(dehs-oh-coo-páh-doh)

upholstery
tapicería
(tah-pee-seh-rée-ah)

upstairs
arriba
(ah-rrée-bah)

vacant
desocupado
(dehs-oh-coo-páh-doh)

vacant and clean
vacío y limpio
(bah-sée-oh ee léem-pee-oh)

vacant and dirty
vacío y sucio
(bah-sée-oh ee sóo-see-oh)

vacant and ready
vacío y listo
(bah-sée-oh ee lées-toh)

(to) vacuum
aspirar
(ahs-pee-ráhr)

vacuum cleaner
aspiradora
(ahs-pee-rah-dóh-rah)

valet
valet
(bah-léh)

vanity
lavabo
(lah-báh-boh)

venetian blind
persiana
(pehr-see-áh-nah)

wall
pared
(pah-réhd)

(to) wash
lavar
(lah-báhr)

washcloth
toalla facial
(toh-áh-yah fah-see-áhl)

washer
lavadora
(lah-bah-dóh-rah)

wastebasket
cesto de basura
(séhs-toh deh bah-sóo-rah)

wastepaper basket
papelera
(pah-peh-léh-rah)

water
agua
(áh-goo-ah)

wax
cera
(séh-rah)

white linen
blancos
(bláhn-cohs)

window
ventana
(vehn-táh-nah)

window cleaner
limpiador de vidrios
(leem-pee-ah-dóhr deh bée-dree-ohs)

window sill
repisón
(reh-pee-sóhn)

wood
madera
(mah-déh-rah)

workload
cuota de trabajo
(coo-óh-tah deh trah-báh-hoh)

writing pad
libreta de apuntes
(lee-bréh-tah deh ah-póon-tehs)

Professional Interaction

Professional Interaccion with Room Attendants

1. Show up to work well groomed and in uniform.
   Preséntese al trabajo debidamente aseada y uniformada.
2. Your eight-hour shift workload is fifteen rooms.
   Su cuota de trabajo por turno de ocho horas es quince cuartos.
3. You are given a daily report by your supervisor.
   Recibe de su supervisor(a) un reporte de camarista.
4. Your supervisor gives you your pass key.
   Recibe de su supervisor(a) la llave de paso.
5. Enter on the control sheet your receipt of the pass key.
   Entre en la bitácora el recibido de la llave de paso.
6. Begin by entering the rooms with the "early service" request.
   Empiece con los cuartos con tarjetas de "early service".
7. Follow with the rooms marked as "checkout" on your report.
   Seguidamente limpie los cuartos indicados en el reporte como "checkout".
8. Finally, clean all the rooms in your section and indicate their status on the daily report.
   Finalmente, limpie todos los cuartos de su sección e indique su situación en el reporte diario.
9. Do not disturb the rooms with the "do not disturb" sign.
   No toque a la puerta de los cuartos con la tarjeta "do not disturb."
10. Knock at doors with your knuckles, not with the room key.
    No toque a la puerta con la llave del cuarto, sino con los nudillos.

11. Knock, wait a few seconds, and announce yourself.
    Llame, espere unos segundos y anúnciese.

12. If there is no answer, knock again, then open the door slightly and look inside.
    Si no recibe contestación, toque otra vez, abra la puerta ligeramente y mire dentro del cuarto.

13. You will receive a service cart with the necessary supplies.
    Recibe un carro de servicio con los suministros necesarios.

14. Verify that the cart is fully equipped.
    Verifique que el carro de servicio cuenta con los suministros necesarios.

15. Your cart must carry:
    a. cleaning supplies,
    b. guest supplies,
    c. bed linens,
    d. mattress pads,
    e. towels and bath mats.
    Su carro de servicio debe contar con:
    a. suministros de limpieza,
    b. suministros para huéspedes,
    c. blancos de cama,
    d. protectores de colchón,
    e. toallas y tapetes para baño.

16. At the end of your shift, give the completed report to your supervisor and restock the cart.
    Al término de su turno, entregue el reporte a su supervisor(a) y coloque nuevos suministros en el carro de servicio.

17. The keys for the status of the rooms are:
    a. **occ** = occupied,
    b. **c/o** = checkout,
    c. **v** = vacant,
    d. **vr** = vacant and ready,
    e. **ooo** = out of order
    Las claves correspondientes al estado físico de los cuartos son:
    *a. **occ** = ocupado,*
    *b. **c/o** = salida,*
    *c. **v** = desocupado,*
    *d. **vr** = desocupado y listo,*
    *e. **ooo** = fuera de servicio.*

18. If the guest is inside, ask if he (she) wants the room serviced now.
    Si el huésped está en la habitación, pregunte si desea el servicio en ese momento.

19. While cleaning a room, place the cart across the door to block the entrance.
    Coloque el carro de servicio en la puerta de la habitación para bloquear la entrada mientras que esté limpiando la habitación.

20. Never close the door while cleaning a room.
    Nunca cierre la puerta mientras esté limpiando el cuarto.

21. Empty the wastebaskets into the trash bag.
    Vacíe la basura de los cestos en la bolsa de basura.

22. Dust the furniture.
    Sacuda los muebles.

23. Clean mirrors and windows.
    Limpie los espejos y vidrios.

24. Vacuum or wash floors, including under the beds.
    Aspire o trapée los pisos, incluyendo debajo de las camas.

25. Make the bed with clean linen.
    Tienda las camas con ropa limpia.

26. Wash the bathtub, tile walls, shower curtain, faucets, and shower head.
    Lave la bañera, las paredes de azulejos, la cortina de baño, los grifos y la regadera.

27. Clean the air-conditioned vents and exhaust fan using a hand brush.
    Limpie las rejillas del aire acondicionado y el extractor con un cepillo de mano.

28. Clean the vanity, towel rack, and mirrors.
    Limpie el lavabo, el toallero y los espejos.

29. Wash the inside of the toilet using toilet bowl cleaner and a johnny mop.
    Lave el inodoro por dentro utilizando líquido limpiador y escobilla.

30. Clean the outside of the toilet with a rag and germicidal.
    Limpie el inodoro por fuera usando un trapo con germicida.

31. Scrub the bathroom floor.
    Friegue el piso del baño.

32. Provide the room with towels, guest supplies, and guest essentials.
    Equipe el cuarto con toallas, suministros de clientes y demás enseres.

33. Check lights, radio, and T.V. set.
    Compruebe las luces, la radio y el televisor.

34. Set thermostat at the right temperature.
    Sitúe el termostato a la temperatura adecuada.

35. Notify your supervisor if anything in the room needs to be repaired.
Reporte a su supervisor(a) si hay alguna anomalía en el cuarto que necesita ser reparada.

36. Replace the toilet paper roll and box of facial tissue if necessary.
Reponga el rollo de papel higiénico y la caja de pañuelos desechables si es necesario.

37. Check the stationery items in the room:
   a. directory of services,
   b. letterheads and envelopes,
   c. note pad and pen,
   d. "do not disturb" sign.
   Compruebe la papelería en el cuarto:
   a. directorio de servicios,
   b. papel membretado y sobres,
   c. block de apuntes y pluma,
   d. tarjeta de "do not disturb".

38. Place the tent card with your name on the dresser.
Coloque la tarjeta de presentación con su nombre sobre el escritorio.

39. For turndown service, follow these procedures:
   a. fold the bed cover and place it in the closet,
   b. fold the corner of bed sheet and blanket, forming a triangle,
   c. draw the curtains and leave one light on,
   d. empty waste baskets,
   e. replace used towels with new ones.
   Para el servicio de cortesías, siga el procedimiento siguiente:
   a. quite la cubierta, dóblela y colóquela en el clóset,
   b. doble la esquina de la sábana y manta formando un triángulo,
   c. cierre las cortinas y deje una luz encendida,
   d. vacíe los cestos de basura,
   e. reponga las toallas usadas con otras limpias.

40. Any items left behind by guests must be brought to the housekeeping office immediately.
Cualquier objeto personal olvidado por huéspedes debe ser depositado en la oficina de ama de llaves inmediatemente.

41. Lost and found items must be identified with your name, date, and the hour and place where it was found.
Los objetos encontrados deben ser marcados con su nombre, fecha y la hora y el lugar donde fueron encontrados.

Professional Interaction with Housepersons

1. Please show up to work well groomed and wearing a clean uniform.
   Por favor, preséntese a trabajar bien aseado(a) y llevando puesto un uniforme limpio.

2. The hotel's main entrance must be swept often.
   Debe barrer la puerta principal del hotel a menudo.

3. Pick up the soiled linen from the floors and bring it to the laundry room.
   Recoja los blancos sucios de los pisos y llévelos a la lavandería.

4. Distribute the clean linen to the floor closets.
   Distribuya los blancos limpios a las estaciones de servicio en los pisos.

5. Check the back stairs early in the morning.
   Inspeccione las escaleras de emergencia por la mañana temprano.

6. The hallways must be vacuumed just before the end of your shift.
   Debe aspirar los pasillos antes del final de su turno.

7. Help the room attendants turn over the mattresses.
   Ayude a las camaristas a voltear los colchones.

8. Bring supplies to the floors throughout the morning.
   Lleve suministros a los pisos a lo largo de la mañana.

9. Mop the public restroom floors every hour or so.
   Trapée los pisos del baño público como cada hora.

10. Clean all glass doors in the lobby.
    Limpie las puertas de cristales en el lobby.

11. Do you know how to shampoo carpets?
    ¿Sabe usted limpiar alfombras?

12. The water fountains must be polished with stainless steel cleaner.
    Debe pulir las fuentes con abrillantador de metales.

13. Please pick up all trash in the parking lot.
    Por favor, recoja la basura en el estacionamiento.

14. Dust and polish the furniture in the lobby.
    Sacuda y abrillante los muebles del lobby.

15. Vacuum sofas and cushions with the hand vacuum.
    Aspire los sofás y cojines con la aspiradora de mano.

16. The lobby ashtrays and trash cans must be cleaned regularly.
    Limpie regularmente los ceniceros y los cestos de basura del lobby.

17. Scrub the urinals with a brush and cleaning powder.
    Friegue los urinarios con cepillo y polvo limpiador.

18. Polish all chrome fixtures and resupply the paper towels.
    Pula los accesorios cromados y reponga las toallas de papel.

19. Leave an extra roll of toilet paper.
    Deje un rollo de papel higiénico de reserva.

20. Wipe the hand set of public telephones with a wet cloth.
    Frote el auricular del teléfono público con un trapo húmedo.

21. The cleaning of public and service elevators is your responsibility.
    La limpieza de los elevadores públicos y de servicio es responsibilidad suya.

22. Dust vending and ice machines and fire extinguishers.
    Sacuda las máquinas vendedoras y de hielo y los extinguidores.

23. Help the room attendants with the floor trash.
    Ayude a las camaristas con el retiro de la basura de los pisos.

24. Pick up room service trays from hallways and place them by the service elevator.
    Retire de los pasillos las charolas del "room service" y colóquelas a la entrada del elevador de servicio.

25. Count and bundle this soiled linen.
    Cuente y ate estos blancos sucios.

Professional Interaction with Floor Supervisors

1. You are in charge of floors seven and eight.
   Usted tiene a su cargo los pisos siete y ocho.

2. Each room attendant should clean fourteen rooms per shift.
   Cada camarista debe limpiar catorce cuartos por turno.

3. In the morning, get the room report for your floors.
   En la mañana, obtenga el reporte de ocupación de cuartos de sus pisos.

4. Distribute the pass keys among your room attendants.
   Distribuya las llaves de paso a sus camaristas.

5. Watch that all room attendants and housepersons are groomed and wearing clean uniforms.
   Compruebe que las camaristas y los mozos estén aseados y lleven uniformes limpios.

6. Check the board and log book for outstanding jobs.
   Compruebe en el pizarrón y la bitácora las labores pendientes del turno anterior.

7. Fill out the room attendant reports from the room occupancy list.
   Rellene los reportes de camaristas usando la lista de ocupación del hotel.

8. Assign each houseperson his (her) job for the day.
   Asigne a cada mozo(a) sus labores del día.

9. Distribute equipment and supplies to each worker.
   Distribuya equipo y suministros a cada empleado(a).

10. Check that there is enough linen to begin the day's work.
    Verifique que haya suficientes blancos para comenzar las labores del día.

11. Assign room attendants the rooms they are to clean.
    Asigne a las camaristas los cuartos que tienen que limpiar.

12. Inspect the carts for supplies.
    Inspeccione los suministros de los carros de servicio.

13. Inspect carefully the rooms that have been cleaned by the room attendants.
    Inspeccione cuidadosamente los cuartos que han sido limpiados por las camaristas.

14. Notify the front desk of the rooms that are ready to be rented.
    Notifique a recepción los cuartos que estén listos para alquilar.

15. If while inspecting the rooms you find an anomaly, write a work order for maintenance.
    Si encuentra alguna anomalía en los cuartos, rellene una orden de trabajo para el departamento de mantenimiento.

16. Please take inventory of all items in your area.
    Por favor, tome inventario de todos los suministros en su área.

17. Resolve the status of the "do not disturb" rooms by two o'clock P.M.
    Resuelva el estado de los cuartos con "do not disturb" antes de las dos de la tarde.

18. Set all thermostats at the proper temperature.
    Sitúe los termostatos a la temperatura adecuada.

19. Take a cot to the fifth floor, room 201.
    Lleve una cama portátil al quinto piso, habitación doscientos uno.

20. The room attendant in the third floor needs more coat hangers.
    La camarista del tercer piso necesita más ganchos.

21. Please take this box of plastic glasses to the store room.
    Favor de llevar esta caja de vasos de plástico al almacén.

22. Don't use towels to dust the furniture; use rags.
    No use toallas para sacudir los muebles; use trapos.

23. Scrape the shower drain well.
    Rasque bien el desagüe de la ducha.

24. Don't use the guest elevators; you may use the service elevator or the stairs.
   No use el elevador de huéspedes; puede usar el elevador de servicio o las escaleras.

25. Please help María deep clean the rooms in her section.
   Favor de ayudar a María a limpiar a fondo los cuartos de su sección.

Professional Interaction with Laundry Attendants

1. We require the wearing of sneakers in the laundry room.
   Requerimos el uso de zapatos tenis en la lavandería.

2. Your job is to sort out the soiled linen coming down from the floors and the food and beverage department.
   Su trabajo consiste en separar la ropa sucia de los pisos y del departamento de alimentos y bebidas.

3. Stained linen must be de-stained before washing.
   La ropa manchada debe desmancharse antes del lavado.

4. We need you to operate the drycleaning machine.
   Debe trabajar en la máquina de limpieza en seco.

5. Sheets and tablecloths must be mangled after washing.
   Las sábanas y los manteles deben ser pasados por el mangle después de ser lavados.

6. Folded linen is stored on these shelves.
   La ropa doblada se coloca en estos estantes.

7. Our bed linen does not need ironing.
   Nuestros blancos no precisan planchado.

8. You must program the washers for each type of linen.
   Debe programar las lavadoras para cada tipo de ropa.

9. Clean the lint traps after each shift.
   Limpie la pelusa de las secadoras después de cada turno.

10. Fill out a weekly storeroom request for laundry products.
   Llene una requisición de suministros para el almacén cada semana.

11. Each type of linen requires a different wash formula.
   Cada tipo de ropa requiere una fórmula de lavado diferente.

12. Sheets and pillowcases, towels and bath mats, and napery are washed in three different groups.
   Los blancos, las toallas y tapetes de baño y la mantelería se lavan en tres grupos diferentes.

13. The laundry floor must be mopped dry constantly.
    El piso de la lavandería debe ser trapeado constantemente para mantenerlo seco.

14. Guest laundry must be given priority.
    La ropa de clientes tiene prioridad de lavado.

15. Spreads, sheets, blankets, mattress pads and shower curtains are folded using the standing sheet folder.
    Los cobertores, sábanas, mantas, protectores de colchón y cortinas de ducha son doblados utilizando el doblador de pie.

Housekeeping Position Descriptions

Room Attendant (Section Housekeeper) (*Camarista*)

Reports to Supervisor or Housekeeping Manager.

Reporta al (a la) Supervisor(a) o al (a la)
Jefe del Departamento de Ama de Llaves.

Position Responsibility

Responsabilidad del Puesto

1. Report in uniform, well groomed, and clock in.
   Presentarse uniformado(a), bien aseado(a), y marcar su tarjeta en el reloj reg-
   istrador.

2. Pick up keys and daily report from supervisor.
   Recoger del (de la) supervisor(a) las llaves y el reporte de camarista.

3. Get service cart and begin cleaning assignments. Checkouts and early
   requests should be cleaned first.
   Recoger el carro de servicio y comenzar las labores de limpieza. Dar preferencia a
   las salidas y los cuartos con tarjetas indicadoras pidiendo servicio.

4. Enter and prepare room for cleaning.
   Entrar y preparar el cuarto para su limpieza.

5. Make the bed.
   Hacer la cama.

6. Dust the room and furniture.
   Sacudir el cuarto y los muebles.

7. Replenish room and bathroom supplies.
   Surtir el cuarto y el baño con suministros.

8. Clean bathroom.
   Limpiar el baño.

9. Vacuum the carpet.
   Aspirar la alfombra.
10. Check room for final appearance.
    Comprobar la apariencia final del cuarto.
11. Fill in the daily report as work progresses.
    Anotar en el reporte diario el trabajo realizado.
12. Check in keys in log book at end of shift.
    Entrar en el libro de bitácora la entrega de llaves al final del turno.
13. Clock out for the day.
    Marcar la tarjeta en el reloj registrador al final de su turno.

Houseperson (*Ayudante de Camarista*)

Reports to Head Houseperson or Housekeeping Manager.

Reporta al (a la) Supervisor(a) de Ayudantes de Camarista o al (a la) Jefe del Departamento de Ama de Llaves.

Position Responsibility

Responsabilidad del Puesto

1. Report in uniform, well groomed, and clock in.
   Presentarse uniformado(a), bien aseado(a), y marcar su tarjeta en el reloj registrador.
2. Clean carpets and upholstered furniture.
   Limpiar alfombras y muebles tapizados.
3. Clean hallways and public restrooms.
   Limpiar corredores y baños públicos.
4. Wash walls and ceilings, move furniture, and turn mattresses.
   Lavar paredes y techos, trasladar muebles y voltear colchones.
5. Sweep, mop, wax, and polish floors.
   Barrer, trapear, encerar y dar brillo a suelos.
6. Dust and polish metal work.
   Sacudir y dar brillo a metales.
7. Collect soiled linen from floors for laundering.
   Recoger blancos sucios de los pisos para su lavado.
8. Distribute clean linen to floors.
   Distribuir blancos limpios a los pisos.
9. Replenish service carts.
   Surtir carros de servicio.

10. Remove trash from floors.
    Recoger la basura de los pisos.

11. Clean elevators, ice and vending machines, and stairwells.
    Limpiar ascensores, máquinas de hielo y de artículos de venta y escaleras.

12. Restock linen and supplies to floor closets.
    Reponer ropa limpia y suministros en el clóset de pisos.

13. Clock out for the day.
    Marcar su tarjeta en el reloj registrador al final del turno.

Floor Supervisor (*Supervisor(a) de pisos*)

Reports to Housekeeping Manager. *Reporta al (a la) Jefe del Departamento de Ama de Llaves.*

Position Responsibility   *Responsabilidad del Puesto*

1. Report to housekeeping in uniform and clock in.
   Presentarse en uniforme y marcar su tarjeta en el reloj registrador.

2. Obtain keys and room occupancy report for your area.
   Obtener llaves y el reporte de ocupación de cuartos de su área.

3. Prepare and distribute room attendant daily reports.
   Preparar y distribuir los reportes de camaristas.

4. Verify attendance, punctuality, grooming, and uniform of room attendants and housepersons.
   Verificar la asistencia, puntualidad, aseo y uniforme de camaristas y ayudantes de camarista.

5. Check all ready rooms in your area, making sure that they are ready to rent.
   Comprobar los cuartos marcados como limpios y asegurarse de que están listos para ser ocupados.

6. Inspect general areas for burned-out lights, spots on carpets or walls, and trash.
   Compruebe que en su área de trabajo no haya focos fundidos, manchas en alfombras o paredes o basura.

7. Check that all room attendants have adequate equipment and supplies.
   Compruebe que las camaristas tengan el equipo y los suministros adecuados.

8. Inspect cleaned rooms and release them to the front desk.
   Inspeccione los cuartos que han sido limpiados y cédalos a recepción.

9. Report any defect or equipment failure to the maintenance department, using a work request form.
   Reporte cualquier desperfecto o rotura al departamento de mantenimiento, utilizando una orden de trabajo.

10. Supervise housepersons.
    Supervisar a los ayudantes de camarista.

11. Make sure that the evening room check is done before the end of the shift.
    Asegurarse de que se efectue el reporte de tarde de ocupación de cuartos antes de finalizar el turno.

12. Ask room service to pick up used trays from hallways.
    Solicitar a room service la retirada de charolas de los pasillos.

13. Send lost and found items to the housekeeping department together with a completed lost-and-found form.
    Envíe los objetos extraviados al departamento de ama de llaves, junto con un comprobante debidamente cumplimentado.

14. Hand in all reports to the housekeeping manager and clock out.
    Entregue los reportes necesarios al (a la) jefe del departamento de ama de llaves y marque su tarjeta en el reloj registrador.

Laundry Attendant (*Empleado(a) de lavandería*)

Reports to Laundry Manager.   *Reporta al (a la) Jefe de Lavandería.*
Position Responsibility   *Responsabilidad del Puesto*

1. Report to work in uniform and clock in.
   Presentarse al trabajo uniformado(a) y marcar su tarjeta en el reloj registrador.

2. Sort soiled linen and check for tears and stains.
   Seleccionar la ropa sucia y separar roturas y artículos manchados.

3. Pretreat heavily stained items before washing.
   Efectuar tratamiento de desmanchado antes de lavar los artículos.

4. Load and set cycles in washers.
   Cargar la ropa en las lavadoras y fijar los ciclos de lavado.

5. Unload washers.
   Descargar las lavadoras.

6. Load and unload dryers.
   Cargar y descargar las secadoras.

7. Fold and stack linen on shelves.
   Doblar y colocar la ropa limpia en los estantes.

8. Keep laundry floor dry and area clean.
   Mantener seco el piso y limpia el área de la lavandería.

9. Check levels of detergents and chemicals.
   Comprobar suministros de detergentes y productos químicos.

10. Report shortages of linen to the laundry manager.
    Comunicar la insuficiencia de ropa al (a la) jefe de lavandería.

11. Clock out.
    Marcar su tarjeta en el reloj registrador.

Housekeeping Procedures

Entering a guestroom *(Entrada al cuarto de clientes)*

1. Do not knock at rooms with "do not disturb" signs.
   No toque en los cuartos con la tarjeta de "do not disturb."

2. Knock at the door with your knuckles and softly announce "Housekeeping."
   Toque con los nudillos a la puerta y anúnciese, diciendo "Housekeeping".

3. Wait a few seconds; knock again. If the guest does not answer, enter the room, leaving the door wide open.
   Espere unos segundos; toque nuevamente. Si el (la) huésped no contesta, entre en el cuarto, dejando la puerta abierta de par en par.

4. For your protection, place the service cart across the door to block the entrance.
   Para su seguridad, coloque el carro de servicio en la puerta para bloquear la entrada .

5. If the guest answers, ask if he (she) wishes you to service the room now or later on.
   Si el (la) huésped contesta, pregunte si desea servicio en ese momento o más adelante.

6. Open the curtains and windows and check that all lights and the T.V. set are in working order.
   Abra las cortinas y ventanas y compruebe que todas las luces y el televisor funcionan.

7. Turn off unnecessary lights and the heating or air-conditioning unit.
   Apague las luces que no necesite y la calefacción o aire acondicionado.

8. Look at the condition of the room and report any damage or missing equipment.
   Compruebe el estado del cuarto y reporte cualquier desperfecto o la falta de equipo.

9. In occupied rooms, pick up newspapers or magazines, fold them neatly, and place them on the desk. Never throw away any materials that are not in the wastebasket.
   En cuartos ocupados, recoja periódicos y revistas, dóblelos cuidadosamente y colóquelos sobre el escritorio. Nunca tire artículos que no estén en el cesto de basura.

10. Empty all trash containers in your trash bag.
    Vacíe los cestos de basura en su bolsa de basura.

11. If there is a room service tray in the room, bring it out and place it in the hallway.
    Si hay una charola de room service en el cuarto, sáquela fuera y colóquela en el pasillo.

Cleaning the Bedroom (*Limpieza del cuarto*)

1. Strip the bed linen, shaking it carefully for guest clothing or valuables. Turn in any items left behind to your supervisor. Place soiled linen and terry cloth in bag.
   Quite los blancos de la cama, sacudiéndolos cuidadosamente por si hubiera prendas o artículos de valor del cliente. Entregue cualquier artículo olvidado a su supervisor(a). Coloque los blancos y la felpa sucios en la bolsa.

2. Make the bed, replacing the bed pad if necessary.
   Haga la cama, reponiendo el protector de colchón si es necesario.

3. Dust bed headboard, pictures, baseboard, and ledges. Dust the night stand, desk, chairs, tables and floor lamp.
   Sacuda la cabecera de la cama, los cuadros, el zócalo y las repisas. Sacuda la mesita de noche, el escritorio, las sillas y mesas y la lámpara de pie.

4. Clean the telephones with a clean rag and cleaning solution.
   Limpie los teléfonos con un trapo limpio y líquido limpiador.

5. Replace the memo pad, pen, stationery, and hotel literature.
   Reponga el bloc de notas, la pluma, la papelería y los folletos del hotel.

6. Place your own name card on the desk.
   Coloque la tarjeta con su nombre sobre el escritorio.

7. Dust the T.V. set, screen, back and stand.
   Sacuda el televisor, la pantalla, la parte trasera y el soporte.

8. Clean the ashtrays and tray and replace the ice bucket, glasses, and matches.
   Limpie los ceniceros y la bandeja y reponga la cubeta para hielo, los vasos y las cerillas.

9. In checkout rooms, clean drawers. In occupied rooms, do not open the drawers.
   En cuartos de salida, limpie los cajones. En cuartos ocupados, no abra los cajones.

10. Dust the coat rack. Replace missing hangers and laundry bags.
    Sacuda la barra para ganchos. Reponga los ganchos que falten y las bolsas de lavandería.

11. Brush lampshades with a dry cloth or feather duster.
    Cepille las pantallas de las luces con un trapo seco o con un plumero.

12. Vacuum the carpet, including under the bed.
    Aspire la alfombra, incluyendo debajo de la cama.

13. Clean window glass and mirrors with window cleaner.
    Limpie los vidrios y espejos con líquido limpiador.

14. Adjust the curtains and sheers to close at the center of the window.
    Ajuste las cortinas y los visillos para que se encuentren en el centro de la ventana.

15. Report anything not working to your supervisor.
    Comunique a su supervisor(a) cualquier desperfecto.

16. Adjust heater or air conditioner thermostat as instructed.
    Ajuste el termostato de la calefacción o el aire acondicionado según instrucciones.

17. If the room has a balcony, dust tables and chairs and sweep the floor. Make sure the balcony door is locked from the inside.
    Si el cuarto tiene terraza, sacuda las sillas y las mesas y barra el suelo. Asegúrese de que la puerta de la terraza está cerrada desde dentro.

18. Give a last look, turn off the lights, lock the door and wipe the door from the outside.
    Eche un vistazo final, apague las luces, cierre la puerta con llave y sacuda el exterior de la puerta.

19. Check the status of the room in your daily report and proceed to make the next room.
    Marque el estado de la habitación en su reporte de camarista y diríjase a hacer el cuarto siguiente.

Making the Bed (*Hacer la cama*)

1. Place the bottom sheet on the mattress. Tuck it in at the head of bed and on the side.
   Coloque la sábana bajera sobre el colchón. Remétala en la cabecera y a lo largo del colchón.

2. Place the top sheet, leaving about six inches at the foot of the bed to be mitered later.
   Coloque la sábana encimera, dejando unas seis pulgadas al pie de la cama para poder hacer ingletes más adelante.

3. Place the blanket over the top sheet, leaving uncovered about nine inches from the head of the bed. Fold the top sheet across the top of the blanket.
   Coloque la manta sobre la sábana encimera, dejando descubiertas unas nueve pulgadas en la cabecera. Doble la sábana encimera sobre el borde de la manta.

4. Tuck the top sheet and blanket and miter both sides of the foot of the bed.
   Remeta la sábana encimera y la manta y haga ingletes en ambos lados del pie de la cama.

5. Place the bedspread so that it just misses touching the floor on the three sides of the bed. Pull it about twelve inches from the headboard and place the pillows about fifteen inches from the headboard on top of the turned back spread.
   Coloque el cobertor de manera que casi toque el suelo por los tres lados de la cama. Vuelva el cobertor en la cabecera de la cama y retírelo unas doce pulgadas, colocando las almohadas unas quince pulgadas de la cabecera sobre el cobertor vuelto.

6. Roll the bedspread and the pillows towards the head.
   Haga rodar el cobertor y las almohadas hacia la cabecera de la cama.

7. Do the opposite side of the bed.
   Haga el lado opuesto de la cama.

Turndown Service *(Servicio de Cortesías)*

1. Pull out the bedspread from the bed and place it on a chair or in the closet.
   Retire el cobertor de la cama y colóquelo sobre una silla o en el clóset.

2. Make a triangle with the corner of the sheet and blanket and fold it back.
   Haga un triángulo con la esquina de la sábana y la manta y dóblelo hacia atrás.

3. Close the drapes and turn on one of the lamps in the room.
   Cierre las cortinas y encienda una de las lámparas de la habitación.

4. Place chocolates, candy, fruit, or cookies in a visible place.
   Coloque chocolates, dulces, fruta o galletas en un sitio visible.

Bathroom Cleaning *(Limpieza del Baño)*

1. Room attendants should use plastic or rubber gloves when cleaning guest or public bathrooms.
   Las camaristas deben usar guantes de goma o plástico en la limpieza de cuartos de baño o baños públicos.

2. Turn on all lights and flush the toilet. Place bowl cleaner and let stand a few minutes.
   Encienda las luces y descargue el tanque del inodoro. Coloque el líquido limpiador de inodoros y déjelo unos minutos para que haga su efecto.

3. Clean the inside of the toilet with a johnny mop, rubbing under the rim.
   Limpie el interior del inodoro con una escobilla, frotando bajo el reborde.

4. Clean under the toilet seat and the outside of the toilet using germicidal.
   Limpie bajo la tapa y el exterior del inodoro usando germicida.

5. Spray cleaning liguid on walls, tub, soap dish, and shower curtain. Scrub all areas with a sponge, particularly the bottom of the shower curtain.
   Rocíe líquido limpiador sobre las paredes, la bañera, la jabonera y la cortina de baño. Frote todas estas áreas con una esponja, particularmente la parte de abajo de la cortina de baño.

6. Wipe chrome fixtures with a dry cloth, including the shower head.
   Frote los accesorios de cromo con un trapo seco, incluyendo la regadera.

7. Use a soft scouring powder to clean the inside of the tub.
   Use polvo limpiador suave para limpiar el fondo de la bañera.

8. Pull the tub stopper out of the tub and clean it. Dry the shower door, if there is one.
   Retire el tapón de la bañera y límpielo fuera de la tina. Seque la puerta de la ducha, si la hubiera.

9. Clean the sink, the sink stopper, and the vanity, and wipe dry all faucets.

   Limpie el lavabo, el tapón del lavabo y el tocador, y seque y dé brillo a todos los grifos.

10. Replace toilet paper and facial tissue as needed.

    Reponga el papel higiénico y los pañuelos de papel si fuera necesario.

11. Clean the mirrors with a damp cloth. Make sure the mirror is spotless.

    Limpie los espejos con un trapo húmedo. Asegúrese de que no quedan manchas en los espejos.

12. Wipe the floor with a damp cloth and germicidal, removing any hair and dirt.

    Frote el suelo con un trapo húmedo y germicida, recogiendo cabellos y suciedad.

13. Restock clean towels, bath mat, and guest supplies. Take a final look before leaving the bathroom.

    Coloque toallas limpias, tapete de baño y suministros de baño. Dé un vistazo final, asegurándose de que todo está en orden.

PART VI

The Engineering Department

Technical Vocabulary

---

air-conditioned
aire acondicionado
(áh-ee-reh ah-cohn-dee-see-oh-náh-doh)

air exhaust
extractor de aire
(ehs-trahc-tóhr deh áh-ee-reh)

algae
algas
(áhl-gahs)

algicide
alguicida
(ahl-guee-sée-dah)

beach
playa
(pláh-yah)

bearing
rodamiento
(roh-dah-mee-éhn-toh)

belt
correa
(coh-rréh-ah)

blade (tool)
hoja
(óh-hah)

113

blower
soplador
(soh-plah-dóhr)

board (wood)
tabla
(táh-blah)

boiler
caldera
(cahl-déh-rah)

branch
rama
(ráh-mah)

breakdown
avería
(ah-beh-rée-ah)

brick
ladrillo
(lah-drée-yoh)

broken
roto
(róh-toh)

broom
escoba
(ehs-cóh-bah)

brush
cepillo
(seh-pée-yoh)

bush
arbusto
(ahr-bóos-toh)

cable
cable
(cáh-bleh)

carpenter
carpintero
(cahr-peen-téh-roh)

carpet
alfombra
(ahl-fóhm-brah)

cement
cemento
(seh-méhn-toh)

chain saw
sierra de cadena
(see-éh-rrah deh cah-déh-nah)

chemicals
productos químicos
(proh-dóoc-tohs kée-mee-cohs)

chlorine
cloro
(clóh-roh)

cockroach
cucaracha
(coo-cah-ráh-chah)

coil
serpentín
(sehr-pehn-téen)

compressor
compresor
(cohm-preh-sóhr)

concrete
concreto
(cohn-créh-toh)

copper sulfate
sulfato de cobre
(sool-fáh-toh deh cóh-breh)

courtyard
patio
(páh-tee-oh)

curtain
cortina
(cohr-tée-nah)

(to) cut
cortar
(cohr-táhr)

(to) dig
cavar
(cah-báhr)

ditch
zanja
(sáhn-hah)

drain
coladera
(coh-lah-déh-rah)

drainage
drenaje
(dreh-náh-heh)

duct
ducto
(dóoc-toh)

electricity
electricidad
(eh-lehc-tree-see-dáhd)

emergency lighting
luces de emergencia
(lóo-sehs deh eh-mehr-héhn-see-ah)

enamel
esmalte
(ehs-máhl-teh)

engineering
ingeniería
(een-heh-nee-eh-rée-ah)

erosion
erosión
(eh-roh-see-óhn)

exit light
luz de salida
(loos deh sah-lée-dah)

fan
ventilador
(behn-tee-lah-dóhr)

faucet
grifo
(grée-foh)

fence
cerca
(séhr-cah)

(to) fertilize
abonar
(ah-boh-náhr)

fertilizer
abono
(ah-bóh-noh)

fire detector
detector de fuego
(deh-tehc-tóhr deh foo-éh-goh)

filter
filtro
(féel-troh)

fire extinguisher
extinguidor
(ehs-teen-guee-dóhr)

flat roof
azotea
(ah-soh-téh-ah)

float
flotador
(floh-tah-dóhr)

flower
flor
(flohr)

flower pot
maceta
(mah-séh-tah)

fluorescent tube
tubo fluorescente
(tóo-boh floo-oh-rehs-séhn-teh)

fountain
fuente
(foo-éhn-teh)

freezer
congelador
(cohn-heh-lah-dóhr)

furniture
muebles
(moo-éh-blehs)

fuse
fusible
(foo-sée-bleh)

game room
salón de juegos
(sah-lóhn deh hoo-éh-gohs)

garbage disposal
triturador
(tree-too-rah-dóhr)

garden
jardín
(hahr-déen)

garden path
andador
(ahn-dah-dóhr)

gardener
jardinero(jardinera)
(hahr-dee-néh-roh) (hahr-dee-néh-rah)

gas
gasolina
(gah-soh-lée-nah)

gloves
guantes
(goo-áhn-tehs)

(to) graft
injertar
(een-hehr-táhr)

grass
hierba
(ee-éhr-bah)

gravel
cascajo
(cahs-cáh-hoh)

grease trap
trampa de grasa
(tráhm-pah deh gráh-sah)

guest room
habitación
(ah-bee-tah-see-óhn)

hammer
martillo
(mahr-tée-yoh)

heating
calefacción
(cah-leh-fahk-see-óhn)

hedge
seto
(séh-toh)

herbicide
herbicida
(ehr-bee-sée-dah)

hinge
bisagra
(bee-sáh-grah)

hoe
azadón
(ah-sah-dóhn)

hole
hoyo
(óh-yoh)

hose
manguera
(mahn-guéh-rah)

insect
insecto
(een-séhc-toh)

insecticide
insecticida
een-sehc-tee-sée-dah)

irrigation water
agua para riego
(áh-goo-ah páh-rah ree-éh-goh)

laundry
lavandería
(lah-bahn-deh-rée-ah)

lawn
césped
(séhs-pehd)

lawn mower
cortadora de césped
(cohr-tah-dóh-rah deh séhs-pehd)

leaf
hoja
(óh-hah)

leak
fuga
(fóo-gah)

light bulb
foco
(fóh-coh)

light plate
placa
(pláh-cah)

light switch
apagador
(ah-pah-gah-dóhr)

lime
cal
(cahl)

lock
cerradura
(seh-rrah-dóo-rah)

locker room
vestidor
(behs-tee-dóhr)

(to) lubricate
lubricar
(loo-bree-cáhr)

maintenance
mantenimiento
(mahn-teh-nee-mee-éhn-toh)

maintenance shop
taller
(tah-yéhr)

manure
estiércol
(ehs-tee-éhr-cohl)

mirror
espejo
(ehs-péh-hoh)

mouse
ratón
(rah-tóhn)

mousetrap
ratonera
(rah-toh-néh-rah)

(to) mow the lawn
cortar el césped
(cohr-táhr ehl séhs-pehd)

nail
clavo
(cláh-boh)

(to) nail
clavar
(clah-báhr)

nozzle
boquilla
(boh-kée-yah)

oil
aceite
(ah-séh-ee-teh)

(to) oil
lubricar
(loo-bree-cáhr)

out of order
fuera de servicio
(foo-éh-rah deh sehr-bée-see-oh)

(to) overwater
poner demasiada agua
(poh-néhr deh-mah-see-áh-dah áh-goo-ah)

packing (faucet)
empaque
(ehm-páh-keh)

paint
pintura
(peen-tóo-rah)

(to) paint
pintar
(peen-táhr)

palm tree
palmera
(pahl-méh-rah)

parking lot
estacionamiento
(ehs-tah-see-oh-nah-mee-éhn-toh)

part
pieza
(pee-éh-sah)

pest control
control de plagas
(cohn-tróhl deh pláh-gahs)

pesticide
pesticida
(pehs-tee-sée-dah)

pipe
tubo
(tóo-boh)

piping
tubería
(too-beh-rée-ah)

plant
planta
(pláhn-tah)

(to) plant
plantar
(plahn-táhr)

plaster
yeso
(yéh-soh)

playground
juegos infantiles
(hoo-éh-gohs een-fahn-tée-lehs)

pliers
alicates
(ah-lee-cáh-tehs)

plumber
plomero
(ploh-méh-roh)

plumbing
plomería
(ploh-meh-rée-ah)

potable water
agua potable
(áh-goo-ah poh-táh-bleh)

pressure
presión
(preh-see-óhn)

pressure gage
manómetro
(mah-nóh-meh-troh)

preventive maintenance
mantenimiento preventivo
(mahn-teh-nee-mee-éhn-toh preh-behn-tée-boh)

(to) prune
podar
(poh-dáhr)

pulley
polea
(poh-léh-ah)

pump
bomba
(bóhm-bah)

rake
rastrillo
(rahs-trée-yoh)

rat
rata
(ráh-tah)

register box
caja de registro
(cáh-hah deh reh-hées-troh)

(to) repair
reparar
(reh-pah-ráhr)

rock
piedra
(pee-éh-drah)

rodent
roedor
(roh-eh-dóhr)

root
raíz
(rah-ées)

rototiller
aflojador de tierra
(ah-floh-hah-dóhr deh tee-éh-rrah)

rubber boots
botas de agua
(bóh-tahs deh áh-goo-ah)

rubber gloves
guantes de goma
(goo-áhn-tehs deh góh-mah)

sand
arena
(ah-réh-nah)

saw
sierra
(see-éh-rrah)

screen
tela de alambre
(téh-lah deh ah-láhm-breh)

screw
tornillo
(tohr-née-yoh)

screwdriver
destornillador
(dehs-tohr-nee-yah-dóhr)

screw nut
tuerca
(too-éhr-cah)

screw valve
válvula de cierre
(báhl-boo-lah deh see-éh-rreh)

(to) seed
sembrar
(sehm-bráhr)

short circuit
cortocircuito
(cohr-toh-seer-coo-ée-toh)

shovel
pala
(páh-lah)

shower
regadera
(reh-gah-déh-rah)

shut-off valve
llave de paso
(yáh-beh deh páh-soh)

sink (kitchen)
fregadero
(freh-gah-déh-roh)

sink (room)
lavamanos
(lah-bah-máh-nohs)

smoke detector
detector de humo
(deh-tehc-tóhr deh óo-moh)

soil
tierra
(tee-éh-rrah)

(to) spray
rociar
(roh-see-áhr)

(to) spray chemicals
fumigar
(foo-mee-gáhr)

sprinkler
regadera
(reh-gah-déh-rah)

stone
piedra
(pee-éh-drah)

storeroom
almacén
(ahl-mah-séhn)

strain
filtro
(féel-troh)

swimming pool
piscina
(pee-seé-nah)

swimming pool
alberca
(ahl-béhr-cah)

tank
tanque
(táhn-keh)

tennis court
cancha de tenis
(cáhn-chah deh téh-nees)

thermostat
termostato
(tehr-mohs-táh-toh)

tile
baldosa
(bahl-dóh-sah)

toilet
inodoro
(ee-noh-dóh-roh)

tool
herramienta
(eh-rrah-mee-éhn-tah)

toolbox
caja de herramientas
(cáh-hah deh eh-rrah-mee-éhn-tahs)

(to) transplant
transplantar
(trahns-plahn-táhr)

trash
basura
(bah-sóo-rah)

trash bag
bolsa de basura
(bóhl-sah deh bah-sóo-rah)

trash can
cubo de basura
(cóo-boh deh bah-sóo-rah)

tree
árbol
(áhr-bohl)

trench
zanja
(sáhn-hah)

(to) vacuum
aspirar
(ahs-pee-ráhr)

valve
válvula
(báhl-boo-lah)

varnish
barniz
(bahr-nées)

(to) varnish
barnizar
(bahr-nee-sáhr)

voltage
voltaje
(bohl-táh-heh)

walk-in freezer
cámara congeladora
(cáh-mah-rah cohn-heh-lah-dóh-rah)

walk-in refrigerator
cámara fría
(cáh-mah-rah frée-ah)

wall
pared
(pah-réhd)

wallpaper
papel tapiz
(pah-péhl tah-pées)

waste
desperdicio
(dehs-pehr-dée-see-oh)

waste water
aguas negras
(áh-goo-ahs néh-grahs)

water
agua
(áh-goo-ah)

(to) water
regar
(reh-gáhr)

(to) weed
escardar
(ehs-cahr-dáhr)

wheelbarrow
carretilla
(cah-rreh-tée-yah)

wire
alambre
(ah-láhm-breh)

wood
madera
(mah-déh-rah)

work order
orden de trabajo
(óhr-dehn deh trah-báh-hoh)

Professional Interaction

Professional Interaction with Maintenance Workers

1. When work is completed, fill in the work request and return it to the initiating department.
   Después de terminar un trabajo, rellene la orden de trabajo, devolviéndola al departamento correspondiente.

2. Give preference to items dealing with guest security and safety.
   Dé preferencia a los trabajos relativos a la protección y seguridad de los clientes.

3. This is the restaurant's gas shut-off valve.
   Esta es la válvula de paso de gas del restaurante.

4. This is the hotel's main electricity switch.
   Este es el interruptor principal de electricidad del hotel.

5. All room thermometers must always be calibrated.
   Los termostatos de las habitaciones deben estar calibrados en todo momento.

6. Do you know how to change air-conditioner filters?
   ¿Sabe usted cambiar los filtros de los acondicionadores de aire?

7. The fans and fan motors must be kept clean and lubricated.
   Los ventiladores y sus motores deben mantenerse limpios y engrasados.

8. Repair the evaporator and condenser of this air-conditioning unit.
   Repare el evaporador y el condensador de esta unidad de aire acondicionado.

9. The drain of the condensation pan is clogged.
   El desagüe del colector de condensación está atascado.

10. There is a leak in the refrigeration system.
    Hay una fuga en el sistema de refrigeración.

11. The lamp switch in room 105 is not working.
    El apagador de lámpara en el cuarto ciento cinco no funciona.

12. Replace the burned-out bulbs in the hallway.
    Cambie los focos fundidos en el corredor.

13. Repair the cord of this vacuum cleaner.
    Repare el cable de esta aspiradora.

14. The plug in the women's restroom is dead.
    El enchufe en el baño de damas no funciona.

15. Replace the wall plate behind the bed.
    Cambie el embellecedor detrás de la cama.

16. Replace the light bulbs with 100-watt ones.
    Cambie los focos por otros de 100 vatios.

17. The sound on the T.V. set in room 106 isn't working.
    El sonido del televisor en la habitación ciento seis no funciona.

18. Call the front desk and put the room out of order.
    Llame a recepción y ponga el cuarto fuera de servicio.

19. Replace the T.V. set in room 107.
    Cambie el televisor en la habitación ciento siete.

20. Adjust the picture of the T.V. set in the lobby.
    Ajuste la imagen en el televisor del vestíbulo.

21. The drawer of this desk does not close.
    El cajón de este escritorio no cierra bien.

22. The door needs a new hinge.
    La puerta necesita una bisagra nueva.

23. Varnish these tables and chairs.
    Barnice estas mesas y sillas.

24. Will you please hang the pictures above the beds?
    Por favor, cuelgue los cuadros sobre las camas.

25. This window needs a new latch.
    Esta ventana necesita un pestillo nuevo.

26. The sliding door is stuck.
    La puerta corrediza está atrancada.

27. Please hang the curtain in room 108.
    Por favor, cuelgue la cortina en la habitación ciento ocho.

28. Clean up the tracks of the sliding doors of the second floor.
    Limpie los carriles de las puertas corredizas del segundo piso.

29. The door handle is loose.
    La perilla de la puerta está floja.

30. Room 102's door lock must be replaced immediately.
    La cerradura del cuarto ciento dos debe ser cambiada inmediatamente.

31. The bathroom door does not fit well.
    La puerta del baño no encaja bien.

32. We are going to install peepholes in all the guest rooms.
    Vamos a instalar mirillas en todas las habitaciones de clientes.

33. The storeroom door needs a door stopper.
    La puerta del almacén necesita un tope.

34. Check all drains in this bathroom.
    Compruebe todos los desagües de este baño.

35. The tub needs a drain plug.
    La bañera necesita un tapón de desagüe.

36. Have you replaced the shower head?
    ¿Ha cambiado la regadera?

37. Replace the missing tiles and grout them.
    Coloque las losetas que faltan y enléchelas.

38. The toilet does not flush and has a leak.
    El inodoro no descarga y tiene una fuga.

39. Replace the toilet seat in the men's bathroom.
    Cambie el asiento del inodoro en el baño de caballeros.

40. The cold water faucet needs a new washer.
    El grifo de agua fría necesita una arandela nueva.

41. The toilet paper holder needs repairing.
    El soporte del rollo de papel higiénico necesita ser reparado.

42. Fix the soap dish in the bathtub.
    Arregle la jabonera de la bañera.

43. The towel rack has fallen down.
    El toallero se ha caído.

44. Paint the walls of the dishwasher area.
    Pinte las paredes en el área del lavaplatos.

45. Check all emergency exit lights.
    Compruebe todas las luces de las salidas de emergencia.

46. Fill the cracks in the walls behind the vanity.
    Rellene las grietas en la pared detrás del tocador.

47. Check the batteries of the smoke detectors.
    Compruebe las pilas de los detectores de humo.

48. Repair the chip on the kitchen counter.
Arregle la desportilladura en el mostrador de la cocina.

49. Bring these work orders to housekeeping.
Lleve estas órdenes de trabajo al departamento de ama de llaves.

50. The packing in this faucet leaks.
La empaquetadura de este grifo tiene una fuga.

51. Do you know how to replace fluorescent tubes?
¿Sabe usted cambiar tubos fluorescentes?

52. All exit lights in the basement must always be on.
Todas las luces de salida en el sótano deben estar siempre encendidas.

53. The garbage disposal in the kitchen is stuck.
El triturador en la cocina está atascado.

Professional Interaction with Swimming Pool Attendants

1. Your responsibility is the swimming pool and its surrounding area.
Su responsabilidad en este puesto es la alberca y el área adyacente.

2. Pick up all trash from the floor and empty the trash cans often.
Recoja la basura del suelo y vacíe los cubos a menudo.

3. Sweep the leaves from pathways.
Barra las hojas en los andadores.

4. Set up long chairs in the morning and fold them up in the evening before ending your shift.
Coloque las tumbonas por la mañana y dóblelas por la tarde antes de teminar su turno.

5. Clean trash from the beach using a rake.
Limpie la basura de la playa usando un rastrillo.

6. Keep a stock of clean towels at all times.
Mantenga un stock de toallas limpias en todo momento.

7. Before giving towels out, ask guests to sign a receipt.
Antes de dar las toallas, pida a los clientes que firmen un recibo.

8. Pick up used towels left behind by guests.
Recoja las toallas abandonadas por los clientes.

9. Bring soiled towels to the laundry room.
Lleve las toallas usadas a la lavandería.

10. Vacuum the pool's inside as soon as you start the shift.
Aspire el interior de la piscina tan pronto como entre de turno.

11. Pick up leaves and floating objects using the pole and net.
    Recoja las hojas y los objetos flotantes usando el palo con la red.

12. Test the water using the chemicals kit.
    Examine el agua utilizando el comprobador químico.

13. Clean the filters as needed to keep the water clean.
    Limpie los filtros cuando sea necesario para mantener el agua limpia.

14. Scrub the pool wall at water level with a hand brush to clean the accumulated grime.
    Frote la pared de la alberca con cepillo de mano para limpiar la suciedad acumulada.

15. The water must be purified daily by adding chemicals.
    El agua es purificada diariamente añadiendo substancias químicas.

16. Pick up plastic glasses and beverage cans left by guests.
    Recoja los vasos de plástico y botes de bebidas dejados por los clientes.

17. Mop up water on the locker room floor regularly.
    Trapée el agua del piso del vestuario regularmente.

18. The boiler temperature is set at seventy degrees.
    La temperatura de la caldera se sitúa a setenta grados.

19. Keep children from running in the pool area.
    Evite que los niños corran en el área de la alberca.

20. Hose down the floor at the end of your shift.
    Lave el suelo con la manguera antes de terminar su turno.

21. Before cleaning the strainers, close the water valve.
    Antes de limpiar los filtros, cierre las llaves de paso del agua.

22. The pH level of the water must be maintained between 7.2 and 7.6.
    El nivel pH del agua debe mantenerse entre 7.2 y 7.6.

23. If the water's pH level gets over 7.6, add muriatic acid to bring it down.
    Si el nivel pH del agua sube más de 7.6, añada ácido muriático para rebajarlo.

24. Always test the water before adding chlorine to the pool.
    Analice siempre el agua antes de añadir cloro a la alberca.

25. To control de growth of algae, use the algicide in this pail.
    Para controlar el crecimiento de algas, utilice el alguicida de este cubo.

26. Keep the water temperature at about seventy-five degrees.
    Mantenga la temperatura del agua a alrededor de setenta y cinco grados.

Personal Interaction with Gardeners and Ground Keepers

1. The garden area must be swept often. Pick up leaves, branches and trash.
   El área de jardines debe ser barrida a menudo. Recoja hojas, ramas y desperdicios.

2. Turn on the sprinklers to water the grass.
   Abra la llave de los rociadores para regar el césped.

3. Bushes and trees are watered using a hose.
   Los arbustos y árboles son regados con manguera.

4. Flower pots are watered by hand.
   Las macetas se riegan a mano.

5. Your job includes pruning trees, including palm trees.
   Su trabajo incluye la poda de árboles y palmeras.

6. Please dig a trench here to install a water pipe for irrigation.
   Por favor, cave una zanja aquí para instalar una tubería de riego.

7. The flower beds are fertilized with manure before planting.
   Los arriates se abonan con estiércol antes de plantarse.

8. Plants and trees are sprayed once a month.
   Las plantas y árboles se fumigan una vez al mes.

9. The fountains are emptied and cleaned to avoid algae growth.
   Las fuentes se vacían y limpian para evitar el crecimiento de algas.

10. You are responsible for the upkeep of the gardening equipment.
    Usted es responsable de la conservación del equipo de jardinería.

11. Cut the hedge to a height of three feet.
    Corte el seto a una altura de tres pies.

12. When spraying insecticides, please use a mouth mask.
    Cuando fumigue con insecticidas, favor de colocarse una mascarilla.

13. Do you know how to graft trees?
    ¿Sabe usted injertar árboles?

14. Dig a hole here to plant this shrub.
    Haga un hoyo aquí para plantar este arbusto.

15. Cut the grass with the lawnmower.
    Corte la hierba con la cortadora de césped.

16. There is not enough pressure in the sprinklers.
    No hay suficiente presión en los rociadores.

17. Remove the snow from sidewalks in front of the restaurant.
    Quite la nieve de las aceras enfrente del restaurante.

18. The entrance to the hotel must be swept very often.
    La entrada del hotel debe ser barrida a menudo.

19. Can you operate a mechanic sweeper?
    ¿Sabe usted maniobrar una barredora mecánica?

20. Use a hose to water the trees in the parking lot.
    Use una manguera para regar los árboles del estacionamiento.

21. Keep the lids of the trash containers shut.
    Mantenga cerradas las tapas de los basureros.

22. Bring a bucket of gravel to fill this empty space.
    Traiga un cubo de cascajo para rellenar este espacio vacío.

23. Paint the fence around the swimming pool.
    Pinte la cerca alrededor de la alberca.

24. Open the tennis court gate early in the morning.
    Abra la entrada de las canchas de tenis por la mañana temprano.

25. If you have any problems, call the engineering department.
    Si tiene problemas, llame al departamento de ingeniería.

26. The weeds on the garden path are killed with herbicide.
    Las malas hierbas en los andadores del jardín se destruyen con herbicida.

27. This is irrigation water; don't drink it.
    Esta agua es para regar; no la beba.

28. Only one-third or less of the grass blades should be cut at any one time.
    Solamente corte un tercio o menos de la altura de la hierba cada vez que la corte.

Engineering Position Descriptions

Maintenance Worker (*Mecánico*)

Reports to Plant Manager   *Reporta al jefe de mantenimiento*
Position Responsibility   *Responsabilidod del Puesto*

1. Keep the guest rooms and public areas in working condition.
   Mantener las habitaciones de clientes y las áreas públicas en condición operativa.

2. Do smaller repair jobs as requested on work orders.
   Hacer reparaciones básicas indicadas en las ordenes de trabajo.

3. Perform smaller repairs in the back-of-the-house areas.
   Realizar trabajos básicos en las áreas de servicio no expuestas al público.

4. Fill in completed work requests, sending one copy to the originating department and one to the engineering file.
   Rellenar las órdenes de trabajos realizados, enviando una copia al departamento correspondiente y otra al archivo de mantenimiento.

5. Keep strict control of tools and material.
   Mantener un control estricto de herramientas y material.

6. Report major defects to the maintenance department.
   Comunicar desperfectos de importancia al departamento de mantenimiento.

7. Perform preventive maintenance in guest rooms and of machinery.
   Realizar mantenimiento preventivo en los cuartos de clientes y la maquinaria.

8. Perform safety checks throughout the property.
   Realizar inspecciones de seguridad en todas las áreas del establecimiento.

9. Note in the log book any anomaly for the attention of the chief engineer.
   Anotar en el libro de bitácora cualquier anomalía para el conocimiento del (de la) jefe de mantenimiento.

Pool Attendant (*Encargado(a) de albercas*)

1. Keep the pool area clean and organized.
   Mantener el área de albercas limpia y en orden.
2. Keep a par stock of chemicals, cleaning supplies, and equipment.
   Mantener un stock adecuado de productos químicos, artículos de limpieza y equipo.
3. Keep control of pool furniture and towels.
   Mantener control de los muebles y toallas de alberca.
4. Keep the proper level of chemicals to ensure cleanliness of the water.
   Mantener un adecuado nivel de productos químicos para asegurar la limpieza del agua.
5. Change filters regularly.
   Cambiar regularmente los filtros.
6. Enforce safety regulations to be followed by guests in the pool area.
   Imponer las reglas de seguridad que deben seguir los clientes en el área de albercas.
7. Keep the water temperature at the right level.
   Mantener la temperatura del agua a nivel adecuado.
8. Request chemicals and cleaning supplies weekly from the storeroom.
   Solicitar productos químicos y suministros de limpieza del almacén semanalmente.
9. Monitor the functioning of the water-processing equipment, notifying maintenance of any breakdown or malfunction.
   Observar el funcionamiento del equipo purificador de agua, notificando al departamento de mantenimiento cualquier rotura o funcionamiento defectuoso.
10. Prohibit alcohol-impaired guests and small children without adult supervision from using the pool.
    Impedir a huéspedes bebidos y a niños pequeños no acompañados de adultos el uso de la alberca.
11. Prohibit glass containers in the pool area.
    Prohibir recipientes de vidrio en el área de albercas.

Gardener/Groundskeeper *(Jardinero(a)/Limpieza Exterior)*

Reports to Plant Manager   *Reporta de jefe de mantenimiento*
Position Responsibility   *Responsabilitad del puesto*

1. Maintain the hotel grounds and garden areas in perfect condition.
   Mantener las áreas exteriores del hotel y los jardines en perfecto estado.

2. Pick up any debris in the hotel grounds, servicing the trash containers often.
   Recoger los desperdicios en el exterior del hotel, ocupándose a menudo de los cubos de basura.

3. Fertilize, irrigate, and mow the lawn.
   Abonar, regar y cortar el césped.

4. Plant, prune, and water trees and shrubs.
   Plantar, podar y regar los arboles y arbustos.

5. Plan the planting of flowers and the property's landscaping.
   Planificar el plantado de flores y de la jardinería ornamental de la propiedad.

6. Use herbicides and pesticides to eliminate plant disease and weeds.
   Usar herbicidas y pesticidas para eliminar las malas hierbas y plagas en las plantas.

7. Keep control of gardening equipment and supplies.
   Controlar el equipo de jardinería y suministros.

8. Turn the irrigation system on and off.
   Conectar y desconectar el sistema de riego.

9. Prepare the soil for planting and transplanting flowers and bushes.
   Preparar la tierra para plantar y transplantar flores y arbustos.

10. Landscape the hotel grounds with rock and gravel.
    Hacer trabajo ornamental con rocas y cascajo en el exterior del hotel.

PART VII

The Restaurant

Technical Vocabulary

appetizer
aperitivo
(ah-peh-ree-tée-boh)

ashtray
cenicero
(seh-nee-séh-roh)

banquet
banquete
(bahn-kéh-teh)

bar
bar
(bahr)

base plate
plato base
(pláh-toh báh-seh)

beer
cerveza
(sehr-béh-sah)

beverages
bebidas
(beh-bée-dahs)

bill
cuenta
(coo-éhn-tah)

bowl
tazón
(tah-sóhn)

bow tie
palomita
(pah-loh-mée-tah)

bread
pan
(pahn)

bread basket
cesta para pan
(séhs-tah páh-rah pahn)

bread plate
plato para pan
(pláh-toh páh-rah pahn)

bread warmer
calentador de pan
(cah-lehn-tah-dóhr deh pahn)

buffet
buffet
(boo-féh)

bus tub
cubeta
(coo-béh-tah)

busperson
ayudante de mesero
(ah-yoo-dáhn-teh deh meh-séh-roh)

butter
mantequilla
(mahn-teh-kée-yah)

canape
canapé
(cah-nah-péh)

cashier
cajero(cajera)
(cah-héh-roh) (cah-héh-rah)

chair
silla
(sée-yah)

cheese
queso
(kéh-soh)

chewing gum
chicle
(chée-cleh)

china
loza
(lóh-sah)

(to) clear the table
retirar el servicio usado
(reh-tee-ráhr ehl sehr-bée-see-oh oo-sáh-doh)

coffee
café
(cah-féh)

coffee break
coffee break
(cóh-fee bréh-eek)

coffee grinder
molino de café
(moh-lée-noh deh cah-féh)

coffee maker
cafetera
(cah-feh-téh-rah)

coffeepot
jarra para café
(háh-rrah páh-rah cah-féh)

coffee warmer
plato caliente
(pláh-toh cah-lee-éhn-teh)

condiments
aderezos
(ah-deh-réh-sohs)

crackers
galletas
(gah-yéh-tahs)

creamer
jarrita para leche
(hah-rrée-tah páh-rah léh-cheh)

crumbs
migajas
(mee-gáh-hahs)

cup
taza
(táh-sah)

customer
cliente
(clee-éhn-teh)

dessert
postre
(póhs-treh)

dessert cart
carro de postres
(cáh-rroh deh póhs-trehs)

dessert plate
plato de postre
(pláh-toh deh póhs-treh)

dining room
comedor
(coh-meh-dóhr)

dishwasher
lavaplatos
(lah-bah-pláh-tohs)

(to) dry
secar
(seh-cáhr)

(to) dust
sacudir
(sah-coo-déer)

fingernails
uñas
(óo-nyahs)

first course
primer plato
(pree-méhr pláh-toh)

food and beverage
alimentos y bebidas
(ah-lee-méhn-tohs ee beh-bée-dahs)

fork
tenedor
(teh-neh-dóhr)

garnish
guarnición
(goo-ahr-nee-see-óhn)

glass
vaso
(báh-soh)

glassware
cristalería
(crees-tah-leh-rée-ah)

goblet
copa
(cóh-pah)

(to) greet
saludar
(sah-loo-dáhr)

grooming
aseo personal
(ah-séh-oh pehr-soh-nahl)

guest
huésped
(oo-éhs-pehd)

high chair
silla de niños
(sée-yah deh née-nyohs)

honey
miel
(mee-éhl)

host (hostess)
host (hostess)
(hohst) (hóhs-tehs)

hot plate
plato caliente
(pláh-toh cah-lee-éhn-teh)

hot water
agua caliente
(áh-goo-ah cah-lee-éhn-teh)

hygiene
higiene
(ee-hee-éh-neh)

ice
hielo
(ee-éh-loh)

ice bucket
hielera
(ee-eh-léh-rah)

ice cream
helado
(eh-láh-doh)

ice cubes
cubitos de hielo
(coo-bée-tohs deh ee-éh-loh)

iced tea
té frío
(teh frée-oh)

jam
mermelada
(mehr-meh-láh-dah)

jam holder
mermeladera
(mehr-meh-lah-déh-rah)

jelly
jalea
(hah-léh-ah)

juice
jugo
(hóo-goh)

ketchup
ketchup
(kéht-choop)

kitchen
cocina
(coh-sée-nah)

knife
cuchillo
(coo-chée-yoh)

lid
tapadera
(tah-pah-déh-rah)

matches
cerillos
(seh-rée-yohs)

meal course
plato
(pláh-toh)

menu
menú
(meh-nóo)

menu item
platillo
(plah-tée-yoh)

microwave oven
microondas
(mee-croh-óhn-dahs)

milk
leche
(léh-cheh)

(to) mop
trapear
(trah-peh-áhr)

mop wringer
escurridor
(ehs-coo-rree-dóhr)

mustard
mostaza
(mohs-táh-sah)

name tag
placa con su nombre
(pláh-cah cohn soo nóhm-breh)

napery
mantelería
(mahn-teh-leh-reé-ah)

napkin
servilleta
(sehr-bee-yéh-tah)

oil and vinegar
aceite y vinagre
(ah-séh-ee-teh ee bee-náh-greh)

orange marmalade
mermelada de naranja
(mehr-meh-láh-dah deh nah-ráhn-hah)

paper towel
toalla de papel
(toh-áh-yah deh pah-péhl)

paperwork
papelería
(pah-peh-leh-rée-ah)

peach jam
mermelada de durazno
(mehr-meh-láh-dah deh doo-ráhs-noh)

pepper
pimienta
(pee-mee-éhn-tah)

pepper shaker
pimentero
(pee-mehn-téh-roh)

place setting
plaqué
(plah-kéh)

plate
plato
(pláh-toh)

(to) refill
rellenar
(reh-yeh-náhr)

requisition
pedido
(peh-dée-doh)

(to) rinse
enjuagar
(ehn-hoo-ah-gáhr)

rim
borde
(bóhr-deh)

rolls
panecillos
(pah-neh-sée-yohs)

room number
número de habitación
(nóo-meh-roh deh ah-bee-tah-see-óhn)

room service
servicio a cuartos
(sehr-bée-see-oh ah coo-áhr-tohs)

room set-up
preparación del salón
(preh-pah-rah-see-óhn dehl sah-lóhn)

salad
ensalada
(ehn-sah-láh-dah)

salad dressing
aderezo para ensaladas
(ah-deh-réh-soh páh-rah ehn-sah-láh-dahs)

salt shaker
salero
(sah-léh-roh)

sanitation
saneamiento
(sah-neh-ah-mee-éhn-toh)

saucer
plato de café
(pláh-toh deh cah-féh)

seafood
mariscos
(mah-rées-cohs)

second course
segundo plato
(seh-góon-doh pláh-toh)

self-service
autoservicio
(ah-oo-toh sehr-bée-see-oh)

(to) serve
servir
(sehr-béer)

service napkin
servilleta de servicio
(sehr-bee-yéh-tah deh sehr-bée-see-oh)

service station
aparador
(ah-pah-rah-dóhr)

service table
mesa de servicio
(méh-sah deh sehr-bée-see-oh)

(to) set the table
poner la mesa
(poh-néhr lah méh-sah)

sheet pan
bandeja
(bahn-déh-hah)

shelf
estante
(ehs-táhn-teh)

shift
turno
(tóor-noh)

side stand
aparador
(ah-pah-rah-dóhr)

silverware
cubertería
(coo-behr-teh-rée-ah)

sink
fregadero
(freh-gah-déh-roh)

soda dispenser
máquina de refrescos
(máh-kee-nah deh reh-fréhs-cohs)

(to) sort
separar
(seh-pah-ráhr)

soup
sopa
(sóh-pah)

soup plate
plato para sopa
(pláh-toh páh-rah sóh-pah)

spoon
cuchara
(coo-cháh-rah)

station
estación
(ehs-tah-see-óhn)

stem
mango
(máhn-goh)

(to) stock
surtir
(soor-téer)

storeroom
almacén
(ahl-mah-séhn)

strawberry jam
mermelada de fresa
(mehr-meh-láh-dah deh fréh-sah)

sugar
azúcar
(ah-sóo-cahr)

sugar bowl
azucarero
(ah-soo-cah-réh-roh)

(to) sweep
barrer
(bah-rréhr)

syrup
jarabe
(hah-ráh-beh)

table
mesa
(méh-sah)

tablecloth
mantel
(mahn-téhl)

(to) take the order
tomar la comanda
(toh-máhr lah coh-máhn-dah)

tea
té
(teh)

teapot
tetera
(teh-téh-rah)

teaspoon
cucharilla
(coo-chah-rée-yah)

tip
propina
(proh-pée-nah)

toaster
tostadora
(tohs-tah-dóh-rah)

to-go cup
vaso "para llevar"
(báh-soh páh-rah yeh-báhr)

tongs
pinzas
(péen-sahs)

tray
charola
(chah-róh-lah)

tray stand
tijeras
(tee-héh-rahs)

uniform
uniforme
(oo-nee-fóhr-meh)

waiter(waitress)
mesero(mesera)
(meh-séh-roh) (meh-séh-rah)

water
agua
(áh-goo-ah)

water glass
vaso para agua
(báh-soh páh-rah áh-goo-ah)

water jar
jarra para agua
(háh-rrah páh-rah áh-goo-ah)

wine
vino
(bée-noh)

wine list
carta de vinos
(cáhr-tah deh bée-nohs)

(to) wipe down
limpiar
(leem-pee-áhr)

(to) wrap
envolver
(ehn-bohl-béhr)

Professional Interaction

Professional Interaction with buspersons/servers

1. Do you prefer to work the morning or evening shift?
   ¿Prefiere trabajar el turno de mañana o el de tarde?

2. Show up for work five minutes before your shift starts.
   Preséntese a trabajar cinco minutos antes de que comience su turno.

3. You must come to work (shaved), well groomed, and wearing shiny black shoes.
   Debe venir a trabajar (afeitado), bien aseado(a) y llevando zapatos negros lustrados.

4. Your fingernails must be very clean.
   Sus uñas deben estar muy limpias.

5. Wear black pants and a white shirt to work. We provide you with a waiter's jacket.
   Lleve pantalones negros y camisa blanca al trabajo. Nosotros le suministramos chaqueta de camarero.

6. Begin your shift by dusting the furniture and vacuuming the carpet.
   Comience su turno sacudiendo los muebles y aspirando la alfombra.

7. Refill salt and pepper shakers and sugar bowls. Prepare salad dressing containers.
   Rellene los saleros, los pimenteros y los azucareros. Prepare los aderezos para ensaladas.

8. Request supplies from the storeroom.
   Solicite suministros del almacén.

9. Prepare the service area: make coffee, bring rolls to the warmer, and get clean silverware for your station.
   Prepare el área de servicio: haga café, ponga panecillos en el calentador y surta su estación de cubertería limpia.

10. Fill several jugs with ice and water.
    Llene varias jarras con hielo y agua.

11. Make iced tea and cut lemon slices.
    Haga té frío y corte rodajas de limón.

12. Set the tables in your station with napery, glassware, and silverware.
    Prepare las mesas en su estación con mantelería, cristalería y cubertería.

13. Carry glasses on a tray or by the base, never touch the rim.
    Transporte los vasos en una charola o por su base, nunca toque el borde.

14. Carry the silverware on a plate, napkin, or tray. Handle it by the stem.
    Transporte la cubertería en un plato, servilleta o charola. Manipule los utensilios siempre por el mango.

15. Keep the service station supplied with the necessary equipment at all times.
    Acomode el aparador de servicio con el equipo necesario en todo momento.

16. Greet guests when you approach the table for the first time.
    Salude a los clientes cuando se acerque inicialmente a la mesa.

17. Take away the extra table settings.
    Retire los plaqués que no se van a utilizar.

18. Bring bread, water, and butter to the table.
    Lleve pan, agua y mantequilla a la mesa.

19. Refill guest glasses with water frequently.
    Rellene los vasos de los clientes con agua frecuentemente.

20. Serve plates from the guests' left and drinks from the right.
    Sirva los platillos por la izquierda de los clientes y las bebidas por la derecha.

21. Clean empty service from the tables and bring it to the dishwashing area.
    Retire el servicio usado de las mesas y llévelo al área de lavaplatos.

22. Use a tray to bring used material to the kitchen.
    Use una charola para llevar a la cocina el material de servicio usado.

23. Change used ashtrays often.
    Cambie los ceniceros usados frecuentemente.

24. Transport soiled china and silverware separate from glassware.
    Transporte la loza y la cubertería usadas separadamente de la cristalería.

25. Empty bottles are not carried on a tray, but by hand.
   No lleve las botellas vacias en charolas, sino a mano.

26. Show the dessert cart to customers.
   Muestre el carro de postres a los clientes.

27. Leave all tips on the table for the server.
   Deje las propinas en la mesa para el (la) mesero(a).

28. Clean the service area. Dump the trash and place new trash bags in the containers.
   Limpie el área de servicio. Tire la basura y ponga bolsas de basura nuevas en los cubos.

29. Clean the soda dispensers well.
   Limpie bien las máquinas de refrescos.

30. Clean the toaster and turn off all electric appliances.
   Limpie la tostadora y apague todos los aparatos eléctricos.

31. Drain and clean the ice bins.
   Vacíe y limpie las cubetas de hielo.

32. Sweep, vacuum, or mop the floor.
   Barra, aspire o trapée el suelo.

33. Clock out after your shift.
   Marque su tarjeta en el reloj registrador al final de su turno.

34. Fold three dozen napkins with place settings inside.
   Doble tres docenas de servilletas con cubiertos dentro.

35. Cut the fruit pies in six triangles each.
   Corte los pasteles de fruta en seis triángulos cada uno.

36. Carry the bus tray and empty it by the dishwashing machine.
   Lleve la cubeta con el material sucio y vacíela en el área del lavaplatos.

37. Wash the service trays at the end of each shift.
   Lave las charolas de servicio al término de cada turno.

38. Pick up empty containers from the salad bar and replace them with full ones from the kitchen.
   Retire los recipientes vacíos del autoservicio de ensaladas y repóngalos con otros llenos de la cocina.

39. Don't carry the menus under your arm.
   No lleve los menús debajo del brazo.

40. The restaurant floor must always be free of papers and debris.
   El piso del restaurante debe estar siempre limpio de papeles y desperdicios.

41. Restock dining room with china, silverware, glassware, and linen.
   Surta el comedor con loza, cubertería, cristalería y mantelería.

Restaurant Position Description

Busperson (*Ayudante de Mesero*)

Reports to Headwaiter   *Su supervisor inmediato es el (la) jefe de meseros.*
Position responsibility   *Responsabilidad del puesto*

1. Maintain cleanliness and sanitation of the dining room and pantry areas, including floors, tables, chairs, walls, windows, sideboards, equipment, and restrooms.
   Mantener la limpieza y saneamiento en las áreas de comedor y despensa, incluyendo suelos, mesas, sillas, paredes, ventanas, aparadores, equipo y baños públicos.

2. Stock dining room with china, silverware, glassware, utensils, condiments, and linen. Restock these supplies in the work stations when service is in progress.
   Surtir el comedor con loza, cubertería, cristalería, utensilios, condimentos y lencería. Reponer estos suministros en las estaciones de servicio durante el servicio.

3. Prepare beverages needed, such as coffee, iced tea, and hot water.
   Preparar las bebidas necesarias, como café, té frío, y agua caliente.

4. Greet and seat guests if neither the hostess or server is available.
   Saludar y acomodar a los huéspedes si la hostess o el (la) mesero(a) no se encuentran en la sala.

5. Serve water, rolls, and butter to guests. Refill as needed.
   Servir agua, panecillos y mantequilla a los huéspedes. Resurtir cuando sea neceasario.

6. Assist servers with table service if necessary.
   Ayudar a los meseros con el servicio de mesa si es necesario.

Restaurant Procedures

| Dining Room Preservice Requirements | *(Preparación del comedor antes del comienzo del servicio)* |

1. Dust tables, chairs, booths, window sills, and sideboards.
   Sacudir mesas, sillas, banquetas, repisas y aparadores.
2. Vacuum carpet or mop floor.
   Aspirar la alfombra o trapear el piso.
3. Refill condiments, salt and pepper shakers, and sugar bowls.
   Rellenar condimentos, saleros, pimenteros y azucareros.
4. Stock service stations with china, glassware, silverware, and napery.
   Surtir las estaciones de servicio con loza, cristalería, cubertería y lencería.
5. Fill pitchers with iced water.
   Llenar las jarras con agua helada.
6. Set tables with table settings, ashtray, salt and pepper shaker, sugar bowl, and cracker basket.
   Montar la mesa con plaqués, cenicero, salero y pimentero, azucarero y cesto con galletas.

Pantry Setup *(Preparacion de la despensa)*

1. Make coffee and iced tea and place a jug of hot water on a hot plate.
   Hacer café y té helado y colocar una jarra de agua caliente en un plato caliente.
2. Set roll warmer at the right temperature and fill with rolls.
   Colocar el calentador de pan a la temperatura adecuada y surtirlo de panecillos.

3. Restock a backup for all supplies: ketchup, mustard, coffee bags, sugar packets, coffee filters, doilies, paper towels, paper napkins, etc.
   Surtir repuestos de todos los suministros: ketchup, mostaza, bolsas de café, paquetes de azúcar, filtros para café, tapetes de papel, toallas de papel, servilletas de papel, etc.

4. Fill salad dressing containers.
   Llenar los envases de aderezos.

5. Cut lemon slices, check juice machines, and fill creamers.
   Cortar rodajas de limón, verificar las máquinas de jugos y llenar cremeras.

6. Fill ice bin with ice cubes.
   Llene el recipiente de hielo con cubitos.

End-of-Shift Procedures *(Procedimientos al Terminar el Turno)*

1. Clean service stations, tables, chairs, and booths by wiping them down with a damp cloth.
   Limpie las estaciones de servicio, mesas, sillas y banquetas con un trapo húmedo.

2. Dump all trash containers and place new trash bags.
   Saque la basura de todos los cubos y ponga nuevas bolsas de basura.

3. Bring soiled linen to laundry room.
   Lleve la mantelería sucia a la lavandería.

4. Change tablecloths in service tables for clean ones.
   Cambie los manteles de las mesitas de servicio por otros limpios.

5. Sweep or vacuum your station.
   Barra o aspire su estación.

6. Bring any used equipment to the pantry or dishwasher area.
   Lleve todos los utensilios sucios a la despensa o al área de lavaplatos.

7. Wash serving trays with soapy water.
   Lave las charolas de servicio con agua jabonosa.

8. Empty and clean the roll warmer, ice bin, juice machine, coffee makers, dessert counter, and any other equipment and utensils.
   Vacíe y limpie el calentador de pan, el recipiente de hielo, la máquina de jugos, las cafeteras, el mostrador de postres y cualquier otro equipo y utensilios.

9. Disconnect all electrical equipment.
   Desconecte todos los aparatos eléctricos.

10. Wash refrigerator doors, gaskets, counters, and soda fountains with soapy water. Rinse and dry.
    Lave las puertas de los refrigeradores, empaques de goma, mostradores y la máquina de refrescos con agua jabonosa. Aclare y seque.

11. Sign off upon ending your shift.
    Marque su tarjeta en el reloj registrador al finalizar su turno.

PART VIII

The Kitchen

Technical Vocabulary

apple
manzana
(mahn-sáh-nah)

apron
delantal
(deh-lahn-táhl)

bacon
tocino
(toh-sée-noh)

bacteria
bacteria
(bahc-téh-ree-ah)

banana
plátano
(pláh-tah-noh)

basket
cesta
(séhs-tah)

beans
frijoles
(free-hóh-lehs)

beef
carne de res
(cáhr-neh deh rehs)

beefsteak
bistec
(bees-téhc)

(to) boil
hervir
(ehr-béer)

bread
pan
(pahn)

(to) bread
empanar
(ehm-pah-náhr)

breaded
empanado
(ehn-pah-náh-doh)

breakfast
desayuno
(deh-sah-yóo-noh)

broiler
parrilla
(pah-rrée-yah)

bus tub
cubeta
(coo-béh-tah)

butter
mantequilla
(mahn-teh-kée-yah)

cake
pastel
(pahs-téhl)

can
bote
(bóh-teh)

can opener
abrelatas
(ah-breh-láh-tahs)

carrots
zanahorias
(sah-nah-óh-ree-ahs)

celery
apio
(áh-pee-oh)

chef
jefe de cocina
(héh-feh deh coh-sée-nah)

cheese
queso
(kéh-soh)

chicken
pollo
(póh-yoh)

chipped
desportillado
(dehs-pohr-tee-yáh-doh)

chocolate
chocolate
(choh-coh-láh-teh)

(to) chop
cortar
(cohr-táhr)

cleaning solution
líquido limpiador
(lée-kee-doh leem-pee-ah-dóhr)

cloth
trapo
(tráh-poh)

coffee
café
(cah-féh)

coffee cup
taza para café
(táh-sah páh-rah cah-féh)

coffee maker
cafetera
(cah-feh-téh-rah)

colander
colador
(coh-lah-dóhr)

cold
frío
(frée-oh)

cover
tapadera
(tah-pah-déh-rah)

(to) cover
cubrir
(coo-bréer)

cucumber
pepino
(peh-pée-noh)

cup
taza
(táh-sah)

(to) cut
cortar
(cohr-táhr)

cutting board
tabla de cortar
(táh-blah deh cohr-táhr)

decaffeinated
descafeinado
(dehs-cah-feh-ee-náh-doh)

deep fryer
freidora
(freh-ee-dóh-rah)

defrost
descongelar
(dehs-cohn-heh-láhr)

degrees
grados
(gráh-dohs)

dessert
postre
(póhs-treh)

detergent
detergente
(deh-tehr-héhn-teh)

dinner
cena
(séh-nah)

dish
plato
(pláh-toh)

dishwasher
lavaplatos
(lah-bah-pláh-tohs)

dishwasher rack
rejilla
(reh-hée-yah)

dishwashing machine
máquina lavaplatos
(máh-kee-nah lah-bah-pláh-tohs)

dough
masa
(máh-sah)

drain
desagüe
(dehs-áh-gooeh)

(to) drain
vaciar/escurrir
(bah-see-áhr)/(ehs-coo-rréer)

drain valve
válvula de desagüe
(báhl-boo-lah deh dehs-áh-gooeh)

dry
seco
(séh-coh)

(to) dry
secar
(seh-cáhr)

dumpster
vertedero
(behr-teh-déh-roh)

egg
huevo
(oo-éh-boh)

filter
filtro
(féel-troh)

fish
pescado
(pehs-cáh-doh)

flour
harina
(ah-rée-nah)

food scraps
desperdicios
(dehs-pehr-dée-see-ohs)

fork
tenedor
(teh-neh-dóhr)

freezer
congelador
(cohn-heh-lah-dóhr)

french fries
papas fritas
(páh-pahs frée-tahs)

fried
frito
(frée-toh)

frozen
congelado
(cohn-heh-láh-doh)

(to) fry
freír
(freh-éer)

frying pan
sartén
(sahr-téhn)

garbage
desperdicios
(dehs-pehr-dée-see-ohs)

garbage can
cubo de basura
(cóo-boh deh bah-sóo-rah)

garbage disposal
triturador
(tree-too-rah-dóhr)

garnish
guarnición
(goo-ahr-nee-see-óhn)

glass
vaso
(báh-soh)

gloves
guantes
(goo-áhn-tehs)

goblet
copa
(cóh-pah)

grease trap
trampa de grasa
(tráhm-pah deh gráh-sah)

greasy
grasiento
(grah-see-éhn-toh)

griddle
plancha
(pláhn-chah)

grill
parrilla
(pah-rrée-yah)

(to) grill
asar
(ah-sáhr)

grind
picar
(pee-cáhr)

ground meat
carne picada
(cáhr-neh pee-cáh-dah)

hair net
redecilla
(reh-deh-sée-yah)

ham
jamón
(hah-móhn)

hamburger
hamburguesa
(ahm-boor-guéh-sah)

handle
asa
(áh-sah)

hard-boiled egg
huevo duro
(oo-éh-boh dóo-roh)

hood
campana
(cahm-páh-nah)

hot
caliente
(cah-lee-éhn-teh)

ice
hielo
(ee-éh-loh)

ice cream
helado
(eh-láh-doh)

juice
jugo
(hóo-goh)

kettle
marmita
(mahr-mée-tah)

kitchen
cocina
(coh-sée-nah)

knife
cuchillo
(coo-chée-yoh)

ladle
cazo
(cáh-soh)

lemon
limón
(lee-móhn)

lettuce
lechuga
(leh-chóo-gah)

lunch
almuerzo
(ahl-moo-éhr-soh)

mayonnaise
mayonesa
(mah-yoh-néh-sah)

meat
carne
(cáhr-neh)

medium
medio hecho
(méh-dee-oh éh-choh)

melon
melón
(meh-lóhn)

microwave oven
microondas
(mee-croh-óhn-dahs)

milk
leche
(léh-cheh)

milk dispenser
surtidor de leche
(soor-tee-dóhr deh léh-cheh)

(to) mince
picar
(pee-cáhr)

minced
picado
(pee-cáh-doh)

(to) mix
mezclar
(mehs-cláhr)

mixer
mezcladora
(mehs-clah-dóh-rah)

mop
trapeador
(trah-peh-ah-dóhr)

(to) mop
trapear
(trah-peh-áhr)

mushrooms
setas
(séh-tahs)

mustard
mostaza
(mohs-táh-sah)

napkin
servilleta
(sehr-bee-yéh-tah)

napkin holder
servilletero
(sehr-bee-yeh-téh-roh)

oil
aceite
(ah-séh-ee-teh)

omelet
tortilla de huevos
(tohr-tée-yah deh oo-éh-bohs)

onion
cebolla
(seh-bóh-yah)

orange
naranja
(nah-ráhn-hah)

oven
horno
(óhr-noh)

over easy
vuelto poco hecho
(boo-éhl-toh póh-coh eh-choh)

oyster
ostra
(óhs-trah)

pan
cazuela
(cah-soo-éh-lah)

pancake
panqueque
(pahn-kéh-keh)

pantry
despensa
(dehs-péhn-sah)

parsley
perejil
(peh-reh-héel)

pastry
pastelería
(pahs-teh-leh-rée-ah)

(to) peel
pelar
(peh-láhr)

peeled
pelado
(peh-láh-doh)

pepper
pimienta
(pee-mee-éhn-tah)

pie
pastel
(pahs-téhl)

(to) plate
emplatar
(ehm-plah-táhr)

poach
hervir a fuego lento
(ehr-béer ah foo-éh-goh léhn-toh)

pork
puerco
(poo-éhr-coh)

pot
olla
(óh-yah)

potato
papa
(páh-pah)

poultry
carne de ave
(cáhr-neh deh áh-beh)

rag
trapo
(tráh-poh)

rare
poco hecho
(póh-coh éh-choh)

rice
arroz
(ah-rróhs)

(to) rinse
enjuagar
(ehn-hoo-ah-gáhr)

(to) roast
asar
(ah-sáhr)

roasted
asado
(ah-sáh-doh)

roll
panecillo
(pah-neh-sée-yoh)

rolling pin
rodillo
(roh-dée-yoh)

rubber mat
estera de goma
(ehs-téh-rah deh góh-mah)

salad
ensalada
(ehn-sah-láh-dah)

salt
sal
(sahl)

sandwich
sandwich
(sáhn-ooeech)

(to) sanitize
sanear
(sah-neh-áhr)

sanitizer
saneador
(sah-neh-ah-dóhr)

sauce
salsa
(sáhl-sah)

saucer
plato de café
(pláh-toh deh cah-féh)

sausage
salchicha
(sahl-chée-chah)

scrambled eggs
huevos revueltos
(oo-éh-bohs reh-boo-éhl-tohs)

(to) scrub
restregar
(rehs-treh-gáhr)

scrub pad
estropajo
(ehs-troh-páh-hoh)

shellfish
mariscos
(mah-rées-cohs)

shrimp
camarón
(cah-mah-róhn)

silverware
cubertería
(coo-behr-teh-rée-ah)

sink
fregadero
(freh-gah-déh-roh)

skimmer
espumadera
(ehs-poo-mah-déh-rah)

slice
rebanada
(reh-bah-náh-dah)

(to) slice
rebanar
(reh-bah-náhr)

(to) smoke
fumar
(foo-máhr)

soap
jabón
(hah-bóhn)

soap dispenser
distribuidor de jabón
(dees-tree-boo-ee-dóhr deh hah-bóhn)

soapy water
agua jabonosa
(áh-goo-ah hah-boh-nóh-sah)

soft-boiled egg
huevo pasado por agua
(oo-éh-boh pah-sáh-doh pohr áh-goo-ah)

(to) sort
separar
(seh-pah-ráhr)

soup
sopa
(sóh-pah)

soup plate
plato sopero
(pláh-toh soh-péh-roh)

spatula
espátula
(ehs-páh-too-lah)

(to) spill
derramar
(deh-rrah-máhr)

spinach
espinacas
(ehs-pee-náh-cahs)

spoon
cuchara
(coo-cháh-rah)

sprayer
rociador
(roh-see-ah-dóhr)

steamer
marmita al vapor
(mahr-mée-tah ahl bah-póhr)

storeroom
almacén
(ahl-mah-séhn)

strawberries
fresas
(fréh-sahs)

sugar
azúcar
(ah-sóo-cahr)

sugar packet
bolsita de azúcar
(bohl-sée-tah deh ah-sóo-cahr)

sunny side up
yema no hecha
(yéh-mah noh éh-chah)

(to) sweep
barrer
(bah-rréhr)

tea bag
bolsita de té
(bohl-sée-tah deh teh)

teaspoon
cucharilla
(coo-chah-rée-yah)

temperature
temperatura
(tehm-peh-rah-tóo-rah)

(to) thaw
descongelar
(dehs-cohn-heh-láhr)

toast
tostada
(tohs-táh-dah)

(to) toast
tostar
(tohs-táhr)

toaster
tostadora
(tohs-tah-dóh-rah)

tomato
tomate
(toh-máh-teh)

tongs
pinzas
(péen-sahs)

(to) towel dry
secar con trapo
(seh-cáhr cohn tráh-poh)

trash
basura
(bah-sóo-rah)

tuna fish
atún
(ah-tóon)

turkey
pavo
(páh-boh)

urn cleaner
limpiador de cafeteras
(leem-pee-ah-dóhr deh cah-feh-téh-rahs)

veal
ternera
(tehr-néh-rah)

vegetables
legumbres
(leh-góom-brehs)

vinegar
vinagre
(bee-náh-greh)

walk-in freezer
cámara congeladora
(cáh-mah-rah cohn-heh-lah-dóh-rah)

walk-in refrigerator
cámara fría
(cáh-mah-rah frée-ah)

warm
caliente
(cah-lee-éhn-teh)

(to) wash
lavar
(lah-báhr)

watermelon
sandía
(sahn-dée-ah)

well done
bien hecho
(bee-éhn éh-choh)

(to) whip
batir
(bah-téer)

wire whip
batidor
(bah-tee-dóhr)

(to) wrap
envolver
(ehn-bohl-béhr)

wringer
escurridor
(ehs-coo-rree-dóhr)

Professional Interaction

Interaction with Dishwashers

1. Your uniform consists of a white shirt, checkered pants, and sneakers, all of which you must buy yourself. A disposable paper cap is worn at all times.
   Su uniforme consiste en una camisa blanca, pantalones a cuadros y zapatos de tenis que usted debe comprarse. Debe llevar siempre una gorra de papel desechable.

2. Your hair must be neatly combed.
   Debe llevar el cabello bien peinado.

3. You must wash your hands after using the restroom.
   Debe lavarse las manos cada vez que use el baño.

4. Scrape food leftovers from plates before placing them in dish racks.
   Retire las sobras de comida de los platos antes de colocarlos en las rejillas.

5. Water spilled on the floor must be wiped up immediately using a mop and wringer.
   El agua derramada en el suelo debe enjugarse inmediatamente usando el trapeador y la escurridora.

6. Watch that silverware is not thrown out with the food scraps into the garbage pail.
   Cuide que la cubertería no se tire con los desperdicios al cubo de basura.

7. Spray the dishes well with the spray nozzle before putting them through the machine.
   Rocíe bien los platos con la regadera antes de pasarlos por la máquina.

183

8. Keep the washing water temperature above 160 degrees F.
   Mantenga la temperatura del agua de lavado por encima de ciento sesenta grados Fahrenheit.

9. After washing, rinse pots and pans in clean, warm water.
   Después del lavado, enjuague las ollas y cacerolas en agua caliente que esté limpia.

10. All utensils must be sanitized by immersing them in very hot water for half a minute.
    Todos los utensilios deben ser saneados sumergiéndolos en agua muy caliente durante medio minuto.

11. Do not towel utensils. Let them drain dry.
    No use trapos para secar los utensilios. Déjelos escurrir hasta que estén secos.

12. Always use rubber gloves and plastic apron when washing.
    Siempre use guantes de goma y delantal de plástico cuando esté lavando.

13. Sort the material before placing it into the corresponding racks.
    Separe el material antes de colocarlo en las rejillas correspondientes.

14. Take the garbage to the dumpster as soon as the pails are full. Wash the pails carefully and cover them with plastic bags.
    Lleve los desperdicios al vertedero cuando los cubos estén llenos. Lave los cubos cuidadosamente y cúbralos con bolsas de plástico.

15. Avoid touching utensils with your hands as much as possible once they are clean.
    Evite tocar los utensilios con las manos lo menos posible una vez que estén limpios.

16. If the dishwashing machine breaks down or the garbage disposal plugs up, call the maintenance department.
    Si la máquina lavaplatos falla o el triturador se atranca, llame al departamento de mantenimiento.

17. Do not run out of detergent. Request supplies from the storeroom ahead of time.
    No se quede sin detergente. Solicite suministros del almacén con antelación.

18. Clean the machine inside out and before ending the shift.
    Limpie la máquina por fuera y por dentro antes de finalizar el turno.

19. Verify the water temperature during service. Keep it to standards.
    Verifique la temperatura del agua durante el servicio. Manténgala según las instrucciones.

20. Brush clean the rubber mats regularly.
    Limpie las esteras de goma con cepillo regularmente.

21. Refill the mobile dish carts as soon as dishes are dry.
    Rellene los carros de platos móviles tan pronto como los platos estén secos.

22. Presoak silver before putting it through the machine.
    Remoje la cubertería antes de pasarla por la máquina.

23. In case of emergency, turn off the switch to stop the dishwasher.
    En caso de emergencia, apague el interruptor para parar el lavaplatos.

24. Use different racks for china, silverware, and glassware.
    Use rejillas diferentes para loza, cubertería y cristalería.

25. Be courteous to dining room and kitchen personnel.
    Sea cortés con el personal de comedor y cocina.

Interaction with Utility Cooks

1. Report to work well groomed and in clean uniform. You must wear sneakers in the kitchen.
   Acuda al trabajo bien aseado(a) y con uniforme limpio. Debe llevar zapatos de tenis en la cocina.

2. Smoking and chewing gum is not allowed while on the job.
   Fumar y mascar chicle no es permitido mientras trabaja.

3. Wash hands with soap very often while on duty.
   Lávese las manos con jabón muy frecuentemente durante el trabajo.

4. Dispose of kitchen oils in the special container for grease.
   Vierta los aceites de la cocina en el contenedor especial para grasas.

5. Sanitize utensils that have been in contact with raw poultry.
   Sanée los utensilios que han estado en contacto con carne de ave cruda.

6. Have you been a breakfast cook before?
   ¿Ha trabajado usted como cocinero(a) de desayunos anteriormente?

7. Prepare the dough for pancakes before the opening of the restaurant.
   Prepare la masa para panqueques antes de que abra el restaurante.

8. Wash these heads of lettuce, chop them, and put it in the refrigerator.
   Lave estas lechugas, córtelas y póngalo en el refrigerador.

9. Prepare two trays of baking potatoes. First, wash and scrub them over the sink.
   Prepare dos bandejas de patatas para asar. Primero lávelas y frótelas en el fregadero.

10. Clean the griddle with the grill brick.
    Limpie la plancha con el grill brick.

11. At lunch time, work the line helping the cook on duty.
Durante el almuerzo, trabaje en la línea de servicio, ayudando al(a la) cocinero(a) de turno.

12. Keep the kitchen floor free from trash and spills.
Mantenga el piso de la cocina seco y limpio de desperdicios.

13. Help the pantry cook prepare sandwiches, salads, and cold dishes.
Ayude al(a la) despensero(a) a preparar sándwiches, ensaladas y platos fríos.

14. Set up five pans with bacon slices for grilling.
Prepare cinco bandejas de tiras de tocino para asar.

15. Bring out an apple pie from the walk-in cooler and cut it into six portions.
Saque un pastel de manzana de la cámara frigorífica y córtelo en seis porciones.

16. Beat three eggs for an omelet.
Bata tres huevos para una tortilla de huevos.

17. Wash and clean the soup kettle.
Lave y limpie la marmita de sopa.

18. Take this requisition to the storeroom. Bring a cart with you.
Lleve este pedido al almacén. Llévese un carro.

19. Change the oil in the deep fryer and dump it in the special container for grease.
Cambie el aceite en la freidora y échelo en el recipiente especial para grasa.

20. Clean the kitchen hood every other day after the dinner service.
Limpie la campana de la cocina cada dos días después del servicio de cena.

21. Peel two pounds of potatoes.
Pele dos libras de papas.

22. I need you to work one of your days off next week.
Necesito que trabaje uno de sus días libres la semana próxima.

23. Can I call you to work when you are off if I am in a jam?
¿Puedo llamarlo(la) a trabajar en sus días libres si me encuentro en un apuro?

24. Checks are handed out by the chef every Friday after lunch service.
Los cheques salariales son entregados por el (la) jefe de cocina cada viernes después del servicio de almuerzo.

25. If you are unable to come to work, call the restaurant two hours before your shift begins.
Si no puede venir a trabajar, llame al restaurante dos horas antes del comienzo de su turno.

Kitchen Position Descriptions

Dishwasher (*Lavaplatos*)

Reports to Executive Chef.

Su supervisor(a) inmediato(a) es el (la) Jefe de Cocina.

Position Responsibility

Responsabilidad del puesto

1. Wash all dishes, silverware, glassware, trays, and service and cooking utensils for the food and beverage department.
   Lavar los platos, cubertería, cristalería, bandejas y utensilios de cocina y servicio del departamento de alimentos y bebidas.

2. Store all the equipment in the proper place.
   Colocar todo el equipo en el lugar apropiado.

3. Maintain the dishwashing machine and the dishwashing area in a clean, sanitary, and efficient manner.
   Mantener la máquina y el área de lavaplatos limpias, saneadas y eficientes.

4. Break down the dishwashing machine to clean and hose down interior.
   Desarmar la máquina lavaplatos para limpiar y lavar con manguera su interior.

5. Keep dishwashing machine de-limed.
   Mantener la máquina lavaplatos decalcificada.

6. Check water temperature to ensure proper level, reporting any problems immediately.
   Comprobar la temperatura del agua, asegurándose de que el nivel es adecuado y dando cuenta de cualquier problema inmediatamente.

7. Remove garbage to the dumpster.
   Llevar los desperdicios al vertedero.

8. Clean and sanitize garbage cans.
   Limpiar y sanear los cubos de desperdicios.

9. Keep dishroom area and equipment clean and in order.
   Mantener el área del lavaplatos y el equipo limpios y en orden.

10. Keep floors free from spills and trash.
    Mantener el suelo seco y limpio de basura.

11. Brush and sanitize floor mats.
    Cepillar y sanear las esteras de goma.

12. Wash pots and pans following the "wash-rinse-sanitize" procedures.
    Lavar ollas y cacerolas siguiendo el procedimiento de "lavado-aclarado-saneamiento".

13. Keep an adequate par stock of detergents and other cleaning materials.
    Mantener un nivel adecuado de detergentes y otros suministros de limpieza.

Utility Cook (*Ayudante de Cocina*)

Reports to Executive Chef   *Su jefe inmediato(a) es el (la) Jefe de Cocina.*

Position Responsibility   *Responsabilidad del puesto*

1. Keep the general kitchen area clean and sanitized.
   Mantener el área de la cocina limpia y saneada.

2. Wash pots and utensils used in the kitchen.
   Lavar cacerolas y utensilios usados en la cocina.

3. Assist in the pre-preparation of food: wash and cut vegetables, grind meats, mix doughs, clean seafood.
   Ayudar en el preparado de alimentos: lavar y cortar legumbres, picar carne, mezclar masas, limpiar mariscos.

4. Assist in the cooking of some dishes, particularly breakfast items and cold orders.
   Ayudar en la preparación de algunos platillos, particularmente de desayuno y fríos.

5. Sweep and mop all floor areas.
   Barrer y trapear los suelos.

6. Remove garbage to dumpster and oils to the grease drum.
   Llevar los desperdicios al vertedero y los aceites al barril de grasas.

7. Requisition foods and paper and cleaning supplies from the storeroom.

Formular pedidos de alimentos y de suministros de papel y limpieza al almacén.

8. Help set up banquet lines away from the kitchen area.

Ayudar a instalar líneas para banquetes en áreas alejadas de la cocina.

Kitchen Procedures

Personal Hygiene

1. Keep hands and fingernails clean at all times. Use soap and water.
   Mantener las manos y las uñas limpias en todo momento. Usar jabón y agua.

2. Wash hands after using the restroom, touching anything that may contain bacteria, and eating.
   Lavarse las manos después de usar el baño, después de tocar algo que pueda contener bacteria o después de comer.

3. Handle food only as required. Avoid touching clean utensils.
   Tocar los alimentos según instrucciones. Evitar tocar utensilios limpios.

4. Do not work around food with open hand cuts or sores.
   No trabajar cerca de alimentos si tiene cortes o llagas en las manos.

5. Do not cough, spit, or sneeze near food. Always cover a cough or sneeze with a handkerchief. Wash hands immediately after using a handkerchief.
   No toser, escupir o estornudar cerca de alimentos. Cubra siempre con un pañuelo su tos o estornudo. Lavar las manos inmediatamente después de usar el pañuelo.

6. Stay home when you have a contagious sickness.
   Quedarse en casa cuando se tenga una enfermedad contagiosa.

7. Wear clean clothing for the job.
   Llevar ropa limpia en el trabajo.

8. Control hair by keeping it neatly trimmed or covered.
   Controlar el cabello, manteniéndolo corto o cubierto.

9. Take a shower or bath daily.
   Tomar una ducha o baño diario.

10. Do not chew gum or smoke on the job.
    No mascar chicle o fumar en el trabajo.
11. Do not use nail polish when working in the kitchen.
    No usar laca de uñas cuando se trabaja en la cocina.
12. Do not allow dirty utensils or equipment to touch food.
    Evitar que utensilios o equipo sucios toquen los alimentos.

Basic Sanitation Rules

1. Always wash hands before starting work, after visiting the bathroom, and after working with poultry or seafood.
   Lavar siempre las manos antes de comenzar el trabajo, después de usar el baño y después de manipular carne de ave o mariscos.
2. Always use clean cooking utensils.
   Utilizar siempre utensilios de cocina limpios.
3. Keep all foods covered as much as possible.
   Mantener los alimentos cubiertos tanto como sea posible.
4. Wash all fruits and vegetables before using.
   Lavar las frutas y legumbres antes de usarlas.
5. Make sure that dented cans have not been punctured.
   Cerciorarse de que los botes que estén hundidos no hayan sido agujereados.
6. Use plastic throwaway gloves when possible.
   Usar guantes de plástico desechables cuando sea posible.
7. Store glasses, cups, pots, and bowls bottom up.
   Colocar vasos, tazas, ollas y escudillas con el borde hacia arriba.

Safety in the Kitchen

1. Never use water on a grease fire.
   Nunca use agua para apagar un fuego causado por grasas.
2. Place a lighted match to gas jets before turning on gas.
   Coloque un cerillo encendido junto a los chorros de gas antes de conectar el gas.
3. Range-top fires can be fought with salt or baking soda.
   Fuegos ocurridos sobre la cocina pueden extinguirse con sal o bicarbonato.
4. Do not smoke in the kitchen.
   No fume en la cocina.

5. Always check to make sure the gas and electricity are shut off before closing down.

   Compruebe siempre que el gas y la electricidad han sido apagados antes de cerrar.

6. Keep towels away from the range. A dangling towel could catch fire.

   Mantenga los trapos de cocina alejados del fuego. Estos pueden prenderse facilmente.

7. Avoid overfilling hot-food containers.

   Evite el rebose de recipientes de alimentos calientes.

8. Keep long handles of saucepans and skillets away from aisles.

   Evite que los mangos de cazuelas y sartenes sobresalgan de la cocina.

9. Lift heavy weights with the legs, not with the back. Bend the knees before lifting.

   Levante objetos pesados con las piernas, no con la espalda. Doble las rodillas antes de levantar el peso.

10. Avoid having glass near food, since it may break or chip.

    Evite colocar objetos de vidrio cerca de alimentos, ya que puede romperse o desportillarse.

11. Never throw objects in the kitchen. Always pass them from hand to hand.

    No arroje objetos en la cocina. Páselos siempre mano a mano.

12. Do not grab for falling knives. When a knife starts to fall, get out of the way.

    No intente atrapar un cuchillo que se cae. Cuando un cuchillo se cae, apártese.

13. Always carry a knife with the tip pointing downward and with the cutting edge turned away from the body.

    Siempre transporte el cuchillo con la punta hacia el suelo y con el filo separado del cuerpo.

14. Never reach into soapy water in search of a knife.

    No trate de recoger un cuchillo inmerso en agua jabonosa.

15. Never cut on metal; use a cutting board.

    Nunca corte sobre metal; utilice una tabla de cortar.

16. When cleaning a knife, keep the sharp edge turned away from the body.

    Cuando limpie el cuchillo, mantenga el filo separado del cuerpo.

17. Pick up knives by the handle only.

    Agarre los cuchillos por el mango solamente.

18. Before cleaning a machine, be sure all electrical switches are in an off position.
    Cuando limpie una máquina, asegúrese de que todos los interruptores están en la posición "off".

19. Do not wear rings or watches when operating electrical power equipment.
    No lleve sortijas ni reloj de pulsera mientras trabaja con máquinas movidas por electricidad.

20. Wear shoes that prevent slipping. Tie shoelaces well.
    Lleve calzado que no resbale. Ate bien los cordones.

21. Tuck in all apron strings.
    Remeta las cintas del delantal.

22. Discard chipped or cracked china and glassware.
    Deseche la loza y cristalería rajada o desportillada.

23. Never force a towel inside a glass to dry it.
    No fuerze el trapo dentro del vaso mientras lo seca.

24. Use a pan and broom to pick up broken china or glassware. Do not use the hands.
    Use recogedor y escoba para limpiar platos o vidrios rotos. No use las manos.

25. Floors must be dry before turning on any electrical equipment.
    Los suelos deben estar secos antes de conectar maquinaria eléctrica.

26. Clean up spills on the floor. If necessary, sprinkle salt on it to prevent slipping.
    Limpie líquidos derramados en el suelo. Si fuera necesario, eche sal para evitar resbalarse.

27. Never leave any pots, pans, or utensils on the floor.
    No deje nunca ollas, cazuelas o utensilios sobre el suelo.

28. Never run in the kitchen; always walk.
    Nunca corra en la cocina; camine.

29. Replace torn or worn rubber mats to avoid falls.
    Reponga las esteras de goma que estén gastadas o rotas para evitar caídas.

Washing Utensils by Hand

1. Keep wash water clean
   Mantenga limpia el agua de lavar.

2. The temperature of wash water should be at least 120 degrees F.
   La temperatura del agua de lavar debe estar por lo menos a ciento veinte grados Fahrenheit.

3. Use proper amount of detergent.
   Use la cantidad de detergente adecuada.

4. Rinse utensils in a different sink.
   Enjuague los utensilios en otro fregadero.

5. Keep rinse water clean.
   Mantenga limpia el agua de enjuagar.

6. Sanitize utensils in a different sink.
   Sanée los utensilios en otro fregadero.

7. Immerse for two minutes in a chlorine rinse with a minimum of fifty ppm or in clean water at 170 degrees F.
   Sumerja los utensilios durante dos minutos en agua clorinada con un mínimo de cincuenta ppm o en agua limpia a ciento setenta grados Fahrenheit.

8. Let the utensils air dry.
   Deje que los utensilios se sequen al aire.

9. Store clean dry utensils in a protected clean place.
   Coloque los utensilio limpios y secos en un sitio donde puedan mantenerse limpios.

Machine Dishwashing

1. Monitor the temperature gauges for wash and rinse water.
   Verifique las temperaturas del agua de lavado y de enjuague en los manómetros.

2. Rinse dishes and flatware before running them through the machine.
   Enjuague los platos y la cubertería antes de pasarlos por la máquina.

3. Rack wares properly so all surfaces are exposed to wash and rinse water.
   Coloque el material apropiadamente en las rejillas de modo que todas las superficies queden expuestas al agua de lavado y aclarado.

4. Air dry wares after washing; never use towels. Towel-drying can recontaminate sanitized material.
   Seque los utensilios al aire; nunca use trapos. Los trapos pueden recontaminar el material saneado.

5. Handle clean dishes and flatware with plastic gloves or clean hands.
   Manipule los platos limpios y la cubertería con guantes de plástico o con las manos limpias.

PART IX

The Employee Handbook
(Sample)

Welcome Statement

Dear Employee: Welcome to the Royal Hotel/Restaurant! You have been carefully selected for your position with our hotel/restaurant because we expect you to play a vital part in the successful operation of our service-oriented company. We are proud to have you as a member of our team, and we are certain that you will receive personal satisfaction from knowing that your efforts will contribute to establishing the fine reputation of the Royal Hotel/Restaurant as an outstanding establishment. Courtesy and hospitality are the two key words in our industry. We are putting hospitality back into the hotel/restaurant business. Our guests return for the warmth, sincerity, and efficient service they enjoy at the Royal. It is our employees who reflect the hospitable attitude to our guests and to fellow employees.

We want you to feel at ease in your new surroundings, and we are providing a handbook of company policies and work rules to help answer any questions you may have. During the next few weeks of orientation, company policies and benefits will be discussed more thoroughly with you. You will have an opportunity to tour the entire facility and become acquainted with coworkers in departments other than your own. Your suggestions, ideas, and comments are always welcome. Please feel free to discuss them with us. We can learn from one another by an exchange of ideas.

We are happy to have you join us as a member of the staff of the exciting Royal Hotel/Restaurant. **Welcome Aboard!**

General Manager

Declaración de bienvenida

*Estimado Empleado(a): ¡Bienvenido(a) al Royal Hotel/Restaurante! Usted ha sido seleccionado(a) cuidadosamente para ocupar su puesto en nuestro hotel/restaurante porque esperamos que usted llegue a ser una parte vital en el entorno operativo de nuestra compañía, la cual tiene como meta servir eficientemente a su clientela. Nos sentimos orgullosos de contarle como un nuevo miembro de nuestro equipo, y estamos seguros de que usted se sentirá personalmente satisfecho(a) de saber que sus esfuerzos contribuirán a continuar la gran reputación que el Royal Hotel/Restaurante tiene como establecimiento excepcional. **Cortesía** y **hospitalidad** son las dos palabras claves en nuestra industria. Esta compañía tiene como objetivo reintegrar el concepto de hospitalidad a la industria. Nuestros clientes vuelven a nuestro establecimiento debido al entusiasmo, a la sinceridad y al eficiente servicio ofrecido por el Royal. Son nuestros empleados quienes reflejan la actitud de hospitalidad que ofrecemos a nuestros clientes, así como a nuestros mismos empleados.*

Deseamos que se sienta confortable en el ambiente que le ofrecemos, a la vez que le entregamos este manual que detalla las reglas de conducta a seguir en el trabajo y que seguramente contestará las preguntas que pueda tener sobre su nuevo empleo. Durante las dos semanas próximas que dedicaremos a su orientación, se le explicarán los requerimientos de la compañía y los beneficios que ésta le ofrece. También tendrá la oportunidad de visitar el establecimiento y conocer a otros empleados que trabajan en departamentos diferentes al suyo. Sus sugerencias, ideas y comentarios son siempre bienvenidos, con el fin de establecer un intercambio de ideas entre usted y la gerencia.

*Nos complace que haya decidido formar parte del equipo del Royal Hotel/Restaurante. ¡**Bienvenido Abordo**!*

Director General

Our Mission

1. To remember that politeness is our most important product.
2. To treat our patrons and fellow employees in an interested, helpful, and gracious manner, as we would want to be treated if the positions were reversed.
3. To judge fairly; to know both sides before taking action.
4. To learn and practice self-control.
5. To keep our properties, buildings, and equipment in excellent condition at all times.
6. To know our job and to become skillful in its performance.
7. To do our duties promptly.
8. To satisfy our patrons or to refer them to our superior.
9. To search constantly to improve our service and standards.
10. To see our guests as the most important persons in our work lives.

Nuestra Misión

1. Recordar que la cortesía es nuestro producto más importante.
2. Tratar a nuestros clientes y compañeros de trabajo de una manera genuina, servicial y amable, de la misma forma que desearíamos ser tratados nosotros.
3. Juzgar equitativamente; analizar ambas partes antes de tomar acción.
4. Aprender y practicar el dominio de sí mismo(a).
5. Mantener nuestros establecimientos, edificios y equipo en condiciones excelentes en todo momento.
6. Conocer nuestro trabajo y adquirir pericia en su cometido.
7. Efectuar nuestros deberes prontamente.
8. Satisfacer a nuestros clientes o dar cuenta a un(a) supervisor(a).
9. Intentar constantemente mejorar nuestro servicio y standards.
10. Imaginar a nuestros clientes como las personas más importantes dentro de nuestra vida laboral.

Employment Policies And Practices

A. Equal Employment Opportunity

It is the policy of the Royal Hotel/Restaurant to conform with and to encourage nondiscrimination in employment and in all other matters in our organization. The Affirmative Action Policy adopted by the company states that the Royal will provide equal opportunity without regard to race, color, religion, sex, national origin, age, or qualified handicap. Such action will include, but will not be limited to, the following: advertising, recruitment, employment, promotion, raise of pay or other forms of compensation, demotion or transfer, and lay-off or termination.

It is the intention and effort of the Royal to comply in all respects with applicable federal, state, and local laws. In addition, we feel a strong, moral obligation to the community to remain committed to this policy.

B. Employee Relations Policy

We believe in the essentials of good relationships: fair employment practices, fair compensation, challenging work, recognition for contributions, pleasant working conditions, opportunity and incentive for advancement, open communications, and the dignity of each individual. These essentials are the foundation upon which our company has built its forward-looking program of ongoing employee relations.

We recognize that, being human, mistakes may be made in spite of our best efforts. We want to correct such mistakes as soon as they happen. The only way we can do this is to know of your problems and complaints. No member of management is too busy to hear the problems or concerns of any employee.

200

Sistemas y Prácticas de Empleo

A. Igualdad de oportunidad de empleo

El Royal Hotel/Restaurante mantiene la política de seguir y fomentar la ley de no discriminación en el empleo. La política de Acción Afirmativa adoptada por la compañía estipula que el Royal ofrecerá igual oportunidad de empleo en materias de raza, color, religión, sexo, nación de origen, edad o desventaja física. Esta política incluye, pero no está limitada a, las actividades siguientes: anuncios, reclutamiento, empleo, promoción, aumento de salario u otras formas de conpensación, descenso de rango o traslado y suspensión de empleo o despido.

El Royal Hotel/Restaurante está comprometido a cumplimentar en todos los aspectos las leyes federales, estatales y locales. Además, nos sentimos obligados con respecto a la comunidad en la cual operamos a mantener nuestra política de Igual Oportunidad de Empleo.

B. Sistema de relaciones laborales

Creemos en los siguientes puntos esenciales determinantes de buenas relaciones entre la empresa y los empleados: una política de empleo razonable, compensación adecuada, trabajo interesante, agradecimiento por los esfuerzos realizados, ambiente laboral agradable, oportunidad y estímulo para ascensos, comunicación abierta y reconocimiento de la dignidad de cada individuo. Estos puntos esenciales son la base sobre la que nuestra compañía ha creado su programa de relaciones laborales.

Reconocemos que, siendo humanos, podemos tener errores a pesar de nuestros mejores esfuerzos. Deseamos corregir estos posibles errores tan pronto como tengan lugar. El único modo de poder conseguir este fin es conocer los problemas y quejas que usted pueda tener. Ningún miembro directivo le dirá que no tiene tiempo para oír sus problemas porque está muy ocupado.

201

C. Company Objectives

The objectives of this company are threefold: to provide a working environment that employees enjoy and are proud of, to market and develop the Royal into the stature of a first class hotel/restaurant, and to remain a profitable organization. Each of these objectives relies on one word: **service**. It is the courteous and professional service we as employees provide to our guests that will place our hotel/restaurant one step ahead of the rest, and in return, will enable us to reach our company goals.

C. Objetivos de la compañía

*Los objetivos de esta compañía son tres: proporcionar un ambiente laboral agradable para los empleados y del cual se sientan orgullosos, proyectar y desarrollar el Royal como un hotel/restaurante de primera categoría y continuar siendo una organización rentable. Cada uno de estos objetivos está basado en una sola palabra: **servicio.** El servicio cortés y profesional que proporcionamos a nuestros clientes es la clave que colocará a nuestro hotel/restaurante por delante de nuestra competencia, y que a la vez hará posible que alcancemos las metas que nuestra compañía se ha fijado.*

Job Specifications

A. Review Period

The first three months (ninety days) of employment are considered a period of review for all new employees. During this period, your abilities and work performance are closely evaluated by your supervisor. If for any reason on or before the end of this three-month period it is determined that you are not suited for the job for which you were hired, you may be reassigned to a different job or terminated. The review period can be extended an additional thirty days by a supervisor if it is felt that the employee's performance is below the department standards, yet with an additional thirty days of training, there is a good chance for improvement.

At the completion of the three-month review period, you will be eligible for employee benefits as described in this handbook.

B. Full-time Employee

A full-time employee is an employee who normally works at least thirty hours per week. Full-time employees are eligible for company fringe benefits as outlined in this handbook after successfully completing the ninety-day review period.

Normas de Empleo

A. Período de prueba

Los primeros tres meses (noventa días) de empleo son considerados como período de prueba para todos los empleados contratados por la compañía. Durante este período, su supervisor(a) observará cuidadosamente su aptitud y el cumplimiento de sus tareas. Si por cualquier razón antes o al término del período de prueba se establece que su capacidad no coincide con el trabajo para el que fue contratado(a), se le asignará otro puesto o será despedido(a). El período de prueba puede ser prolongado por otros treinta días si se considera que su rendimiento está por debajo de la media del departamento y que con otros treinta días de entrenamiento existe la posibilidad de mejorar su efectividad.

Al término de los tres meses de prueba se le considerará elegible para recibir los beneficios de empleados especificados en este manual.

B. Empleado(a) de Tiempo Completo

Un(a) empleado(a) de tiempo completo ha de trabajar normalmente un mínimo de treinta horas por semana. Los empleados de tiempo completo son elegibles para recibir los beneficios suplementarios detallados en este manual, después de haber completado los noventa días del período de prueba.

C. Part-Time Employee

A part-time employee is an employee who normally works less than thirty hours per week. After successfully completing their ninety-day review period, part-time employees are eligible for company fringe benefits, with an option to participate in the health and life insurance at their own expense.

C. Empleado(a) de Tiempo Parcial

Un(a) empleado(a) de tiempo parcial es aquel que trabaja normalmente menos de treinta horas por semana. Después de haber completado satisfactoriamente los noventa días del período de prueba, los empleados de tiempo parcial son elegibles para recibir los beneficios suplementarios ofrecidos por la compañía, teniendo opción a participar en el seguro de enfermedad y de vida a su propio cargo.

Pay Procedures

A. Payday

Payday is every Friday. You can pick up your paycheck from your supervisor any time after eleven o'clock A.M. If you are not scheduled to work on a Friday and wish to pick up your paycheck, please do not linger or visit in the work areas. This causes a disruption in the work flow, which in return affects the service to our guests.

Each pay period starts on Sunday at twelve o'clock A.M. and ends on Sunday at twelve o'clock the following week. You will receive a new time card every Sunday for the upcoming week. You should punch your time card as follows: punch in no earlier than five minutes before the beginning of your regular scheduled work time and punch out immediately after quitting work for the day. All overtime work must be approved in advance by your supervisor. Punching in or out for any other employee is prohibited and if done for any reason will result in immediate disciplinary action.

Tipped employees must declare their tips as income on the back of their timecard each week. All employees must sign the time card every week. Failure to do so will result in holding the check until the time card is signed.

If an employee loses his (her) paycheck, there is a two-week waiting period before a replacement check is issued.

Pago De Salarios

A. Día de pago

El día de pago es el viernes. Los empleados pueden recoger los cheques de su supervisor(a) a partir de las once de la mañana. Si usted no trabaja los viernes y desea recoger su cheque, no se entretenga con otros empleados en el área de trabajo. Esto causa interrupciones en el desempeño de las tareas, lo que puede afectar el servicio a nuestros clientes.

Cada período salarial comienza el domingo a las doce de la noche y termina el domingo de la semana siguiente a la misma hora. Usted recibirá una tarjeta cada domingo para ser utilizada durante la semana. Marque la tarjeta en el reloj registrador siguiendo las indicaciones siguientes: no marque con más de cinco minutos de antelación antes de comenzar su turno designado y marque la tarjeta inmediatamente después de terminar su turno. Las horas extras deben ser aprobadas con antelación por su supervisor(a). Queda prohibido marcar la tarjeta de otro(a) empleado(a) y en caso de que se haga, el (la) causante recibirá inmediatamente medidas disciplinarias.

Los empleados que reciben propinas deben declarar éstas cada semana, utilizando la parte de atrás de sus tarjetas respectivas. Todos los empleados deben firmar su tarjeta cada semana. Si no se hiciese, los cheques serán retenidos hasta que el (la) empleado(a) firme su tarjeta.

Si un(a) empleado(a) pierde su cheque salarial, deberá esperar dos semanas hasta que el cheque sea nuevamente emitido.

B. Deductions

Deductions from your paycheck are made for federal, state, local, and Social Security taxes. No other deductions will be made from your checks without authorization from you.

C. Overtime

Should it become necessary to work overtime, all hours actually worked in excess of forty in any one work week will be paid on the basis of one-and-one-half times the regular hourly rate of pay. All overtime work must be approved in advance by your immediate supervisor. At times, it may be necessary for you to work at a time other than the regularly scheduled hours. Should this change be made, your supervisor will notify you as far in advance as possible so that you may plan accordingly.

B. Descuentos

Los descuentos reflejados en su cheque salarial son para cubrir los impuestos federales, estatales y locales, así como la Seguridad Social. No se harán otros descuentos sin su autorización personal.

C. Horas extras

Si es necesario trabajar horas extra, el tiempo que exceda las cuarenta horas normalmente trabajadas por semana será pagado con un suplemento del cincuenta por ciento del salario base por hora. Las horas extra deben ser aprobadas previamente por su supervisor(a). En ciertas ocasiones, puede ser necesario que usted trabaje horas diferentes a las que tiene asignadas. El cambio de horas le será anunciado por su supervisor(a) tan pronto como sea posible con objeto de que pueda usted estar preparado(a).

Time Off The Job

A. Meals

The Royal provides one free meal for each employee who works a minimum of a four-and-one-half hour shift. All meals must be eaten in the employee cafeteria which has been provided specifically for this purpose. Employees are not allowed to consume hotel/restaurant-supplied food or beverages when not on duty.

B. Leave of Absence

The Hotel/Restaurant understands that sometimes under very unusual circumstances it is imperative that an employee take a leave of absence for either personal, medical, or military reasons. The following provisions apply.

1. Any employee, with the exception of review-period employees, may request a leave of absence. The decision whether or not to grant the leave of absence will be determined by the department manager based upon the urgency of the situation, the need for the leave, the department's workload, and an understanding with the employee that he (she) will return to work at the end of the leave. Requests for a leave of absence must be made in writing.
2. Normally, an employee may not take a leave of absence for more than thirty days. Leave extensions are granted only under extraordinary circumstances.

Ausencias Del Trabajo

A. Comidas

El Royal proveé una comida gratuita a cada empleado(a) que trabaja un turno mínimo de cuatro horas y media. Todas las comidas deben consumirse en la cafetería de empleados, la cual ha sido instalada especificamente para este cometido. Los empleados no deben consumir comidas o bebidas del hotel/restaurante no estando de servicio.

B. Ausencia con Permiso

El hotel/Restaurante entiende que a veces, bajo circunstancias muy especiales, es imperativo que los empleados se ausenten con permiso debido a razones personales, médicas o militares. A este fin, se deben seguir las estipulaciones siguientes.

1. *Cualquier empleado(a), a excepción de aquellos en período de prueba, puede solicitar ausencia con permiso. La decisión de si ésta es concedida o nó dependerá del (de la) jefe de departamento, basada en lo urgente de la situación, la necesidad de la ausencia, el nivel de trabajo en el departamento y el acuerdo de que el (la) empleado(a) se reincorporará al trabajo al término del período de ausencia. La solicitud de ausencias con permiso deben hacerse por escrito.*

2. *Normalmente, los empleados no pueden ausentarse con permiso por más de treinta días. La prolongación de ausencias por más de treinta días es concedida solamente en circunstancias extraordinarias.*

3. It should be understood that, except for military service leave, return to work after a leave will be dependent upon the availability of open positions. The Hotel/Restaurant will make a good-faith effort to provide a position of like, or equal status, as soon as such a position becomes available.
4. An employee may continue to participate in the company's medical insurance plan, provided prior arrangements are made to remit the required premiums in full in advance of the period of coverage.
5. If an employee who has been granted a leave of absence fails to return to work at the expiration of the leave, unless prior arrangements are made for an extension, his (her) employment will be terminated as of the original date such leave was granted.

C. Jury Duty

Jury duty is an obligation and a most important element in the democratic process. The Royal believes that everyone should meet his (her) civic responsibilities and urges you to serve on city, state and federal juries when summoned. If you are a full-time employee, you will receive full pay for the first fifteen days while serving on jury duty or as a subpoened witness, as well as governmentally supplied jury duty pay or subpoena witness pay to help with expenses incidental to jury duty. Jury duty cannot be used in determining overtime.

3. *Se hace constar que, excepto en ausencias por motivos militares, la vuelta al trabajo dependerá de la disponibilidad de puestos de trabajo vacantes. El Hotel/Restaurante hará todo lo posible para ofrecer un puesto similar, o de igual rango, tan pronto como dicho puesto quede libre.*

4. *Los empleados pueden continuar con su seguro de enfermedad con la compañía siempre que coticen la prima en su totalidad por adelantado.*

5. *Si el (la) empleado(a) a quien se le concedió ausencia con permiso no vuelve al trabajo al termino de su ausencia (al menos que se hubiera concedido una extensión del plazo) su empleo será terminado retroactivo a la fecha del comienzo de la ausencia.*

C. Miembro de Jurado

Ejercer como miembro de jurado es una obligación y elemento importante en el proceso democrático. El Royal entiende que cada individuo debe ejercer sus responsibilidades cívicas, por lo que le insta a servir en jurados locales, estatales y federales cuando sea convocado(a). Si usted es un (a) empleado(a) de tiempo completo, se le otorgará su salario total durante los primeros quince días que ejerza como miembro del jurado o como testigo oficial, además de la remuneración que recibirá oficialmente, con el fin de resarcirle por los gastos adicionales que resultan en estos casos. El tiempo empleado como miembro de jurado no puede computarse para efectos de horas extra.

What You Can Expect from the Company

A. Group Insurance

The Royal Hotel/Restaurant provides group insurance programs to protect you and your family. The group coverage becomes effective the first day of the month following completion of your first review period (three months).

1. Medical and Hospital

The company offers group medical and hospitalization insurance to full-time employees and their families. The company pays an established single premium rate toward the plan and a payroll deduction is available for the balance. This coverage is available to part-time employees at their own expense.

2. Life Insurance

The company provides life insurance in the amount of $ _____, with an additional $ _____ for accidental death and dismemberment for full-time employees at no charge. In the situation of a leave of absence, the company will continue to contribute to the employee's group health and life insurance for the first three months of the leave of absence. If a leave of absence extends over three months and the employee wishes to remain on the company group insurance, he (she) is responsible for paying for the total cost of such coverage.

Lo que le Ofrece la Compañía

A. Seguro Colectivo

El Hotel/Restaurante Royal mantiene un seguro colectivo para su protección y la de su familia. La protección colectiva entra en vigor el primer día del mes siguiente al período de prueba (tres meses).

1. **Seguro médico y de hospitalización**

   La compañía ofrece un seguro colectivo y de hospitalización a empleados de tiempo completo y sus familias. La compañía paga una prima establecida y descuenta de la nómina salarial la diferencia para cubrir el coste. Este seguro se ofrece también a empleados de tiempo parcial que deseen pagar el total de la prima.

2. **Seguro de vida**

   La compañía ofrece un seguro de vida por la cantidad de $_____, con $_____ adicionales por muerte accidental y desmembramiento a empleados de tiempo completo sin cargo alguno. En el caso de ausencia con permiso, la compañía continuará cubriendo la prima del seguro de enfermedad y de vida durante los primeros tres meses de la ausencia. Si la ausencia con permiso se prolonga más de tres meses y el (la) empleado(a) desea continuar en el seguro colectivo, éste será responsable de pagar el total del costo de la prima.

B. Worker's Compensation

Employees are covered by the Worker's Compensation laws of the state. To be properly protected, all accidents for injuries on the job must be reported to a supervisor within forty-eight hours. Supervisors will make arrangements for employees to be examined. Failure to report an injury immediately could cause a claim to be disallowed.

C. Parking

The hotel/restaurant provides free, patroled parking for all employees. Because of the limited parking surrounding of the hotel/restaurant, all employees are required to park as far away from the building as possible. A parking authorization sticker will be issued per car to each employee. The sticker must be displayed on the left rear bumper. The company will not be liable for fire, theft, damage, or personal injury involving employee automobiles.

D. Lockers

The hotel/restaurant provides lockers for employees to use for uniforms and personal belongings. Each employee requesting a locker must provide his (her) own lock.

E. Payroll Savings Program

The Royal provides you the opportunity to set up a payroll savings plan. Our accounting office can deduct a specified amount from your paycheck, authorized by you, and then automatically deposit that amount in your name into an account with a savings institution of your choice.

B. Seguro de accidente en el trabajo

Los empleados están protegidos por las leyes del Seguro de Trabajo del estado. Para estar debidamente protegidos, cualquier daño sufrido en accidente de trabajo deberá ser comunicado a su supervisor(a) antes del transcurso de cuarenta y ocho horas. Los supervisores se encargarán de que el (la) empleado(a) sea examinado(a) físicamente. En caso de no comunicar inmediatamente la lesión se podría denegar la cobertura.

C. Aparcamiento

El hotel/restaurante ofrece aparcamiento gratuito vigilado a todos los empleados. Debido al número limitado de aparcamientos, los empleados deben aparcar tan lejos del edificio como sea posible. Cada empleado(a) recibirá una pegatina por carro. La pegatina deberá ser colocada en la parte izquierda del parachoques trasero. La compañía no se hace responsable en caso de fuego, robo, daño o lesiones personales relativas a automóviles de empleados.

D. Roperos

El hotel/restaurante provée roperos a los empleados para guardar uniformes y objetos personales. Cada empleado(a) que use un ropero debe suplir su propio candado.

E. Programa de Ahorro Salarial

El Royal le ofrece la oportunidad de mantener un plan de ahorro salarial. Nuestra oficina de contabilidad puede deducir de su salario una cantidad acordada, autorizada por usted, y depositarla automaticamente en su nombre en la caja de ahorros que usted escoja.

F. Educational Assistance

The Royal Hotel/Restaurant strongly supports and encourages the continuing education of employees. The hotel/restaurant will reimburse employees 50% of the tuition and book cost up to $200 for those courses that are job related and/or pertain to the employee's current or future career path. The following provisions apply.

1. Employees must be employed at least six months before a request can be made for tuition reimbursement.
2. Only one request can be submitted per semester.
3. Employees must have at least a C grade at the completion of the course(s) or the request will be denied. Report cards must be submitted for documentation before the reimbursement is awarded.
4. Courses must be offered through an accredited educational institution.

G. Employee suggestions

The Royal is interested in employee suggestions aimed at improving working conditions, service to our guests, energy conservation, and safety. Suggestions should be placed in the box near the employee cafeteria. These suggestions go directly to the General Manager. Cash awards of $20 are given to those employees whose suggestions are judged beneficial to the hotel/restaurant.

H. Use of Hotel Food and Beverage Facilities

Employees are welcome to take advantage of and enjoy the food and beverage outlets with the following restrictions.

1. Employees may eat in the food outlets any day of the week with the approval of their department manager, except between the hours of twelve o'clock noon and one o'clock p.m. Approval must be obtained in advance. Employees cannot be in uniform and must be appropriately dressed.
2. When using the food and beverage outlets, do not interfere with the normal course of business, i.e. chatting with employees who are on duty or being disruptive in the area.
3. Employees are not allowed to call room service at any time for a meal or drink. Room service is available for our guests only.

F. Ayuda Educacional

El Hotel/Restaurante Royal apoya y fomenta el proceso educativo de sus empleados. El hotel/restaurante reembolsará a los empleados el 50% del costo de la enseñanza y de los libros hasta un máximo de 200 dólares para cursos relacionados con el trabajo o con la profesión actual o futura del (de la) empleado(a). Este beneficio se ofrece con las condiciones siguientes.

1. *Empleados deben haber trabajado un mínimo de seis meses en el momento de solicitar el reembolso.*
2. *Solamente puede solicitarse una petición por semestre.*
3. *Los empleados deben tener por lo menos una nota de C al término del curso; en caso contrario la petición será denegada. Las notas deben ser entregadas para su verificación antes de que el reembolso pueda ser aprobado.*
4. *Los cursos deben ser tomados en instituciones de enseñanza acreditadas.*

G. Sugerencias de Empleados

El Royal está interesado en recibir sugerencias de sus empleados a fin de mejorar las condiciones de trabajo, el servicio a nuestros huéspedes, el ahorro de energía y la seguridad. Las sugerencias deben ser colocadas en el buzón situado en la cafetería de empleados. Estas sugerencias llegan directamente al (a la) Gerente General. Se darán premios en metálico de 20 dólares a aquellos empleados cuyas sugerencias se consideran beneficiosas al hotel/restaurante.

H. Uso de los Servicios de Alimentos y Bebidas

Los empleados pueden utilizar los servicios de alimentos y bebidas con las condiciones siguientes.

1. *Los empleados pueden comer a su cargo en los servicios de alimentos y bebidas cualquier día de la semana con la aprobación de su supervisor(a), excepto entre las doce del mediodía y la una de la tarde. La aprobación debe ser obtenida con antelación. Los empleados no pueden estar de uniforme y deben estar apropiadamente vestidos.*
2. *Cuando utilice los servicios de alimentos y bebidas, no deberá interferir con el normal desenvolvimiento del servicio, es decir, no charlar con otros empleados que estén trabajando o causar interrupciones.*
3. *No es permitido a los empleados llamar a "room service" en ningún momento para ordenar comida o bebida. El "room service" es para el uso exclusivo de nuestros huéspedes.*

What the Company Expects from You

A. Punctuality and Absenteeism Policy

Regular and punctual attendance is an important requirement of your position here at the Royal Hotel/Restaurant. We understand there will be times when illness and emergencies will cause you to be absent or late; however, it is your responsibility to report your tardiness or absences as outlined in your department policy. Habitual absence and tardiness are discourteous to your fellow employees and will result in disciplinary procedures, including termination.

B. Hotel/Restaurant Security

The security and protection of our employees and guests are very important to our company. For this reason, the hotel/restaurant is electronically monitored and patroled by security personnel. To ensure a safe and secure workplace, the following provisions apply.

1. **Entrances and exits:** All employees entering and exiting the hotel/ restaurant who need to punch in or out using the time clock must do so through the employee entrance.
2. **Uniforms and name tags:** Employees must wear the required uniforms and name tags while on duty. This will enable Security to ensure that only our employees are in the hotel/restaurant.

Lo que la Compañía Espera de Usted

A. Reglas sobre Puntualidad y Ausencia

La asistencia y puntualidad en el trabajo es un requisito importante para los emplea-dos del Hotel/Restaurante Royal. La compañía es consciente de que a veces es nece-sario ausentarse o llegar tarde al trabajo debido a enfermedad o emergencia. Sin embargo, será su responsabilidad comunicar la tardanza o la ausencia según consta en las reglas de conducta de su departamento. Ausencias y tardanzas habituales son falta de cortesía para con sus compañeros de trabajo y serán causa de procedimientos disciplinarios e incluso despido.

B. Seguridad del Hotel/Restaurante

La seguridad de nuestros empleados y huéspedes es muy importante para nuestra compañía. Por esta razón, el hotel/restaurante está electronicamente controlado y es patrullado por el Departamento de Seguridad. Con objeto de mantener un centro de trabajo seguro, se deben seguir las disposiciones siguientes.

1. **Entradas y salidas:** Todos los empleados que entren o salgan del hotel/restau-rante y que tengan que marcar el reloj registrador deberán hacerlo por la entrada de servicio.
2. **Uniformes y tarjetas con su nombre:** Los empleados deben llevar puestos sus uniformes de trabajo y las tarjetas con sus nombres cuando estén de servicio. Esta medida permite al Departamento de Seguridad asegurarse de que sólo nues-tros empleados están en el hotel/restaurante.

3. **Packages:** All parcels, packages, knapsacks, and purses will be subject to a random search at the Security Department's discretion. Parcel passes must accompany all items leaving the hotel/restaurant.

The Security Department is for your protection. All employees are encouraged to report any unusual activities within the hotel/restaurant to a security guard at once.

C. Telephone and Elevator Use

Telephone use: Telephones are an important part of our business and should therefore be restricted to business use. Incoming telephone calls, except emergencies, are not permitted while you are on duty. Any calls you may receive will be held by your supervisor until you are off duty. There is a public telephone available which may be used for outgoing calls. Emergency calls may be made with the permission of your supervisor.

Elevator use: A service elevator is provided for all employees who are required to go to the floors to perform their duties. Under no circumstances should any employee use the guest elevators. The only exceptions are those who work in the bell stand, front desk, and security.

D. Personal Appearance

Each employee is a representative of the Royal Hotel/Restaurant, and in a business such as ours, personal appearance and cleanliness are extremely important. Neatness and good taste in your dress and manner contribute much to the impression you make on your fellow employees, and more importantly, on our guests. On your first day of employment, you will receive a dress-code policy for your department from your supervisor.

E. Name Tags

Each employee is issued a name tag the first day of employment. Name tags are a requirement of each position and must be worn visibly at all times while on duty; this includes during breaks, meals, etc. Cafeteria privileges will not be extended to any employee not wearing a name tag. Replacement name tags are supplied at the cost of $1.00 to the employee and must be ordered through your supervisor.

3. **Paquetes:** *Todos los paquetes, envoltorios, mochilas y bolsas serán registrados al azar por el Departamento de Seguridad. Cualquier objeto sacado del hotel/restaurante necesitará un pase.*

El Departamento de Seguridad existe para protegerle. Todos los empleados deben dar parte al (a la) guarda de seguridad de cualquier actividad sospechosa dentro del hotel/restaurante.

C. Uso de Teléfonos y Elevadores

Uso de teléfonos: *Los teléfonos son un componente importante de nuestro negocio y por lo tanto deben utilizarse unicamente para fines comerciales. Las llamadas desde fuera, excepto en caso de emergencia, no son permitidas durante su turno. Las llamadas recibidas serán retenidas por su supervisor(a) hasta que termine su turno. Existe un teléfono público para sus llamadas al exterior. Las llamadas de emergencia pueden hacerse con el permiso de su supervisor(a).*

Uso de Elevadores: *Existe un elevador de servicio para todos los empleados que deban trasladarse a los pisos. Bajo ningún concepto deben los empleados utilizar los elevadores de huéspedes. Se exceptúan aquellos empleados del Departamento de Botones, Recepción y Seguridad.*

D. Apariencia Personal

Cada empleado(a) representa al Hotel/Restaurante Royal, y en un negocio como es el nuestro, la apariencia y el aseo personal son extremadamente importantes. La pulcritud y el buen gusto en su atuendo y aspecto contribuyen en gran modo a la impresión que usted proyecta a otros empleados, y lo que es más importante, a nuestros huéspedes. En el primer día de empleo recibirá del (de la) supervisor(a) de su departamento instrucciones sobre su atuendo de trabajo.

E. Placa con su Nombre

En el primer día de empleo cada empleado(a) recibe una placa con su nombre. Estas placas son necesarias en cada puesto de trabajo y deben llevarse bien visibles en cualquier momento, incluyendo durante sus descansos, comidas, etc. Los privilegios en la cafetería serán denegados a los empleados que no lleven su placa. Para reponer su placa los empleados deben dirigirse a su supervisor(a) pagando un dólar por cada nueva placa que necesiten.

F. Smoking Policy

Smoking by employees is prohibited in all public areas of the hotel/restaurant. For the purpose of good public relations, employees should consider the comfort and convenience of our guests and fellow employees, to whom smoking may be a source of irritation.

G. Disciplinary Action Procedures

The Royal Hotel/Restaurant takes pride in all its employees and attempts to provide a work environment to satisfy the personal and professional needs of every worker. Teamwork and service are important in the hospitality industry and both are interrelated. If there is a breakdown in the teamwork between employees or departments, a disruption in the service to our guests occurs. When this disruption in teamwork and service is caused by employee substandard performance, behavior, or actions, procedures, which can include termination, have been designed to eliminate the problem. The following provisions outline the step-by-step procedures managers will follow if disciplinary measures are necessary.

1. Counseling with the employee by the immediate supervisor who explains the problem and how it affects coworkers, the department, and the hotel/restaurant. Solutions are discussed and agreed upon.
2. If the problem persists, a written documentation by the supervisor is submitted to inform the employee of the problem and its seriousness. Solutions are agreed upon and documented with a time frame in which the problem must be corrected.
3. The third written documentation on any one problem or a combination of problems within a six-month period can result in immediate termination.
4. When hired, all employees read and sign the Company Conduct Policy Form. This form lists offenses which are considered quite severe and which, in most instances and when documented, will result in immediate dismissal.

F. Consumo de Tabaco

Queda prohibido el consumo de tabaco en todas las áreas públicas del hotel/restaurante. Con objeto de mantener buenas relaciones públicas, los empleados deben considerar el confort y la comodidad de nuestros huéspedes y de otros empleados a quienes el humo puede causarles irritación.

G. Procedimientos de Acción Disciplinaria

El Hotel/Restaurante Royal se enorgullece de todos sus empleados y trata de crear un ambiente laboral que satisfaga las necesidades personales y profesionales de cada trabajador(a). El trabajo en equipo y el servicio son importantes en la industria hotelera y ambos están interrelacionados. Si existe una interrupción en el trabajo de equipo entre empleados o departamentos, se crean fallas en el servicio a nuestros clientes. Cuando la interrupción en el trabajo de equipo y en el servicio es causada por la ejecución, acción o comportamiento inaceptable de un(a) empleado(a) se recurrirá a determinados procedimientos para eliminar el problema, incluyéndose la posibilidad de despido. Los procedimientos siguientes determinan los pasos a seguir en caso de acciones disciplinarias.

1. *Asesoramiento del (de la) supervisor(a) con el (la) empleado(a) con objeto de explicar el problema y cómo afecta a otros empleados, al departamento y al hotel/restaurante. Se discutirán las soluciones posibles y se llegará a un acuerdo.*

2. *Si persiste el problema, el (la) supervisor(a) entregará al (a la) empleado(a) un informe por escrito detallando la seriedad del caso. Se llegará a un acuerdo sobre la solución y quedará constancia del período de tiempo en el que el problema debe ser corregido.*

3. *El tercer informe por escrito de cualquier problema o combinación de problemas dentro de un período de tiempo de seis meses puede ser causa de despido inmediato.*

4. *Los empleados, al ser contratados, leen y firman las Reglas de Comportamiento de la Compañía. Estas reglas enumeran las ofensas consideradas como severas, las que en la mayoría de los casos serán causa de despido inmediato.*

You and Our Guests

A. Service

Service is our product. The quality of service we provide to our guests determines the success of the Royal. We all share the responsibility of maintaining and improving the high quality of service that our hotel/restaurant is known for. In every direct sense, the guest is the employer of all of us. They return because of the professional and courteous service employees exhibit day in and day out.

B. Confidentiality

Information about the hotel/restaurant, the guests, or your fellow employees is not to be passed on or discussed with other employees. Be especially careful about divulging names or room numbers of one guest to another. As an employee, you are in a position to observe the personal lives of many people. Refrain from discussing your observations either within or outside the hotel/restaurant.

C. Lost and Found Items

Protect the property of guests against loss, damage, or theft. Report found items immediately to your supervisor. The found items are taken to the Security Department and are recorded in a log book. If the found item is not claimed within ninety days, it belongs to the finder. Failure to report items found is considered theft and immediate termination will result.

Usted y Nuestros Huéspedes

A. Servicio

Nuestro producto es el servicio. La calidad del servicio que ofrecemos a nuestros clientes determina el éxito del Royal. Todos compartimos la responsabilidad de mantener y mejorar la alta calidad del servicio por el que nuestro hotel/restaurante es conocido. En realidad, el huésped es quien nos emplea a todos nosotros. Los huéspedes vuelven debido al servicio cortés y profesional que nuestros empleados muestran día tras día.

B. Confidencialidad

Información sobre el hotel/restaurante, los huéspedes u otros empleados no debe ser divulgada o discutida con otros empleados. Hay que prestar particular atención para no dar nombres o número de habitación de un(a) cliente a otro(a). Como empleado(a), usted podrá observar la vida personal de un gran número de personas. Absténgase de discutir sus observaciones dentro o fuera del hotel/restaurante.

C. Objetos Extraviados

Proteja las pertenencias de los huéspedes contra daños, deterioro o robo. Comunique los objetos encontrados inmediatamente a su supervisor(a). Los objetos encontrados se entregarán al Departamento de Seguridad y serán registrados en el libro de bitácora. Si el objeto encontrado no es reclamado en el plazo de noventa días, pertenecerá a quien lo encontró. La negligencia en comunicar los objetos encontrados será considerada como robo, resultando en despido inmediato.

Your Career with the Company

A. Performance Appraisal

All employees receive a performance appraisal three months after their hire date and every six months thereafter. Wage increases accompany the appraisals and are based on a percentage of wages which relates to performance. The performance appraisal process concentrates on the development of necessary technical knowledge, and if necessary, behavioral changes. In other words, the process includes a review of past performance but emphasizes future objectives and improvements which will be beneficial to the employee and the company.

B. Transfer and Promotion

It has long been a company policy to encourage career growth through transfer and promotion among our employees. The hotel/restaurant will first attempt to fill vacant positions in house before using outside sources. All vacant positions are posted in the Personnel Department and on the bulletin board outside the employee cafeteria. The following steps outline the procedures employees should follow if interested in transfer or promotion.

1. An individual must be employed at least three months before a transfer or promotion will be considered.
2. Employees must go to the Personnel Department and inform the clerk of their interest in the vacant position. The position will be explained in detail and an interview will be scheduled with the manager of the vacant position.

Su Carrera Profesional en la Compañía

A. Evaluación de Rendimiento

Todos los empleados reciben una evaluación de rendimiento tres meses después de la fecha de contratación y cada seis meses después. Los aumentos de salario son basados en las evaluaciones y su porcentaje depende del rendimiento en el trabajo. La evaluación de rendimiento se centra en el desarrollo de los conocimientos técnicos y en cambios de actitud necesarios para el desempeño de funciones. En otras palabras, el proceso incluye un análisis del rendimiento anterior pero también determinará objetivos y mejoramiento en el futuro, lo cual beneficiará al (a la) empleado(a) y a la compañía.

B. Traslado o Promoción

La compañía siempre ha seguido la política de fomentar el avance en el puesto de trabajo por medio de traslados y promociones. El hotel/restaurante intentará cubrir las vacantes con sus empleados antes de con personal ajeno. Las vacantes serán anunciadas en el Departamento de Personal y en el tablón de anuncios situado en la cafetería de empleados. Los empleados deberán seguir el procedimiento siguiente si están interesados en traslados o promociones dentro del hotel/restaurante.

1. *Los empleados deberán haber trabajado un mínimo de tres meses antes de ser considerados para traslado o promoción.*
2. *Los empleados deberán notificar al Departamento de Personal sobre su intención de cubrir la vacante anunciada. El puesto les será explicado detalladamente y se fijará una entrevista con el (la) jefe del departamento que tenga la vacante.*

3. The decision whether to approve a transfer or promotion will be based on the employee's performance in present and previous positions, on his (her) ability to take on added responsibility, and on his (her) initiative, merit, attendance, and length of service.
4. Once a transfer or promotion is approved, a two-week resignation of the present position must be submitted to the employee's present manager.
5. The first three months of the new position will be considered a period of review, regardless of length of employment prior to the transfer or promotion.

This company foresees an unlimited growth potential for individuals with initiative, drive, and ambition.

3. La decisión de aprobar el traslado o la promoción estará basada en el comportamiento del (de la) empleado(a) en su puesto actual y en puestos anteriores, en su abilidad para asumir responsabilidad y en su iniciativa, merecimiento, asistencia al trabajo y tiempo de empleo.

4. Si el traslado o la promoción es aprobada, el (la) empleado(a) deberá entregar a su jefe inmediato(a) su decisión de dimitir de su puesto actual en dos semanas.

5. Los primeros tres meses en el nuevo puesto serán considerados como período de prueba, sin tener en cuenta la duración del puesto ocupado con anterioridad al traslado o promoción.

El hotel/restaurante ofrece enormes posibilidades de avance a aquellos empleados que demuestren iniciativa, deseos y ambición personal.

How the Employees Keep in Touch

A. Bulletin Boards

Bulletin boards are an excellent means of communication and should be read regularly by all employees. Each department has a bulletin board, and a central one is located in the employee cafeteria. Make it a habit to read posted material on these boards to keep up with what's happening.

B. Department Meetings

At least once a month you will be required to attend a scheduled department meeting. These meetings are designed to pass along information to you concerning hotel policies, department changes, etc. These meetings also allow you to communicate any concerns you may have about your position, department policies, etc. Attendance is mandatory, and each employee will be paid for the duration of the meeting, with tipped employees receiving minimum wage.

Cómo Mantenerse en Contacto

A. Tablones de Anuncios

Los tablones de anuncios son un medio excelente de comunicación y deberían ser leídos regularmente por todos los empleados. El tablón de anuncios principal está localizado en la cafetería de empleados, además, cada departamento cuenta con el suyo propio. Lea habitualmente los anuncios colocados en los tablones con objeto de quedar informado de lo que está ocurriendo.

B. Juntas de Departamento

Por lo menos una vez al mes será requerido(a) a asistir a una junta de su departamento. Estas juntas tienen por objeto transmitirle información sobre el hotel, cambios en el departamento, etc. Estas juntas también le ofrecen la oportunidad para exponer cualquier preocupación que usted pueda tener sobre su trabajo, sobre la política de su departamento, etc. La asistencia es obligatoria y se pagará a cada empleado(a) el tiempo que dure la junta; los empleados que reciben propinas serán remunerados con salario mínimo.

Things Employees Should Know

A. Employment of Relatives and Referrals

The company will employ relatives of its employees; the only restriction is that one relative cannot supervise another, since we feel that this may cause a conflict of interest. A relative is defined as father, mother, son, daughter, brother, sister, grandmother, grandfather, granddaughter, grandson, aunt, uncle, cousin, or any family relationship resulting from marriage. If you recommend a friend or relative, and that individual is hired, you will be awarded $25.00 six months after the referral hire date if you both are still employed. It's the company's way of saying "thank you."

B. Visitors

Visiting with friends and relatives during your shift is strongly discouraged. We feel this will cause a disruption in the service to our guests. If out-of-town friends and relatives stay in the hotel, make prior arrangements with your supervisor, who will accommodate both you and the hotel.

C. Check Cashing

It is the hotel/restaurant's policy not to cash either employee payroll checks or personal checks.

Para su Información

A. Empleo de Familiares y Recomendaciones

La compañía da empleo a familiares de los empleados; la única restricción es que un familiar no puede supervisar a otro(a), ya que creemos que esto podría ser causa de conflicto de intereses. Un familiar queda definido como padre, madre, hijo, hija, hermano, hermana, abuela, abuelo, nieta, nieto, tía, tío, primo(a) u otra relación familiar que resulte por matrimonio. Si usted recomienda a un(a) amigo(a) o familiar y éste(a) es contratado(a), se le abonarán $25.00 seis meses después de la fecha de contratación si ambos continúan al servicio de la empresa. De este modo la compañía le agradece su recomendación.

B. Visitantes

La visita personal de amigos y familiares durante su turno no está permitida. Creemos que esto causaría interrupciones en el servicio a nuestros huéspedes. En el caso de que amigos o familiares vengan de fuera y se hospeden en el hotel, debe comunicarlo a su supervisor(a), quien tratará de acomodar a usted y a las necesidades del hotel.

C. Cobro de Cheques

Es política del hotel/restaurante no cobrar cheques salariales o personales.

D. Personal Information Changes

If you change your name, marital status, number of dependents, address, or telephone number, you should immediately notify your supervisor, who will notify the Personnel Department.

E. Sexual Harrasment

It is the intent of the company to provide its employees with the best possible working environment. As part of this effort we want employees to know that this establishment prohibits personal harassment. This includes, but is not limited to, harassment based on sex, race, or national origin.

> Supervisors, male or female, shall not use their authority to solicit subordinates for sexual favors when failure to submit would result in an adverse working environment. No employee, whether or not a supervisor, shall physically or verbally harass or intimidate any other employee.

Employees are urged to contact the Personnel Department if they feel there is a violation of this policy. The matter will be fully investigated and, if appropriate, immediate action taken. Every effort will be made to keep the employee's identity confidential if requested.

F. No Solicitation Rule

Solicitations are not permitted by employees for any purpose during working time. An employee may not engage in solicitation of other employees during their working shift. Employees may not engage in solicitation of other employees in customer service areas. Distribution of literature by employees is not permitted for any purpose during working time or in working areas. Working time does not include meal breaks or rest periods or other specified times during the work shift when employees are not engaged in performing their work tasks. Working areas are defined as areas of the premises where employees perform their work tasks, but do not include break rooms, employee restrooms or parking lots. Off-duty employees are prohibited from entering any area not open to the public and are prohibited from interfering with an on-duty employee's performance of his (her) work tasks.

Nonemployees may not solicit for any purpose or engage in distribution of literature of any kind on the premises at any time. Solicitation or distribution of literature to nonemployees by employees is prohibited.

D. Cambio de Información Personal

Si usted cambia su nombre, su estado civil, su número de dependientes su dirección o su número de teléfono, debe comunicarlo inmediatamente a su supervisor(a), quien lo comunicará a su vez al Departamento de Personal.

E. Acoso Sexual

La compañía desea proporcionar a sus empleados el mejor ambiente laboral posible. Como parte de este esfuerzo, hacemos constar que este establecimiento prohibe cualquier forma de acoso personal. Esto incluye, aunque no está limitado a, acoso basado en sexo, raza o nacionalidad de origen.

Los supervisores, hombres o mujeres, no deberán usar su autoridad para solicitar de sus subordinados favores de carácter sexual cuando la negativa resulte en condiciones de trabajo o salario adversas o cuando creen un ambiente laboral adverso. Ningún(a) empleado(a), sea o no supervisor(a), acosará física o verbalmente o intimidará a otro(a) empleado(a).

Los empleados podrán dirigirse al Departamento de Personal si creen que existe una violación de esta política. El caso será investigado en su totalidad y si procede, se tomarán medidas oportunas. También se intentará mantener la identidad del (de la) empleado(a) confidencialmente si así éste(a) lo prefiere.

F. Solicitación por parte de Empleados

Las solicitaciones por parte de los empleados no están permitidas en caso alguno durante las horas de trabajo. Los empleados no pueden solicitar de otros empleados mientras estén trabajando. Los empleados no pueden solicitar en el área de servicio a clientes. La distribución de literatura por parte de los empleados no está permitida en ningún caso durante las horas de trabajo o en áreas de trabajo. Las horas de trabajo no incluyen las comidas o períodos de descanso o cualquier otro tiempo en el que los empleados no estén cumpliendo sus tareas. Las áreas de trabajo están definidas como áreas donde los empleados trabajan, pero no incluyen los cuartos para descansar, los vestuarios de empleados o el aparcamiento. Los empleados que no estén de servicio no podrán entrar en áreas no abiertas al público y se les prohibe interferir con los empleados de servicio que estén desempeñando sus funciones.

Aquellos que no fueran empleados no podrán hacer solicitaciones por ningún motivo o distribuir literatura de ningún tipo en el establecimiento. Las solicitaciones o distribución de literatura a no empleados por parte de los empleados no está permitida.

Resignation

A. Two-Week Written Notice

Though we hope you remain with the company for a long time, sometimes personal affairs force a change in occupation or residence. In such case, a two-week written resignation is requested. This courtesy of advance notice allows us to adjust working schedules and attempt to secure a replacement. On the employee's last day of employment, all company property must be returned. Upon the receipt of such property, a separation interview will be conducted, health insurance coverage conversion will be discussed, and the final pay check will be issued the following week on the normal payday.

B. References

The Personnel Department will issue a letter of reference to any employee requesting such. This letter will only indicate length of employment and position.

C. Re-employment

Should an individual wish to seek re-employment with the hotel/restaurant, he (she) may do so by filling out an application in the Personnel Department. Reemployment will be based on the employee's performance when he (she) was employed at the hotel/restaurant and whether the qualifications meet the requirements of the desired position.

Dimisión

A. Aviso por Escrito de Dos Semanas

Aunque esperamos que usted continúe trabajando en la compañía, a veces ocurren asuntos personales que requieren cambio de empleo o de residencia. En este caso, requerimos un aviso por escrito de dos semanas. Esta cortesía de aviso adelantado nos permitirá ajustar nuestros horarios y tratar de encontrar un substituto. En el último día de trabajo, usted deberá devolver todos los artículos pertenecientes a la compañía. Una vez recibidos dichos artículos se le hará una entrevista de salida donde se discutirá la continuación de su póliza de seguro, entregándole el cheque salarial el día de pago de la semana siguiente.

B. Recomendaciones

El Departamento de Personal emitirá una carta de recomendación a aquellos empleados que lo soliciten. Esta carta solamente indicará la duración del empleo y el puesto desempeñado.

C. Reempleo

Si algún(a) trabajador(a) desea volver a colocarse en el hotel/restaurante, éste(a) deberá rellenar un formulario de empleo en el Departamento de Personal. El reempleo será considerado basándose en el desempeño de sus funciones cuando estuvo empleado(a) en el hotel/restaurante y si su capacidad corresponde al puesto deseado.

Employee Conduct

The following acts will result in disciplinary action or termination.

1. Reporting to work under the influence of drugs or alcohol.
2. Carrying a firearm or any other deadly weapon while on the premises.
3. Fraternizing with any guest.
4. Leaving work during working hours without the permission of an immediate supervisor.
5. Using the telephones without authorization.
6. Smoking in uniform in public areas.
7. Willfully altering a job application information.
8. Demonstrating excessive tardiness or absenteeism.
9. Sleeping while on duty.
10. Parking a vehicle in nondesignated areas.
11. Drinking alcohol or using drugs on the job.
12. Eating or drinking while not on break or in nondesignated areas.
13. Socially or sexually harassing employees, supervisors, or guests.
14. Soliciting employees or guests during working hours.
15. Behaving in an insubordinate manner.
16. Leaving the work area without authorization from a supervisor.
17. Clocking in before or after the designated time. Tampering with time cards.
18. Intimidating employees, supervisors, or guests.
19. Stealing, abusing or destroying intentionally guest or company property.
20. Gambling while on duty.
21. Being absent for three consecutive days without acknowledgment of a supervisor.
22. Lacking due respect to guests or supervisors.

Conducta de los Empleados

Las acciones siguientes serán causa de acción disciplinaria o despido.

1. Acudir al trabajo bajo la influencia de drogas o alcohol.
2. Estar en posesión de arma de fuego u otra arma mortal en el local de trabajo.
3. Fraternizar con los huéspedes.
4. Abandonar el área de trabajo durante las horas de servicio sin el permiso de un(a) supervisor(a) inmediato(a).
5. Usar los teléfonos sin autorización.
6. Fumar de uniforme en áreas públicas.
7. Alterar intencionalmente la información en la solicitud de empleo.
8. Incurrier en excesiva tardanza o absentismo.
9. Dormir estando de servicio.
10. Aparcar el vehículo en áreas no designadas.
11. Beber alcohol o usar drogas en el trabajo.
12. Comer o beber fuera de los descansos o en áreas no designadas.
13. Acosar social o sexualmente a empleados, supervisores o huéspedes.
14. Solicitar a empleados o huéspedes durante las horas de trabajo.
15. Comportarse de una manera insubordinada.
16. Abandonar el área de trabajo sin la autorizacion de un(a) supervisor(a).
17. Marcar el reloj registrador antes o después del tiempo designado. Falsificar la tarjeta registradora.
18. Intimidar a empleados, supervisores o huéspedes.
19. Robar, abusar o destruir la propiedad de huéspedes o de la compañía.
20. Participar en juegos de azar en horas de servicio.
21. Estar ausente durante tres días consecutivos sin el conocimiento de un(a) supervisor(a).
22. Mostrar falta de respeto a huéspedes o supervisores.

Spanish-English Hospitality Vocabulary

Abbreviations:
(a.) adjective; (m.) masculine noun; (f.) feminine noun; (v.) verb
(infinitive); (ue) *ue* stem-changing verb; (ie) *ie* stem-changing verb;
(i) *i* stem-changing verb; (irreg.) irregular verb

abajo downstairs
abonar (v.) fertilize
abono (m.) fertilizer
abrelatas (m.) can opener
abril (m.) April
abuso de substancias (m.)
   substance abuse
aceite (m.) oil
aceite y vinagre (m.) oil and
   vinegar
acoso sexual (m.) sexual
   harassment
acostarse (v.) (ue) go to bed
actitud (f.) attitude
adentro inside
aderezo (m.) dressing; condiment

aderezo para ensalada (m.)
   salad dressing
adiós goodbye
aflojador de tierra (m.)
   rototiller
afuera outside
agosto (m.) August
agua (f.) water
agua caliente (f.) hot water
agua jabonosa (f.) soapy
   water
agua para riego (f.) irrigation
   water
agua potable (f.) drinking
   water
aguas negras (f.) waste water
aguja (f.) needle

ahí there
ahora now
aire acondicionado (m.) air-
   conditioning
alambre (m.) wire
alberca (f.) swimming pool
alcohólico (a.) alcoholic
alegrarse (v.) be glad
alegría (f.) joy
alfombra (f.) carpet
algas (f.) algae
alguicida (m.) algicide
alicates (m.) pliers
alimentos y bebidas (m.) food
   and beverage
allá there
allí there

almacén (m.) storeroom
almidón (m.) starch
almidonar (v.) starch
almohada (f.) pillow
almorzar (v.) (ve) have lunch
almuerzo (m.) lunch
alto (a.) tall
ama de llaves (f.) executive housekeeper
amarillo (a.) yellow
anaranjado (a.) orange
andador (m.) garden path
anoche last night
antes earlier
anunciar (v.) announce
año (m.) year
apagador (m.) light switch
aparador (m.) service station; service stand
aparcamiento (m.) parking
apariencia personal (f.) grooming
apellido (m.) last name
aperitivo (m.) appetizer; aperitif
apio (m.) celery
apodo (m.) nickname
aprendizaje (m.) apprenticeship
aquel that
aquí here
árbol (m.) tree
arbusto (m.) bush
áreas públicas (f.) public areas
arena (f.) sand
arma (f.) weapon
arriba upstairs
arroz (m.) rice
asa (f.) handle
asar (v.) roast, grill
aseo personal (m.) grooming
así thus
asistente (m., f.) assistant
aspiradora (f.) vacuum cleaner
aspirar (v.) vacuum
asustarse (v.) get frightened
atún (m.) tuna fish
aumento (m.) raise

aunque although
ausencia excesiva (f.) absenteeism
autoservicio (m.) self-service
avería (f.) breakdown
ayer yesterday
ayudante de mesero (m., f.) busperson
azadón (m.) hoe
azotea (f.) flat roof
azúcar (m.) sugar
azucarero (m.) sugar bowl
azul (a.) blue
azulejo (m.) tile

bacteria (f.) bacteria
bajar (v.) come down
bajo (a.) low
bajo under
balde (m.) bucket
baldosa (f.) tile
bandeja (f.) charola; sheet pan
banquete (m.) banquet
bañera (f.) bathtub
baño (m.) bath; bathroom, restroom
baño público (m.) public bathroom
bar (m.) bar
barniz (m.) varnish
barnizar (v.) varnish
barrer (v.) sweep
bastante enough
basura (f.) trash
bata (f.) frock; robe
batir (v.) beat
bebida (f.) beverage
beber (v.) drink
bien well
bien hecho (a.) well done
bisagra (f.) hinge
bistec (m.) beefsteak
bitácora (f.) log book
blanco (a.) white
blancos (m.) bed linen
bloc de notas (m.) note pad
bloqueado (a.) blocked
bloquear (v.) block
bolsa de basura (f.) trash bag

bolsa de lavandería (f.) laundry bag
bolsa sanitaria (f.) sanitary bag
bolsita de azúcar (f.) sugar packet
bolsita de té (f.) tea bag
bomba (f.) pump
boquilla (f.) nozzle
borde (m.) rim
botas de agua (f.) rubber boots
bote (m.) can
botón (m.) button
buffet (m.) buffet
buzón de sugerencias (m.) suggestion box

cable (m.) cable
caerse (v. irreg.) fall down
café (m.) coffee
cafetera (f.) coffee maker
cafetería (f.) cafeteria
caja (f.) cash register; box
caja de herramientas (f.) toolbox
caja de registro (f.) register box
cajero(a) (m., f.) cashier
cajón (m.) drawer
cal (f.) lime
caldera (f.) boiler
calefacción (f.) heating
calentador de pan (m.) bread warmer
caliente (a.) hot
callarse (v.) stop talking
calle (f.) street
calmarse (v.) calm down
cama (f.) bed
cama matrimonial (f.) queen-sized bed
cama portátil (f.) cot
cámara congeladora (f.) walk-in freezer
cámara fría (f.) walk-in refrigerator
camarista (m., f.) housekeeper; room attendant
camarón (m.) shrimp

cambiarse (v.) change clothes
cambio (m.) change
cambio de turno (m.) shift turnover
campana (f.) kitchen hood
canapé (m.) canape
canasta de frutas (f.) fruit basket
cancha de tenis (f.) tennis court
cansarse (v.) get tired
¡caramba! Good gracious!
carne (f.) meat
carne de ave (f.) poultry
carne de res (f.) beef
carne picada (f.) ground meat
carpintero(a) (m., f.) carpenter
carretilla (f.) wheelbarrow
carro (m.) car; cart
carro de postres (m.) dessert cart
carro de servicio (m.) housekeeping cart
carta (f.) letter
carta de vinos (f.) wine list
casa (f.) house
casarse (v.) get married
cascajo (m.) gravel
casi almost
castaña (f.) chestnut
castaño (a.) chestnut
catorce fourteen
cavar (v.) dig
cazo (m.) ladle; pot
cazuela (f.) pan; casserole
cebolla (f.) onion
cemento (m.) cement
cena (f.) dinner
cenicero (m.) ashtray
cenizas (f.) ashes
cepillo (m.) brush
cepillo de mano (m.) hand brush
cera (f.) wax
cerca near
cerillos (m.) matches
cero zero
cerrado (a.) closed

cerradura (f.) lock
cerrar (v.) (ie) close, shut
cerrar con llave (v.) lock
cerveza (f.) beer
césped (m.) lawn
cesta (f.) basket
cesta para pan (f.) bread basket
cesto de basura (m.) wastebasket
champú (m.) shampoo
charola (f.) tray
cheque (m.) check
chicle (m.) chewing gum
chocolate (m.) chocolate
cien hundred
cinco five
cincuenta fifty
cita (f.) appointment
ciudad (f.) city
ciudadano(a) (m., f.) citizen
claro (a.) light
clavar (v.) nail
clavo (m.) nail
cliente (m. f.) customer
cloro (m.) chlorine
closet (m.) closet
cobertor (m.) bedspread
cocina (f.) kitchen
código postal (m.) ZIP Code
coffee break (m.) coffee break
cojín (m.) cushion
coladera (f.) drain
colador (m.) colander
colcha (f.) quilt
colchón (m.) mattress
colgar (v.) (ue) hang
colilla (f.) cigarette butt
comedor (m.) dining room
comenzar (v.) (ie) begin
comer (v.) eat
comida (f.) meal
cómo how
como as, like
compañía (f.) company
competente (a.) competent
comprender (v.) understand
compresor (m.) compressor
comprobar (v.) (ve) check

con with
concreto (m.) concrete
congelado (a.) frozen
congelador (m.) freezer
contra against
contratar (v.) hire
contar (v.) (ve) count
control de plagas (m.) pest control
control de ropa (m.) linen control
convoy de mesa (m.) cruet
copa (f.) goblet
correa (f.) belt
correr la cortina (v.) draw the curtain
cortadora de césped (f.) lawnmower
cortar (v.) cut, chop, mow
cortar el césped (v.) mow the lawn
cortés (a.) courteous
cortesía, servicio de (f.) turndown service
cortina (f.) curtain
cortina de ducha (f.) shower curtain
cortocircuito (m.) short circuit
costar (v.) (ve) cost
coser (v.) sew
cristalería (f.) glassware
cuadro (m.) picture, painting; square
cual which
cuando when
¿cuánto? How much?
cuarenta forty
cuarto (m.) guestroom
cuarto de repaso (m.) pick-up room
cuarto de salida (m.) checkout room
cuarto listo (m.) room ready for check-in
cuatro four
cubertería (f.) flatware
cubeta (f.) bus tub
cubeta para hielo (f.) ice bucket

cubitos de hielo (m.) ice cubes
cubo (m.) bucket
cubo de basura (m.) trash can
cubrir (v.) cover
cucaracha (f.) cockroach
cuchara (f.) spoon
cucharilla (f.) teaspoon
cuchillo (m.) knife
curriculum vitae (m.) resume
cuota de trabajo (f.) workload

dar (v.) (irreg.) give
de of
decir (v.) (irreg.) tell, say
dedo (m.) finger
delantal (m.) apron
delito mayor (m.) felony
demasiado too much
departamento (m.) department
departamento de ama de llaves (m.) housekeeping department
derramar (v.) spill
desagüe (m.) drain
desayuno (m.) breakfast
descafeinado (a.) decaffeinated
descanso (m.) rest; break
descongelar (v.) thaw, defrost
desde from
desinfectante (m.) disinfectant
desmanchar (v.) de-stain
desmayarse (v.) faint
desocupado (a.) unoccupied, vacant
desodorante (m.) deodorant
despacio slowly
despedirse (v.) (i) say goodbye
despensa (f.) pantry
desperdicio (m.) waste; garbage; food scraps
despertarse (v.) (ie) wake up
despido (m.) termination
desportillado (a.) chipped
después after
destapador (m.) bottle opener
destornillador (m.) screwdriver

detector de fuego (m.) fire detector
detector de humo (m.) smoke detector
detergente (m.) detergent
devolver (v.) (ue) give back; return
día (m.) day
día festivo (m.) holiday
día laborable (m.) working day
diciembre (m.) December
diez ten
difícil (a.) difficult
dirección (f.) address
dirección postal (f.) mailing address
director(a) (m., f.) director; manager
directorio telefónico (m.) telephone book
directorio de servicios (m.) service directory
distribuidor de jabón (m.) soap dispenser
divertirse (v.) (ie) have a good time
división cuartos (f.) rooms division
doblar (v.) fold
doblador (m.) folder
doce twelve
domicilio (m.) residence; address
domingo (m.) Sunday
¿dónde? Where?
dorado (a.) golden
dormir (v.) (ue) sleep
dormirse (v.) (ue) fall asleep
dos two
drenaje (m.) drainage
droga (f.) drug
ducha (f.) shower
ducharse (v.) take a shower
ducto (m.) duct
durante during
duro (a.) hard

el the
él he

ella she
ellas (f.) they
ellos they (m. or mixed group)
electricidad (f.) electricity
elevador (m.) elevator
empanado (a.) breaded
empanar (v.) bread
empapar (v.) soak
empaque (m.) packing
empezar (v.) (ie) begin; start
emplatar (v.) plate
empleado (m.) employee
empleo (m.) employment; job
empresa (f.) company, firm
en in
en seguida at once
encender (v.) (ie) light; turn on
encontrar (v.) (ve) find
enero (m.) January
enfadarse (v.) get angry
enfermo (a.) sick
enfrente opposite
enjuagar (v.) rinse
ensalada (f.) salad
entender (v.) (ie) understand
entrada (f.) entrance; entree
entrada principal (f.) main entrance
entre between
entrenamiento (m.) training
entrenar (v.) coach; train
entrevista (f.) interview
envolver (v.) (ue) wrap
equipaje (m.) luggage
equipo (m.) equipment; team
equipo de limpieza (m.) cleaning team
equipo de relevo (m.) swing team
equivocarse (v.) make a mistake
erosión (f.) erosion
escalera (f.) ladder
escalera de servicio (f.) service stairs
escaleras (f.) staircase; steps
escardar (v.) weed

escoba (f.) broom
escobilla (f.) johnny mop
escolaridad (f.) education
esconder (v.) hide
escribir (v.) write
escribir a máquina (v.) type
escritorio (m.) desk;
escuela secundaria (f.) high
   school
escurridor (m.) mop wringer
escurrir (v.) drain; wring
ese(a) that
esmalte (m.) enamel
español (a.) Spanish
espátula (f.) spatula
espejo (m.) mirror
espinacas (f.) spinach
esponja (f.) sponge
espumadera (f.) skimmer
estación (f.) station; season
estación de servicio (f.) service station
estacionamiento (m.) parking
estado (m.) state
estante (m.) shelf
estar (v.) (irreg.) be
este(a) this
estera de goma (f.) rubber
   mat
estiércol (m.) manure
estropajo (m.) scrubbing pad
etiqueta (f.) tag; label
evaluación (f.) evaluation;
   appraisal
excusa (f.) excuse
éxito (m.) success
experiencia (f.) experience
expreso (a.) express
extintor (m.) fire extinguisher
extractor de aire (m.) air
   extractor

favor (m.) favor
febrero (m.) February
fecha (f.) date
fechar (v.) date
felpa (f.) terry cloth
filtro (m.) filter; strainer
fin de semana (m.) weekend
firma (f.) signature

firmar (v.) sign
flor (f.) flower
flotador (m.) float
foco (m.) light bulb
fontanero(a) (m., f.) plumber
fregadero (m.) kitchen sink
freidora (f.) deep fryer
freír (v.) fry
fresa (f.) strawberry
frijoles (m.) beans
frío (a.) cold
frito (a.) fried
fuego (m.) fire
fuente (f.) fountain
fuera de servicio (a.) out of
   order
fuga (f.) leak
fumigar (v.) fumigate
funda de almohada (f.) pillowcase
fusible (m.) fuse

galleta (f.) cracker
gana (f.) desire
gancho (m.) clothes hanger
gasolina (f.) gasoline
gente (f.) people
gerente (m., f.) manager
gerente general (m., f.) general manager
germicida (m.) germicide
ginebra (f.) gin
gorro de baño (m.) shower
   cap
gota (f.) drop
gracias (f.) thank you
grados (m.) degrees
grasiento (a.) greasy
gratis (a.) gratis, free
grifo (m.) faucet, tap
gris (a.) gray
guantes (m.) gloves
guantes de goma (m.) rubber
   gloves
guarnición (f.) garnish
guía de televisión (f.) T.V.
   guide
guía telefónica (f.) telephone
   book
guinda (f.) cherry

habitación (f.) guest room
hablar (v.) speak; talk
hacer (v.) (irreg.) do; make
hacer ingletes (v.) (irreg.)
   miter
hamburguesa (f.) hamburger
harina (f.) flour
hasta until
helado (m.) ice cream
herbicida (m.) herbicide
herramienta (f.) tool
hervir (v.) (ie) boil
hervir a fuego lento (v) (ie)
   poach
hielo (m.) ice
hielera (f.) ice bucket
hierba (f.) grass
higiene (f.) hygiene
hoja (f.) leaf; sheet of paper
¡hola! Hi!
hongos (m.) fungi
honradez (f.) honesty
horario de trabajo (m.) work
   hours
horas extra (f.) overtime
horno (m.) oven
host (m.) host
hostess (f.) hostess
hotel (m.) hotel
hoy today
hoyo (m.) hole
huésped (m., f.) guest
huevo (m.) egg
huevo duro (m.) hard-boiled
   egg
huevo pasado por agua (m.)
   soft-boiled egg
huevos revueltos (m.) scrambled eggs
humo (m.) smoke

ingeniería (f.) engineering
inglés (m.) English
injertar (v.) graft
inmigrante (m., f.) immigrant
inodoro (m.) toilet
insecticida (m.) insecticide
insecto (m.) insect
inspección (f.) inspection
inspeccionar (v.) inspect

insubordinación (f.) insubordination
inventario (m.) inventory
invierno (m.) winter
ir (irreg.) to go
irse (irreg.) to go away

jabón (m.) soap
jabón de baño (m.) bath soap
jabón de tocador (m.) hand soap
jabón líquido (m.) liquid soap
jabonera (f.) soap dish
jalea (f.) jelly
jamón (m.) ham
jarabe (m.) syrup
jardín (m.) garden
jardinero(a) (m., f.) gardener
jarra (f.) jug; jar
jarra para agua (f.) water jar
jarra para café (f.) coffee jar
jarrita para leche (f.) creamer
jefe de cocina (m., f.) chef; head cook
jerez (m.) sherry
jornada de trabajo (f.) workday
juegos infantiles (m.) playground
jueves (m.) Thursday
jugo (m.) juice
julio (m.) July
junio (m.) June
junta de departamento (f.) department meeting

ketchup (m.) ketchup
kilo (m.) kilogram
kiwi (m.) kiwi

la the
ladrillo (m.) brick
lámpara (f.) lamp
lámpara de pie (f.) floor lamp
lápiz (m.) pencil
lástima (f.) pity
lastimarse (v.) get hurt
lavabo (m.) room sink; vanity
lavado a seco (m.) drycleaning

lavandería (f.) laundry room
lavamanos (m.) bathroom sink
lavaplatos (m.) dishwasher
lavar (v.) wash
leche (f.) milk
lechuga (f.) lettuce
legal (a.) legal
legumbres (f.) vegetables
lejos far
lencería (f.) linens
levantarse (v.) get up
libreta de apuntes (f.) note pad
libro (m.) book
licencia para manejar (f.) driver's license
limón (m.) lemon
limpiador de cafeteras (m.) urn cleaner
limpiador de vidrios (m.) window cleaner
limpiar (v.) clean; wipe down
limpiar a fondo (v.) deep clean
líquido limpiador (m.) cleaning solution
lista de espera (f.) waiting list
lista de lavandería (f.) laundry list
listo para alquilar (a.) ready for rent
litro (m.) liter
llamar (v.) call
llave (f.) key
llave de paso (f.) shut-off valve
llave maestra (f.) master key
llegar tarde (v.) tardiness
lluvia (f.) rain
lobby (m.) lobby
loza (f.) china
lubricar (v.) lubricate; oil
luces de emergencia (f.) emergency lights
lunes (m.) Monday
luz de salida (f.) exit light

maceta (f.) flower pot
madera (f.) wood

mal badly
maleta (f.) suitcase
mancha (f.) stain
mangle (m.) mangle
mango (m.) handle; stem; mango
manguera (f.) hose
mano (f.) hand
manómetro (m.) pressure gage
manta (f.) blanket
mantel (m.) tablecloth
mantelería (f.) napery
mantenimiento (m.) maintenance
mantequilla (f.) butter
manual (m.) manual; handbook
manzana (f.) apple
mañana tomorrow
mañana (f.) morning
máquina de hacer hielo (f.) ice machine
máquina de refrescos (f.) soda dispenser
máquina lavaplatos (f.) dishwashing machine
máquina para lavar alfombras (f.) rug shampooer
marcar el reloj registrador (v.) clock in; clock out
marcharse (v.) go away
mariscos (m.) seafood, shellfish
marmita (f.) kettle
marmita al vapor (f.) steam kettle
marrón (a.) brown
martes (m.) Tuesday
martillo (m.) hammer
marzo (m.) March
más more
masa (f.) dough
material (m.) material
mayo (m.) May
mayonesa (f.) mayonnaise
medio de locomoción (m.) transportation
medio hecho (a.) medium done

mejor better
mejorarse (v.) get better
melón (m.) melon
menos less
mensaje (m.) message
menú (m.) menu
mermelada (f.) jam
mermelada de durazno (f.) peach jam
mermelada de fresa (f.) strawberry jam
mermelada de naranja (f.) marmalade
mermeladera (f.) jam pot
mes (m.) month
mesa (f.) table
mesa de noche (f.) night table
mesa de servicio (f.) service table
mesero(a) (m., f.) waiter, waitress
mezcladora (f.) mixer
mezclar (v.) mix
mi my
microondas (m.) microwave oven
miel (f.) honey
miércoles (m.) Wednesday
migajas (f.) breadcrumbs
mil thousand
molino de café (m.) coffee grinder
morado (a.) purple
moreno (a.) dark; brown
mostaza (f.) mustard
mostrador (f.) counter
mover (v.) (ve) move
mozo(a) de limpieza (m., f.) janitor
mozo(a) de pisos (m., f.) housekeeping houseperson
mucho much
muebles (m.) furniture
mugre (f.) dirt

nada nothing
nadie nobody
naranja (f.) orange
naranja (a.) orange

negro (a.) black
ni...ni neither...nor
nieve (f.) snow
ninguno no one
niñera (f.) babysitter
niño(a) (m., f.) child
no no; not
noche (f.) night
nombre (m.) name
nosotras (f.) we
nosotros (m., mixed group) we
notificar (v.) notify
noventa ninety
noviembre (m.) November
nuestro our
nueve nine
número (m.) number
número de habitación (m.) room number
nunca never

objetos extraviados (m.) lost & found items
ochenta eighty
ocho eight
octubre (m.) October
ocupado (a.) occupied
oficina (f.) office
oír to hear
olla (f.) pot
once eleven
orden de trabajo (f.) work order
ordenanzas (f.) rules and regulations
oscuro (a.) dark
ostra (f.) oyster
otoño (m.) autumn, fall

paga (f.) pay, salary
pala (f.) shovel
pálido (a.) pale
palmera (f.) palm tree
palomita (f.) bow tie
pan (m.) bread
panecillo (m.) bread roll
panqueque (m.) pancake
pantalla (f.) screen
paño (m.) cloth, fabric

pañuelo (m.) handkerchief
pañuelos desechables (m.) facial tissues
papa (f.) potato
papas fritas (f.) fried potatoes
papel (m.) paper
papel de escribir timbrado (m.) hotel stationery papel
papel higiénico (m.) toilet paper
papel tapiz (m.) wallpaper
papelera (f.) wastepaper basket
papelería (f.) paperwork
para for
parar (v.) stop
pardo (a.) brown
pared (f.) wall
parrilla (f.) broiler; grill
pasillo (m.) hallway
pastel (m.) cake; pie
pastelería (f.) pastry selection
patio (m.) patio; courtyard
patrón (m., f.) boss, employer
patrona (f.) boss, employer
pavo (m.) turkey
pedido (m.) requisition
pedir (v.) (i) ask
pelar (v.) peel
pena (f.) sorrow
peor worse
pepino (m.) cucumber
pera (f.) pear
perder (v.) (ie) lose
¡perdón! pardon me!
perejil (m.) parsley
periódico (m.) newspaper
pero but
perro (m.) dog
persiana (f.) venetian blind
personal (m.) personnel
pescado (m.) fish
pesticida (m.) pesticide
picado (a.) ground; minced
picar (v.) grind; mince
piedra (f.) rock; stone
pimentero (m.) pepper shaker
plomería (f.) plumbing
plomero(a) (m., f.) plumber

pluma (f.) pen
poco little
poco hecho (a.) rare
podar (v.) prune
poder (v.) (ve) can
polea (f.) pulley
pollo (m.) chicken
polvo (m.) dust
polvo limpiador (m.) cleaning powder
poner (v.) (irreg.) put
poner demasiada agua (v.) (irreg.) overwater
poner la mesa (v.) (irreg.) set the table
por by
¡Por favor! Please!
¿Por qué? Why?
porque because
portamaletas (m.) luggage rack
postre (m.) dessert
preferir (v.) (ie) prefer
preocuparse (v.) worry
preparación del salón (f.) room set-up
primavera (f.) spring
primero first
primer plato (m.) first course
probar (v.) (ve) try; taste
productos de lavandería (m.) laundry products
productos químicos (m.) chemicals
propina (f.) tip
protector de colchón (m.) mattress pad
puerco (m.) pork
puerta (f.) door
puesto (m.) position
pulir (v.) polish
puntual (a.) punctual

¿Qué? What
que that
quedarse (v.) stay; remain
quejarse (v.) complain
quemar (v.) burn
querer (v.) (ie) want; love
queso (m.) cheese

quien who
quince fifteen
quitarse (v.) take off clothing

radio (f.) radio
raíz (f.) root
rama (f.) branch
rápido quick; fast
rascar (v.) scrape
rastrillo (m.) rake
rata (f.) rat
rato (m.) short period of time
ratón (m.) mouse
ratonera (f.) mousetrap
rebanada (f.) slice
rebanar (v.) slice
recepción (f.) front desk
reclutamiento (m.) recruiting
recogedor (m.) dustpan
recomendación (f.) references
recordar (v.) (ve) remember
recursos humanos (m.) human resources
redecilla (f.) hairnet
refrigerador (m.) refrigerator
regadera (f.) shower
regar (v.) (ie) water
reír (v.) (i) laugh
rejilla (f.) air vent; grill; dishwasher rack
rellenar (v.) fill out; refill
reloj registrador (m.) time-clock
reparar (v.) repair, fix
repetir (v.) (i) repeat
repisa (f.) shelf
repisón (m.) window sill
reporte (m.) report
reporte de camarista (m.) room attendant report
reporte de mañana (m.) A.M. report
reporte de ocupación (m.) occupancy report
reporte de tarde (m.) P.M. report
requisición (f.) requisition
residente (m.) resident
responsabilidad (f.) responsibility

restregar (v.) scrub
retirar el servicio usado (v.) clear the table
robo (m.) theft
rociador (m.) sprayer
rociar (v.) to spray
rodamiento (m.) bearing
rodillo (m.) rolling pin; roller
roedor (m.) rodent
rogar (v.) (ue) ask; beg
rojo (a.) red
romper (v.) break
room service (m.) room service
ropa (f.) linens; clothes
ropa limpia (f.) clean linen
ropa sucia (f.) soiled linen
rosado (a.) pink
rotar (v.) rotate
roto (a.) broken
rubio (a.) blond
rueda (f.) wheel

sábado (m.) Saturday
sábana (f.) sheet
sábana bajera (f.) bottom sheet
sábana encimera (f.) top sheet
saber (v.) (irreg.) know
sacudir (v.) dust
sal (f.) salt
sala (f.) living room
salario (m.) salary, wage
salchicha (f.) sausage
salero (m.) salt shaker
salida (f.) exit; checkout room
salir (v.) (irreg.) go out; exit
salón de juegos (m.) game room
salsa (f.) sauce, hot sauce
saludar (v.) greet
sandía (f.) watermelon
sandwich (m.) sandwich
saneador (m.) sanitizer
saneamiento (m.) sanitation
sanear (v.) sanitize
sartén (f.) frying pan
secadora (f.) dryer

secar (v.) dry
secar con trapo (v.) towel dry
sección de cuartos (f.) room section
seco (a.) dry
segundo second
segundo plato (m.) second course
seguridad (f.) security
Seguridad Social (f.) Social Security
seguro (a.) sure; reliable
seguro (m.) insurance
seguro de enfermedad (m.) health insurance
seguro de vida (m.) life insurance
seis six
selección (f.) screening
semana (f.) week
sembrar (v.) (ie) seed, sow
sentar (v.) (ie) seat
sentir (v.) (ie) feel
separar (v.) sort; separate
septiembre (m.) September
ser (v.) (irreg.) be
serpentín (m.) coil
servicio (m.) service
servicio de cuartos (m.) room service
servilleta (f.) napkin
servilleta de papel (f.) paper napkin
servilleta de servicio (f.) service napkin
servilletero (m.) napkin holder
servir (v.) (i) serve
sesenta sixty
seta (f.) mushroom
setenta seventy
seto (m.) hedge
sexo (m.) sex
si if
sí yes
siempre always
sierra (f.) saw
sierra de cadena (f.) chain saw
siete seven

silla (f.) chair
silla de niño (f.) high chair
sillón (m.) armchair
sin without
sin equipaje (a.) without luggage
sobre on
sobre (m.) envelope
sofá (m.) sofa, couch
solicitud (f.) application
sopa (f.) soup
soplador (m.) blower
stock (m.) stock
subir (v.) go up
sucio (a.) dirty
suelo (m.) floor
suficiente sufficient; enough
sulfato de cobre (m.) copper sulfate
suministros de clientes (m.) guest supplies
suministros de limpieza (m.) cleaning supplies
supervisor(a) (m., f.) supervisor
supervisor(a) de cuartos (m., f.) room supervisor
surtidor de leche (m.) milk dispenser
surtir (v.) stock

tabla (f.) board
tabla de cortar (f.) cutting board
tabla de planchar (f.) ironing board
taller (m.) maintenance shop
tampoco neither
tanque (m.) tank
tapadera (f.) cover; lid
tarde late
tarde (f.) afternoon; evening
tarjeta (f.) card
tarjeta de comentarios (f.) comment card
tarjeta de no molestar (f.) do not disturb card
tarjeta de presentación (f.) housekeeper room table tent

tarjeta postal (f.) postcard
tarjeta registradora (f.) time card
tapadera (f.) lid; cover
tapete de baño (m.) bath mat
tapicería (f.) upholstery
taza (f.) cup
taza para café (f.) coffee cup
tazón (m.) bowl
té (m.) tea
té frío (m.) iced tea
techo (m.) ceiling; roof
tela de alambre (f.) screen
teléfono (m.) telephone, phone
televisión (f.) television
televisor (m.) T.V. set
temperatura (f.) temperature
temporal (a.) temporary
temprano early
tender la cama (v.) (ie) make the bed
tenedor (m.) fork
tener (v.) (irreg.) have
tercero third
termostato (m.) thermostat
ternera (f.) veal
terraza (f.) balcony
test (m.) test
tetera (f.) teapot
tiempo completo (a.) fulltime
tiempo parcial (a.) parttime
tierno (a.) tender
tierra (f.) soil
tijera (f.) tray stand
tina (f.) bathtub
toalla (f.) towel
toalla de baño (f.) bath towel
toalla de mano (f.) hand towel
toalla de papel (f.) paper towel
toalla facial (f.) washcloth
toallero (m.) towel rack
tocador (m.) dresser
tocar a la puerta (v.) knock at the door
tocino (m.) bacon
todavía yet; still
tomar (v.) take; drink

tomar la comanda (v.) take the order
tomate (m.) tomato
tope de puerta (m.) doorstop
torcer (v.) (ue) to twist
tornillo (m.) screw
tortilla de huevos (f.) omelet
tostada (f.) toast
tostadora (f.) toaster
trabajar (v.) work
trabajo (m.) job; employment, work
traer (v.) (irreg.) bring
trampa de grasa (f.) grease trap
transplantar (v.) transplant
trapeador (m.) floor mop
trapear (v.) mop
trapo (m.) rag
trece thirteen
treinta thirty
tres three
triturador (m.) garbage disposal
tubo (m.) pipe
tubo fluorescente (m.) fluorescent tube
tubería (f.) piping
tuerca (f.) screw nut
turno (m.) shift

un a, an
uno one
uniforme (m.) uniform

uña (f.) fingernail
usted you

vacaciones (f.) vacations
vacante (f.) job opening
vaciar (v.) empty
vacío (a.) empty
vacío y limpio (a.) vacant and clean
vacío y listo (a.) vacant and ready
vacío y sucio (a.) vacant and dirty
valet (m.) valet
válvula (f.) valve
válvula de cierre (f.) screw valve
válvula de desagüe (f.) drain valve
vaso (m.) glass
vaso de plástico (m.) plastic glass
vaso para agua (m.) water glass
vaso para llevar (m.) to-go cup
vaso para vino (m.) wine glass
veinte twenty
vela (f.) candle
veneno (m.) poison
venir (v.) (irreg.) come; arrive
ventana (f.) vindow

ventilador (m.) fan
ver (v.) see
verano (m.) summer
verdad (f.) truth
verde (a.) green
verificar (v.) verify
vertedero (m.) dumpster
vestidor (m.) locker room
vestidor de empleados (m.) employee locker room
vestirse (v.) (i) get dressed
viernes (m.) Friday
vinagre (m.) vinegar
vino (m.) wine
violeta (a.) violet
visillos (m.) sheers
voltaje (m.) voltage
volteo de colchón (m.) mattress rotation
volver (v.) (ve) come back
vuelto poco hecho (a.) over easy

y and
yarda (f.) yard
yema (f.) yolk
yema blanda (a.) sunny-side up
yeso (m.) plaster
yo I

zanja (f.) ditch
zapato (m.) shoe
zumo (m.) juice

English-Spanish Hospitality Vocabulary

Abbreviations:
(a.) adjective; (m.) masculine noun; (f.) feminine noun; (v.) verb
(infinitive); (ue) *ue* stem-changing verb; (ie) *ie* stem-changing verb;
(i) *i* stem-changing verb; (irreg.) irregular verb

a un, una

absenteeism ausencia excesiva (f.)

address domicilio (m.), dirección (f.)

afternoon tarde (f.)

against contra

air-conditioned aire acondicionado (m.)

air exhaust extractor de aire (m.)

air vent rejilla (f.)

alcoholic alcohólico (a.)

alcoholic beverages bebidas alcohólicas (f.)

algae algas (f.)

algicide alguicida (m.)

almost casi

although aunque

A.M. report reporte de mañana (m.)

and y

announce anunciar (v.)

appetizer aperitivo (m.)

apple manzana (f.)

application solicitud (f.)

application form solicitud de ingreso (f.)

appointment cita (f.)

appraisal evaluación (f.)

apprenticeship aprendizaje (m.)

April abril (m.)

apron delantal (m.)

aptitude test test de aptitud (m.)

armchair sillón (m.)

ashes cenizas (f.)

ashtray cenicero (m.)

ask pedir (v.); rogar (v.) (ue)

assistant asistente (m., f.)

at once en seguida

attitude actitud (f.)

August agosto (m.)

babysitter niñera (f.)

bacon tocino (m.)

bacteria bacteria (f.)

badly mal

balcony terraza (f.)

banana plátano (m.)

banquet banquete (m.)
bar bar (m.)
base plate plato base (m.)
basket cesto (m.), cesta (f.)
bath baño (m.)
bath mat tapete de baño (m.)
bath soap jabón de baño (m.)
bath towel toalla de baño (f.)
bath tub bañera (f.); tina (f.)
bathroom baño (m.), servicio (m.), cuarto de aseo (m.)
be ser; (v.) (irreg.) estar (v.) (irreg.)
be glad alegrarse (v.)
beach playa (f.)
beans frijoles (m.)
bearing rodamiento (m.)
because porque
bed cama (f.)
bed cover cobertor (m.)
bed linen blancos (m.)
bedspread cobertor (m.)
beef carne de res (m.)
beefsteak bistec (m.)
beer cerveza (f.)
beg rogar (v.) (ue), pedir (v.) (i)
begin comenzar (v.) (ie), empezar (v.) (ie)
belt correa (f.)
better mejor
between entre
beverages bebidas (f.)
bill cuenta (f.)
birthday cumpleaños (m.)
black negro (a.)
blackboard pizarrón (m.)
blade hoja (f.)
blanket manta (f.)
blocked bloqueado (a.)
blond rubio (a.)
blower soplador (m.)
blue azul (a.)
board tabla (f.)
boil hervir (v.) (ie)
boiler caldera (f.)
book libro (m.)
bottle botella (f.)
bottle opener destapador (m.)

bottom sheet sábana bajera (f.)
bow tie palomita (f.)
bowl tazón (m.)
box caja (f.)
branch rama (f.)
bread pan (m.)
bread empanar (v.)
breaded empanado (a.)
bread basket cesta para pan (f.)
bread plate plato para pan (m.)
bread warmer calentador de pan (m.)
break descanso (m.)
break romper (v.)
breakdown avería (f.)
breakfast desayuno (m.)
brick ladrillo (m.)
bring traer (v.) (irreg)
broiler parrilla (f.)
broken roto (a.); averiado (a.)
broom escoba (f.)
brown marrón (a.), moreno (a.), pardo (a.)
brush cepillo (m.)
bucket cubo (m.)
buffet buffet (m.)
burn quemar (v.)
bush arbusto (m.)
busperson ayudante de camarero (m., f.); garrotero(a) (m., f.)
bus tub cubeta (f.)
but pero
butter mantequilla (f.)
button botón (m.)
by por

cable cable (m.)
cafeteria cafetería (f.)
cake pastel (m.)
call llamar (v.)
calm down calmarse (v.)
can bote (m.), lata (f.)
can poder (v.) (ue)
can opener abrelatas (m.)
canape canapé (m.)

candle vela (f.)
car carro (m.), automóvil (m.)
card tarjeta (f.)
carpenter carpintero(a.) (m., f.)
carpet alfombra (f.)
carrots zanahorias (f.)
cart carro (m.)
cashier cajero (m.)
cash register caja registradora (f.)
ceiling techo (m.)
celery apio (m.)
cement cemento (m.)
chain saw sierra de cadena (f.)
chair silla (f.)
change cambio (m.)
change cambiar (v.)
change clothes cambiarse de ropa (v.)
check comprobar (v.) (ue)
check cheque (m.)
cheese queso (m.)
chef chef (m., f.); jefe de cocina (m., f.)
checkout room cuarto de salida (m.)
chemicals productos químicos (m.)
cherry guinda (f.), cereza (f.)
chestnut castaña (f.)
chestnut castaño (a.)
chewing gum chicle (m.)
chicken pollo (m.)
child niño(a) (m., f.)
chile chile (m.)
china loza (f.)
chipped desportillado (a.)
chlorine cloro (m.)
chocolate chocolate (m.)
chop cortar (v.)
cigarette cigarrillo (m.)
cigarette butt colilla (f.)
citizen ciudadano(a) (m., f.)
city ciudad (f.)
clean limpiar (v.)
clean linen ropa limpia (f.)

cleaning equipment equipo de limpieza (m.)
cleaning solution líquido limpiador (m.)
cleaning supplies suministros de limpieza (m.)
clear the table retirar el servicio usado (v.)
clock in or out marcar el reloj registrador (v.)
close cerca
close cerrar (v.) (ie)
closet closet (m.)
cloth trapo (m.)
coach entrenar (v.)
cockroach cucaracha (f.)
coffee café (m.)
coffee break coffee break (m.)
coffee cup taza para café (f.)
coffee grinder molino de café (m.)
coffee maker cafetera (f.)
coffee pot jarra para cafe (f.)
coffee warmer calentador (m.), plato caliente (m.)
coil serpentín (m.)
colander colador (m.)
cold frío (a.)
come venir (v.) (irreg.)
come back volver (v.)
come down bajar (v.)
comment card tarjeta de comentarios (f.)
company empresa (f.), compañía (f.)
competent competente (a.)
complain quejarse (v.)
compressor compresor (m.)
concrete concreto (m.)
condiment aderezo (m.)
copper sulfate sulfato de cobre (m.)
cost costar (v.) (ue)
cot cama portátil (f.)
couch sofá (m.)
count contar (v.) (ue)
counter mostrador (m.)
county condado (m.)
courteous cortés (a.)

courtyard patio (m.)
cover tapadera (f.)
cover cubrir (v.); tapar (v.)
cracker galleta (f.)
creamer jarrita para leche (f.)
crib cuna (f.)
crumbs migajas (f.)
cucumber pepino (m.)
cup taza (f.)
curtain cortina (f.)
cushion cojín (m.)
customer cliente (m., f.)
cut cortar (v.)
cutting board tabla para cortar (f.)

dark oscuro (a.)
date fecha (f.)
date fechar (v.)
day día (m.)
decaffeinated descafeinado (a.)
December diciembre (m.)
deep clean limpiar a fondo (v.)
deep fryer freidora (f.)
defrost descongelar (v.)
degrees grados (m.)
dental insurance seguro dental (m.)
deodorant desodorante (m.)
department departamento (m)
department head jefe de departamento (m., f.)
department meeting junta de departamento (f.)
departure room cuarto de salida (m.)
desire deseo (m.); ganas (f.)
desk escritorio (m.)
dessert postre (m.)
dessert plate plato de postre (m.)
de-stain desmanchar (v.)
detergent detergente (m.)
difficult difícil (a.)
dig cavar (v.)
dining room comedor (m.)
dinner cena (f.)

director director(a) (m., f.)
dirt mugre (f.)
dirty sucio (a.)
disciplinary action acción disciplinaria (f.)
dish plato (m.)
dishwasher lavaplatos (m.)
dishwasher rack rejilla (f.)
dishwashing machine lavaplatos (m.)
disinfectant desinfectante (m.)
ditch zanja (f.)
do hacer (v.) (irreg.)
do not disturb sign tarjeta de no molestar (f.)
dog perro (m.)
door puerta (f.)
door stopper tope de puerta (m.)
dough masa (f.)
downstairs abajo
drain desagüe (m.); coladera (f.)
drain vaciar (v.); escurrir (v.)
drainage drenaje (m.)
drawer cajón (m.)
dress vestir (v.) (i)
dresser tocador (m.)
drink bebida (f.)
drink beber (v.), tomar (v.)
driver's license licencia para manejar (f.), permiso de conducir (m.)
drop gota (f.)
drug droga (f.)
dry seco (a.)
dry secar (v.)
drycleaning limpieza en seco (f.)
dryer secadora (f.)
duct ducto (m.)
dumpster vertedero (m.)
during durante
dust polvo (m.)
dust sacudir (v.)
dustpan recogedor (m.)

early temprano
eat (v.) comer

education educación (f.); escolaridad (f.)
egg huevo (m.)
eight ocho
eighty ochenta
electricity electricidad (f.)
elevator elevador (m.), ascensor (m.)
eleven once
emergency lighting luces de emergencia (f.)
employee empleado(a) (m., f.)
employee appraisal evaluación de empleados (f.)
employee cafeteria cafetería de empleados (f.)
employee entrance entrada de empleados (f.)
employee exit salida de empleados (f.)
employee handbook manual de empleados (m.)
employee lounge salón de empleados (m.)
employer patrón (m.), patrona (f.)
empty vacío (a.)
empty vaciar (v.)
enamel esmalte (m.)
engineering ingeniería (f.)
English inglés (m.)
enough bastante, suficiente
entrance entrada (f.)
envelope sobre (m.)
equal opportunity employer empresa de igual oportunidad (f.)
erosion erosión (f.)
evening tarde (f.); noche (f.)
exact exacto (a.)
excuse excusa (f.)
executive housekeeper ama de llaves (f.)
exit salida (f.)
exit salir (v.) (irreg.)
exit light luz de salida (f.)
experience experiencia (f.)
express expreso (a.)

facial tissue pañuelos desechables (m.)
faint desmayarse (v.)
fall otoño (m.)
fall asleep dormirse (v.) (ue)
fall down caerse (v.) (irreg.)
fan ventilador (m.)
far lejos
fast rápido
faucet grifo (m.)
favor favor (m.)
February febrero (m.)
feel sentir (v.) (i)
felony delito mayor (m.)
fence cerca (f.)
fertilize fertilizar (v.)
fertilizer abono (m.)
fifteen quince
fifty cincuenta
fill out rellenar (v.)
filter filtro (m.)
find encontrar (v.) (ue)
finger dedo (m.)
fingernail uña (f.)
fire fuego (m.)
fire detector detector de fuego (m.)
fire extinguisher extintor de incendios (m.)
first primero
first course primer plato (m.)
first interview entrevista previa (f.)
first name nombre (m.)
fish pescado (m.)
five cinco
flat roof azotea (f.)
float flotador (m.)
floor piso (m.); suelo (m.)
floor closet estación de servicio (f.)
floor lamp lámpara de pie (f.)
floor mop trapeador (m.)
flour harina (f.)
flower flor (f.)
fluorescent tube tubo fluorescente (m.)
fold doblar (v.)
folder doblador (m.)

food comida (f.)
food and beverage alimentos y bebidas (m.)
food scraps desperdicios (m.)
for por
fork tenedor (m.)
forty cuarenta
fountain fuente (f.)
four cuatro
fourteen catorce
free gratis (a.); libre (a.)
free meal comida gratis (f.)
freezer congelador (m.)
french fries papas fritas (f.)
Friday viernes (m.)
fried frito (a.)
frock bata (f.)
from de; desde
front desk recepción (f.)
front of the house áreas públicas (f.)
frozen congelado (a.)
fruit basket cesta de frutas (f.)
fry freír (v.) (i)
frying pan sartén (f.)
full time tiempo completo (a.)
full-time job empleo de tiempo completo (m.)
fungi hongos (m.)
furniture muebles (m.)
fuse fusible (m.)

game room salón de juegos (m.)
garbage basura (f.)
garbage can cubo de basura (m.)
garbage disposal triturador (m.)
garden jardín (m.)
garden path andador (m.)
gardener jardinero(a) (m., f.)
garnish guarnición (f.)
gasoline gasolina (f.)
general manager gerente general (m., f.)
germicidal germicida (m.)
get angry enfadarse (v.)

get better mejorarse (v.)
get dressed vestirse (v.) (i)
get frightened asustarse (v.)
get hurt lastimarse (v.)
get married casarse (v.)
get tired cansarse (v.)
get up levantarse (v.)
gin ginebra (f.)
give dar (v.) (irreg.)
give back devolver (v.) (ue)
glass vaso (m.); vidrio (m.)
glassware cristalería (f.)
gloves guantes (m.)
go ir (v.) (irreg.)
go away irse (v.) (irreg.); mar-
    charse (v.)
go out salir (v.) (irreg.)
go to bed acostarse (v.) (ue)
go up subir (v.)
goblet copa (f.)
golden dorado (a.)
goodbye adiós
graft injertar (v.)
grass hierba (f.)
gravel cascajo (m.)
gray gris (a.)
grease trap trampa de grasa
    (f.)
greasy grasiento (a.)
green verde (a.)
green card tarjeta verde (f.)
greet saludar (v.)
griddle plancha (f.)
grill parrilla (f.)
grill asar a la parrilla (v.)
grind picar (v.); moler (v.)
    (ue)
grooming apariencia personal
    (f.); aseo personal (m.)
ground meat carne picada (f.)
guest huésped (m., f.)
guest supplies suministros de
    clientes (m.)
guestroom habitación (f.),
    cuarto (m.)

hair pelo (m.)
hair net redecilla (f.)
hallway pasillo (m.)
ham jamón (m.)

hamburger hamburguesa (f.)
hammer martillo (m.)
hand mano (f.)
hand brush cepillo de mano
    (m.)
hand soap jabón de tocador
    (m.)
hand towel toalla de manos
    (f.)
handbook manual (m.)
handle asa (f.), mango (m.)
hang up colgar (v.) (ue)
hanger gancho (m.)
hard duro (a.)
hard-boiled egg huevo duro
    (m.)
have tener (v.) (irreg.)
have a good time divertirse
    (v.) (ie)
he él
hear oír (v.) (irreg.)
heating calefacción (f.)
hedge seto (m.)
her su
herbicide herbicida (m.)
here aquí
Hi! ¡Hola!
hide esconder (v.)
high chair silla para niños (f.)
high school escuela secun-
    daria (f.)
high school diploma diploma
    de educación secundaria
    (m.)
hinge bisagra (f.)
hire contratar (v.)
hiring contratación (f.)
his su
hood campana (f.)
hoe azadón (m.)
hole agujero (m.)
holiday día festivo (m.)
honesty honradez (f.)
honey miel (f.)
hose manguera (f.)
host host (m.), capitán de
    meseros (m.)
hostess hostess (f.)
hot caliente (a.)
hot plate plato caliente (m.)

hotel hotel (m.)
house casa (f.)
housekeeper camarista (f.)
housekeeper report reporte
    de camarista (m.)
housekeeper room table tent
    tarjeta de presentación (f.)
housekeeping department
    departamento de ama de
    llaves (m.)
housekeeping supervisor
    supervisor(a) de cuartos
    (m., f.)
How? ¿Cómo?
How much? ¿Cuánto?
human resources recursos
    humanos (m.)
hundred cien
hygiene higiene (f.)

I yo
ice hielo (m.)
ice bucket hielera (f.)
ice cream helado (m.)
ice cubes cubitos de hielo
    (m.)
ice machine máquina de hielo
    (f.)
ice water agua con hielo (f.)
iced tea té helado (m.), té frío
    (m.)
identification card tarjeta de
    identificación (f.)
if si
immigrant inmigrante (m., f.)
in en
insect insecto (m.)
insecticide insecticida (m.)
inside dentro
inspect inspeccionar (v.);
    comprobar (v.) (ue)
inspection inspección (f.)
insubordination insubordi-
    nación (f.)
insurance seguro (m.)
interview entrevista (f.)
inventory inventario (m.)
iron plancha (f.)
iron planchar (v.)
ironer planchador (m.)

ironing board tabla de planchar (f.)
irrigation water agua de riego (f.)

jam mermelada (f.)
jam holder mermeladera (f.)
janitor mozo(a) de limpieza (m., f.)
January enero (m.)
jelly jalea (f.)
job trabajo (m.), empleo (m.)
job application solicitud de empleo (f.)
job description descripción del puesto (f.)
job experience experiencia en esta clase de trabajo (f.)
job opening vacante (f.)
johnny mop escobilla (f.)
joy alegría (f.)
juice jugo (m.), zumo (m.)
July julio (m.)
June junio (m.)

ketchup ketchup (m.)
kettle marmita (f.)
key llave (f.)
key holder llavero (m.)
kilogram kilo (m.)
kitchen cocina (f.)
kiwi kiwi (m.)
knife cuchillo (m.)
knock at the door tocar a la puerta (v.)
know saber (v.) (irreg.)

ladle cazo (m.)
last name apellido (m.)
last night anoche
late tarde
later después
laugh reír (v.) (i)
laundry lencería (f.), lavandería (f.)
laundry bag bolsa de lavandería (f.)
laundry list lista de lavandería (f.)

laundry products productos de lavandería (m.)
laundry room lavandería (f.)
lawn césped (m.)
lawnmower cortador de césped (m.)
leaf hoja (f.)
leak fuga (f.)
legal legal (a.)
legal immigrant inmigrante legal (m., f.)
legal resident residente legal (m., f.)
lemon limón (m.)
less menos
letter carta (f.)
letterhead papel de escribir timbrado (m.)
lettuce lechuga (f.)
lid tapadera (f.)
life insurance seguro de vida (m.)
light luz (f.)
light claro (a.)
light encender (v.) (ie)
light bulb foco (m.)
light plate placa (f.)
light switch apagador (m.)
lime cal (f.)
linen lencería (f.)
linen folder doblador (m.)
liquid soap jabón líquido (m.)
liter litro (m.)
little poco
living room sala (f.)
lobby vestíbulo (m.), lobby (m.)
lock cerradura (f.)
lock cerrar (v.) (ie)
locker room vestidor de empleados (m.)
log book bitácora (f.)
lose perder (v.) (ie)
lost perdido (a.), extraviado (a.)
lost and found items objetos extraviados (m.)
low bajo
lubricate lubricar, engrasar (v.)

luggage equipaje (m.)
luggage rack portamaletas (m.)
lunch almuerzo (m.)
lunch break descanso para el almuerzo (m.)

mailing address dirección postal (f.)
main entrance entrada principal (f.)
maintenance mantenimiento (m.)
maintenance shop taller (m.)
make hacer (v.) (irreg.)
make a mistake equivocarse (v.)
make the bed tender la cama (v.) (ie)
manager director (m., f.), gerente (m., f.)
mangle mangle (m.), planchadora (f.)
manure estiércol (m.)
March marzo (m.)
master key llave maestra (f.)
matches cerillos (m.)
material material (m.)
mattress colchón (m.)
mattress pad protector de colchón (m.)
mattress rotation volteo de colchón (m.)
May mayo (m.)
mayonnaise mayonesa (f.)
meal comida (f.)
meal course plato (m.), platillo (m.)
meat carne (f.)
medical insurance seguro de enfermedad (m.)
medium medio hecho (a.)
melon melón (m.)
menu menú (m.)
menu item plato (m.), platillo (m.)
message mensaje (m.)
microvave oven microondas (m.)
milk leche (f.)

milk dispenser surtidor de leche (m.)
mince picar (v.)
minced picado (a.)
minimum wage salario mínimo (m.)
mirror espejo (m.)
miter hacer ingletes (v.) (irreg.)
mix mezclar (v.)
mixer mezcladora (f.)
Monday lunes (m.)
month mes (m.)
mop trapeador (m.)
mop trapear (v.)
mop wringer escurridor (m.)
more más
morning mañana (f.)
mouse ratón (m.)
mousetrap ratonera (f.)
move mover (v.) (ue)
mow the lawn cortar el césped (v.)
much mucho
mushroom seta (f.)
mustard mostaza (f.)
my mi

nail clavo (m.)
nail clavar (v.)
name nombre (m.)
name tag etiqueta (f.)
napery mantelería (f.)
napkin servilleta (f.)
napkin holder servilletero (m.)
near cerca
needle aguja (f.)
neither tampoco
neither...nor ni...ni
never nunca
newspaper periódico (m.)
nickname apodo (m.)
night noche (f.)
night stand mesita de noche (f.)
nine nueve
ninety noventa
no no
no baggage sin equipaje (a.)

no one ninguno
no smoking no fumar
nobody nadie
note pad bloc de notas (m.)
nothing nada
notify notificar (v.)
November noviembre (m.)
nozzle boquilla (f.)
number número (m.)

occupancy ocupación (f.)
occupancy report reporte de ocupación (m.)
October octubre (m.)
of de
office oficina (f.)
oil aceite (m.)
oil lubricar, (v.) engrasar (v.)
oil and vinegar aceite y vinagre (m.)
omelet tortilla de huevos (f.)
on sobre
one uno
onion cebolla (f.)
opening vacante (f.)
opposite enfrente
orange naranja (f.)
orange anaranjado (a.), naranja (a.)
orange marmalade mermelada de naranja (f.)
our nuestro
out of order fuera de servicio (a.)
outside afuera
oven horno (m.)
over easy vuelto poco hecho (a.)
overtime horas extra (f.)
overwater poner demasiada agua (v.) (irreg.)
oyster ostra (f.)

packing empaque (m.), empaquetadura (f.)
paint pintura (f.)
paint pintar (v.)
pale pálido (a.)
palmtree palmera (f.)
pan cazuela (f.)

pancake panqueque (m.), tortas (f.)
pantry despensa (f.)
paper papel (m.)
paper napkin servilleta de papel (f.)
paper towel toalla de papel (f.)
paperwork papelería (f)
Pardon me! ¡Perdón!
parking aparcamiento (m.)
parking lot aparcamiento (m.)
parsley perejil (m.)
part pieza (f.)
part time tiempo parcial (a.)
part-time job empleo de tiempo parcial (m.)
pass key llave de paso (f.)
pastry pastelería (f.)
pay paga (f.); sueldo (m.)
pay pagar (v.)
pay raise aumento salarial (m.)
paycheck cheque salarial (m.)
payday día de pago (m.)
peach jam mermelada de durazno (f.)
pear pera (f.)
peel pelar (v.)
peeled pelado (a.)
pen pluma (f.)
pencil lápiz (m.)
people gente (f.)
pepper pimienta (f.)
pepper shaker pimentero (m.)
permanent job empleo permanente (m.)
personal information información personal (f.)
personnel personal (m.)
personnel department departamento de personal (m.)
pest control control de plagas (m.)
pesticide pesticida (m.)
phone teléfono (m.)
physical examination examen médico (m.)

pickup room cuarto de repaso (m.)
picture cuadro (m.)
pie pastel (m.)
pillow almohada (f.)
pillowcase funda de almohada (f.)
pineapple piña (f.)
pink rosado (a.)
pipe tubo (m.)
piping tubería (f.)
pity lástima (f.)
plant planta (f.)
plant plantar (v.)
plaster yeso (m.)
plastic apron delantal de plástico (m.)
plastic glass vaso de plástico (m.)
plate plato (m.)
plate emplatar (v.)
plate setting plaqué (m.)
plated emplatado (a.)
playground juegos infantiles (m.)
please por favor
pliers alicates (m.)
plumber plomero(a) (m., f.); fontanero(a) (m., f.)
plumbing plomería (f.)
P.M. report reporte de tarde (m.)
poach hervir a fuego lento (v.) (ie)
poison veneno (m.)
polish pulir (v.)
pork puerco (m.)
position puesto (m.)
postcard tarjeta postal (f.)
pot olla (f.)
potato papa (f)
poultry carne de ave (f.)
potable water agua potable (f.)
prefer preferir (v.) (ie)
pressure presión (f.)
pressure gage manómetro (m.)
preventive maintenance mantenimiento preventivo (m.)

probationary period período de prueba (m.)
professional test test profesional (m.)
prove probar (v.) (ue)
prune podar (v.)
public areas áreas públicas (f.)
public restroom baño público (m.)
pulley polea (f.)
pump bomba (f.)
punctual puntual (a.)
punctuality puntualidad (f.)
purple morado (a.)
put poner (v.) (irreg.)

queen-sized bed cama matrimonial (f.)
quick rápido (a.)
quickly rapidamente
quilt colcha (f.)

radio radio (f.)
rag trapo (m.)
rain lluvia (f.)
raise aumento (m.)
rake rastrillo (m.)
rare poco hecho (a.)
rat rata (f.)
ready room cuarto listo (m.)
ready to rent listo para alquilar (a.)
recruiting reclutamiento (m.)
red rojo (a.)
reference recomendación (f.)
refill rellenar (v.)
refrigerator refrigerador (m.)
register box caja de registro (f.)
reliable seguro (a.)
remain quedarse (v.)
remember recordar (v.) (ue)
repair reparar (v.)
repit repetir (v.) (i)
report reporte (m.)
requisition requisición (f.), pedido (m.)
resident residente (m.)

responsibility responsibilidad (f.)
restroom baño (m.), servicio (m.)
resume curriculum vitae (m.)
retirement plan plan de retiro (m.)
rice arroz (m.)
rim borde (m.)
rinse enjuagar (v.)
roast asar (v.)
rock roca (f.), piedra (f.)
rodent roedor (m.)
roll panecillo (m.)
rolling pin rodillo (m.)
room cuarto (m.), habitación (f.)
room attendant camarista (m., f.)
room division división cuartos (f.)
room number número de habitación (m.)
room section sección de cuartos (f.)
room service room service (m.), servicio a cuartos (m.)
room set-up preparación del salón (f.)
root raíz (f.)
rotate rotar (v.)
rototiller aflojador de tierra (m.)
rubber boots botas de agua (f.)
rubber gloves guantes de goma (m.)
rubber mat estera de goma (f.)
rug alfombra (f.), tapete (m.)
rug shampooer máquina para lavar alfombras (f.)
rules and regulations ordenanzas (f.)

salad ensalada (f.)
salad dressing aderezo de ensaladas (m.)
salary salario (m.)

salt sal (f)
salt shaker salero (m.)
sand arena (f.)
sandwich sandwich (m.)
sanitary bag bolsa sanitaria (f.)
sanitation saneamiento (m.)
sanitize sanear (v.)
sanitizer saneador (m.)
Saturday sábado (m.)
sauce salsa (f.)
saucer plato de café (m.)
sausage salchicha (f.)
saw sierra (f.)
say decir (v.) (irreg.)
say goodbye despedirse (v.) (i)
scrambled eggs huevos revueltos (m.)
scrape rascar (v.)
screen pantalla (f.); tela de alambre (f.)
screening selección (f.)
screw tornillo (m.)
screw valve válvula de cierre (f.)
screwdriver destornillador (m.)
scrub restregar (v.)
scrub pad estropajo (m.)
seafood mariscos (m.)
season estación (f.)
seasonal work trabajo temporal (m.)
seat sentar (v.) (ie)
second segundo (m.)
second segundo (a.)
second course segundo plato (m.)
section housekeeper camarista (m., f.)
security seguridad (f.)
see ver (v.)
seed semilla (f.)
seed sembrar (v.) (ie)
selection process proceso selectivo (m.)
self-service autoservicio (m.)
September septiembre (m.)
serve servir (v.) (i)

service servicio (m.)
service cart carro de servicio (m.)
service directory directorio de servicios (m.)
service napkin servilleta de servicio (f.)
service stairs escalera de servicio (f.)
service station estación de servicio (f.)
service table mesa de servicio (f.)
set the table montar la mesa (v.), poner la mesa (v.) (irreg.)
seven siete
seventy setenta
sew coser (v.)
sex sexo (m.)
sexual harassment acoso sexual (m.)
shampoo champú (m.)
shampooer (rug) máquina para lavar alfombras (f.)
she ella
sheers visillos (m.)
sheet sábana (f.)
sheet pan bandeja (f.)
shelf estante (m.)
shellfish mariscos (m.)
sherry jerez (m.)
shift turno (m.)
shift turnover cambio de turno (m.)
shoe zapato (m.)
short circuit cortocircuito (m.)
shovel pala (f.)
shower ducha (f.); regadera (f.)
shower cap gorro de baño (m.)
shower curtain cortina de baño (f.)
shrimp camarón (m.)
shut cerrar (v.) (ie)
shut-off valve válvula de paso (f.)
sick enfermo (a.)

side stand aparador (m.)
sign firmar (v.)
signature firma (f.)
silver plata (f.)
silver plateado (a.)
silverware cubertería (f.)
sink lavabo (m.); fregadero (m.)
six seis
sixty sesenta
skill experiencia (f.)
skimmer espumadera (f.)
sleep dormir (v.) (ue)
slice rebanada (f.)
slice rebanar (v.)
slowly despacio
smoke fumar (v.)
smoke humo (m.)
smoke detector detector de humo (m.)
snow nieve (f.)
soak empapar, remojar (v.)
soap jabón (m.)
soap dish jabonera (f.)
soap dispenser distribuidor de jabón (m.)
soap holder jabonera (f.)
soapy water agua jabonosa (f.)
Social Security Seguridad Social (f.)
soda dispenser máquina de refrescos (f.)
sofa sofá (m.)
soft-boiled egg huevo pasado por agua (m.)
soil tierra (f.)
soiled linen ropa sucia (f.)
sorrow pena (f.)
sort separar (v.)
soup sopa (f.)
soup plate plato para sopa (m.)
soup spoon cuchara de sopa (f.)
Spanish español (m.)
spatula espátula (f.)
speak hablar (v.)
spill derramar (v.)
spinach espinacas (f.)

sponge esponja (f.)
spoon cuchara (f.)
spray rociar (v.)
spray chemicals fumigar (v.)
sprayer rociador (m.)
spring primavera (f.)
sprinkler regadera (f.)
stain mancha (f.)
starch almidón (m.)
starch almidonar (v.)
state estado (m.)
station estación (f.)
stationery papelería (f.)
steam vapor (m.)
steam kettle marmita al
   vapor (f.)
stem mango (m.)
still todavía
stock stock (m.), surtido (m.)
stock surtir (v.)
stone piedra (f.)
stool inodoro (m.)
stop parar (v.)
stop talking callarse (v.)
storeroom almacén (m.)
strain filtro (m.)
strawberries fresas (f.)
strawberry jam mermelada de
   fresa (f.)
street calle (f.)
substance abuse abuso de
   substancias (m.)
success éxito (m.)
sugar azúcar (m.)
sugar bowl azucarero (m.)
sugar packet bolsita de azúcar
   (f.)
suggestion box buzón de sugerencias (m.)
suitcase maleta (f.)
summer verano (m.)
Sunday domingo (m.)
sunny side up yema blanda
   (a.), yema no hecha (a.)
supervisor supervisor(a) (m.,
   f.)
supplies suministros (m.)
sweep barrer (v.)
swimming pool alberca (f.),
   piscina (f.)

swing team equipo de relevo
   (m.)
syrup jarabe (m.)

table mesa (f.)
tablecloth mantel (m.)
take tomar (v.)
take a shower ducharse (v.)
take off clothing quitarse (v.)
take the order tomar la
   comanda (v.)
tall alto (a.)
tank tanque (m.)
tardiness llegar tarde (v.)
taste probar (v.) (ue)
tea té (m.)
tea bag bolsita de té (f.)
teapot tetera (f.)
teaspoon cucharilla (f.)
team equipo (m.)
telephone teléfono (m.)
telephone book directorio
   telefónico (m.), guía telefónica (f.)
television televisión (f.)
tell decir (v.) (irreg.)
temperature temperatura (f.)
temporary temporal (a.)
temporary job empleo temporal (m.)
ten diez
tender tierno (a.)
tennis court cancha de
   tenis (f.)
termination despido (m.)
terry cloth felpa (f.)
test test (m.)
thank you gracias
that ese, esa, aquel, aquella
thaw descongelar (v.)
the el, la, los, las
theft robo (m.)
there allá; allí
thermostat termostato (m.)
they ellos, ellas
third tercero
thirteen trece
thirty treinta
this este, esta
thousand mil

three tres
Thursday jueves (m.)
thus así
tile baldosa (f.); azulejo (m.)
time la hora (f.)
time card tarjeta registradora
   (f.)
time clock reloj registrador
   (m.)
tip propina (f.)
toast tostada (f.)
toast tostar (v.)
toaster tostadora (f.)
today hoy
to-go cup vaso para llevar
   (m.)
toilet inodoro (m.)
toilet paper papel higiénico
   (m.)
toilet paper holder portarrol-
   los (m.)
tomato tomate (m.)
tomorrow mañana
tongs pinzas (f.)
too much demasiado
tool herramienta (f.)
toolbox caja de herramientas
   (f.)
towel toalla (f.)
towel dry secar con trapo (v.)
towel rack toallero (m.)
train entrenar (v.)
training entrenamiento (m.)
transplant transplantar (v.)
transportation medio de locomoción (m.)
trash basura (f.)
trash bag bolsa de basura (f.)
trash can cubo de basura (m.)
tray charola (f.), bandeja (f.)
tray stand tijeras (f.)
tree árbol (m.)
trench zanja (f.)
truth verdad (f.)
tub tina (f.)
Tuesday martes (m.)
tuna fish atún (m.)
turkey pavo (m.)
turndown service servicio de
   cortesía (m.)

turn off apagar (v.)
turn on encender (v.) (ie)
T.V. set televisor (m.)
T.V. guide guía de televisión (f.)
twelve doce
twenty veinte
twist torcer (v.) (ue)
two dos
type escribir a máquina (v.)

uniform uniforme (m.)
unoccupied desocupado (a.)
upholstery tapicería (f.)
upstairs arriba
urn cleaner limpiador de cafeteras (m.)

vacant vacío (a.)
vacant and clean vacío y limpio (a.)
vacant and dirty vacío y sucio (a.)
vacant and ready vacío y listo (a.)
vacation vacación (f.)
vacuum aspirar (v.)
vacuum cleaner aspiradora (f.)
valet valet (m.)
valve válvula (f.)
vanity tocador (m.)
varnish barniz (m.)
varnish barnizar (v.)
veal ternera (f.)
vegetables legumbres (f.)
venetian blinds persiana (f.)
verify verificar (v.)
vinegar vinagre (m.)
violet violeta (a.)
voltage voltaje (m.)

wage salario por horas (m.)
wait esperar (v.)

waiter mesero (m.)
waiting list lista de espera (f.)
waitress mesera (f.)
wake up despertarse (v.) (ie)
walk-in freezer cámara congeladora (f.)
walk-in refrigerator cámara fría (f.)
wall pared (f.)
wallpaper papel tapiz (m.)
want querer (v.) (ie)
warm caliente (a.)
wash lavar (v.)
washer lavadora (f.)
waste desperdicios (m.)
waste water aguas negras (f.)
wastebasket cesto de basura (m.)
wastepaper basket papelera (f.)
water agua (f.)
water glass vaso para agua (m.)
water jar jarra para agua (f.)
watermelon sandía (f.)
wax cera (f.)
we nosotros, nosotras
weapon arma (f.)
Wednesday miércoles (m.)
weed cizaña (f.), mala hierba (f.)
weed escardar (v.)
week semana (f.)
weekend fin de semana (m.)
well bien
well done bien hecho (a.)
wheel rueda (f.)
wheelbarrow carretilla (f.)
When? ¿Cuándo?
Where? ¿Dónde?
Which? ¿Cuál?
whip batir (v.)
white blanco (a.)

white linen blancos (m.)
Who? ¿quién?
Why? ¿por qué?
window ventana (f.)
window sill repisón (m.)
wine vino (m.)
wine list lista de vinos (f.)
winter invierno (m.)
wipe down limpiar (v.)
wire alambre (m.)
wire whip batidor (m.)
with con
without sin
wood madera (f.)
work trabajo (m.)
work trabajar (v.)
work contract contrato de trabajo (m.)
work hours horario de trabajo (m.)
work order orden de trabajo (f.)
workday jornada de trabajo (f.)
working days días laborables (m.)
workload cuota de trabajo (f.)
worry preocuparse (v.)
wrap envolver (v.) (ue)
wringer escurridor (m.)
write escribir (v.)
writing pad libreta de apuntes (f.)

yard yarda (f.)
year año (m.)
yellow amarillo (a.)
yesterday ayer
yet todavía
yolk yema (f.)
you usted, ustedes
your su, sus

ZIP Code código postal (m.)

Exercises

Pronunciation Exercises

A. Write the phonetic pronunciation for the following words.

Example: *cocina* = **coh-sée-nah**

almacén	*botella*
casa	*cena*
dinero	*entrar*
fuego	*goma*
gente	*guisar*
hotel	*chocolate*
tina	*jabón*
kilo	*lata*
llave	*menú*
noviembre	*ocupado*
pedir	*querer*
rama	*silla*
tierra	*tener*
uniforme	*vacío*
extensión	*examen*
soy	*yeso*
zócalo	*taza*

267

B. Pronounce and divide the following words into syllables.
Example: *mano = **ma/no***

hablar	*escribir*
abierto	*ahora*
temprano	*después*
agua	*camarista*
ayudante	*mesero*
cocina	*despensa*
día	*semana*
año	*mañana*
yeso	*azúcar*
huevo	*fresa*

C. Underline the stressed syllables of the following words.
Example: frega*de*ro

gerente	*recepción*
área	*alberca*
desagüe	*destornillador*
visillo	*alfombra*
rapidamente	*árboles*
menú	*guisantes*
cremera	*después*
día	*elevador*
sábana	*cobertor*
tina	*periódico*

Definite Article Exercises

A. Give the appropriate definite article for each of the following words. Choose from el, la, los, and las

1. *cuchillo*   2. *manzana*   3. *agua*   4. *bolsas de plástico*   5. *grifos*

6. *espátula*   7. *día*   8. *trapeador*   9. *huéspedes*   10. *hotel*

11. *reloj registrador*   12. *tazas*   13. *almacén*   14. *lavadora*   15. *congeladores*

B. Change to plural.
Example: *el plato = los platos*

1. *el restaurante*   2. *la estera de goma*   3. *el ayudante*
4. *la alberca climatizada*   5. *la cocinera mexicana*   6. *el piso*
7. *la alfombra*   8. *la solicitud de empleo*   9. *la mano*
10. *el turno de noche*   11. *el menú*   12. *la habitación*
13. *la ventana*   14. *el elevador*   15. *el autobús*

C. Translate the following words into English.

1. *el ayudante de mesero*   2. *los condimentos*   3. *el restaurante*   4. *los cocineros*
5. *los platillos*   6. *el almuerzo*   7. *los clientes*   8. *el hotel*   9. *el autobús*
10. *las meseras*   11. *los vasos*   12. *el agua fría*   13. *los aderezos*
14. *el elevador*   15. *las toallas*

D. Translate the following words into Spanish.
1. the housemen   2. the bread   3. the oranges   4. the bed covers
5. the dishwasher (person)   6. the soap   7. the detergents
8. the children   9. the frying pans   10. the doors   11. the door knob
12. the car   13. the company   14. the flowers   15. the bathrooms

Indefinite Article Exercises

A. Give the appropriate indefinite article for each of the following words. Choose from un, una, unos, and unas

1. *tenedores*   2. *limón*   3. *café*   4. *papel higiénico*   5. *tubería*   6. *sartenes*
7. *noche*   8. *escobas*   9. *cliente*   10. *restaurantes*   11. *libro de bitácora*
12. *tetera*   13. *azoteas*   14. *secadora*   15. *refrigeradores*

B. Change the following words to plural.
Example: *un plato = **unos platos***

1. *un hotel*   2. *una azada*   3. *un mozo*   4. *un lavaplatos*
5. *un aparcamiento*   6. *un carro de servicio*   7. *una mesa*   8. *una máquina*
9. *una cajera*   10. *una supervisora*   11. *un plomero*   12. *un cuarto*
13. *una repisa*   14. *un piso*   15. *una pared*

C. Translate the following Spanish words into English.

1. *unas cucharas*   2. *un vaso*   3. *unos hoteles*   4. *una cafetera*
5. *un plato de café*   6. *un desayuno*   7. *una señora*   8. *unos tomates*
9. *unas flores*   10. *un gancho*   11. *un teléfono*   12. *unas cervezas*
13. *una botella de vino*   14. *unos colchones*   15. *un sillón*

D. Translate the following words into Spanish.

1. some chairs   2. a desk   3. a sink   4. some onions   5. some pots
6. a hose   7. a johnny mop   8. a napkin   9. some detergents
10. some rags   11. an ashtray   12. a glass of water   13. an oven
14. some ice buckets   15. a supervisor

Gender Exercises

A. Indicate whether the following nouns are masculine or feminine.
Example: *papel* = **masculine**

1. *azúcar*   2. *mantequilla*   3. *mano*   4. *colador*   5. *miel*   6. *campana*
7. *restaurante*   8. *mantel*   9. *camas*   10. *manta*   11. *jarra*   12. *freidora*
13. *pan*   14. *mostaza*   15. *mirilla*

B. Translate the following words into Spanish.

1. the napkin   2. some trash bags   3. the day   4. a day
5. some matches   6. the radios   7. some hangers   8. the Bible
9. some drawers   10. an orange juice   11. the flour   12. some utensils
13. the equipment   14. a hallway   15. the vanity

C. Change the following names of people into their feminine forms.
Example: *supervisor* = **supervisora**

1. *mesero*   2. *cocinero*   3. *portero*   4. *lavador*   5. *jardinero*   6. *plomero*
7. *limpiador*   8. *cajero*   9. *doctor*   10. *director*   11. *ciudadano*
12. *empleado*   13. *planchador*   14. *mexicano*   15. *español*

Plural Exercises

A. Change the following nouns from singular to plural.
Example: *cortina* = **cortinas**

1. *uniforme*   2. *comedor*   3. *cafetería*   4. *pasillo*   5. *regadera*   6. *jabonera*

7. *cucharilla*   8. *césped*   9. *arbusto*   10. *panqueque*   11. *pescado*

12. *carne*   13. *legumbre*   14. *tortilla*   15. *frijol*   16. *cena*

17. *polvo limpiador*   18. *foco*

B. Translate the following words into Spanish.
1. appraisals   2. beverages   3. attitudes   4. birthdays   5. addresses

6. companies   7. cities   8. dates   9. drugs   10. department heads

11. documents   12. names   13. jobs   14. employee handbooks

15. letters

C. Change the following nouns from plural to singular.
1. *cables*   2. *carpinteros*   3. *ladrillos*   4. *ramas*   5. *calderas*   6. *escobas*

7. *patios*   8. *serpentines*   9. *zanjas*   10. *macetas*   11. *filtros*   12. *bisagras*

13. *hoyos*   14. *guantes*   15. *clavos*

Pronoun Exercises

A. Supply the correct subject pronoun to match the verb form given. Choose from yo, usted, él, ella, nosotros, nosotras, ustedes, ellos, and ellas.

1. ... *limpio el cuarto.*   2. ... *comemos en la cafetería.*   3. ... *fríe papas.*

4. ... *barren el suelo.*   5. ... *ponen la mesa.*   6. ... *friegan la cubertería.*

7. ... *lavo los vasos.*   8. ... *cortan la carne.*   9. ... *sacude los muebles.*

10. ... *hablamos español.*   11. ... *trapeo la cocina.*   12. ... *pinta la pared.*

13. ... *sirven el desayuno.*   14. ... *aspiro la alfombra.*   15. ... *llamo por teléfono.*

B. Change each noun in bold to a direct object pronoun.
Example: *Yo trapeo el suelo.* = *Yo lo trapeo.*

1. *Usted lava **la ropa**.*   2. *Ella sacude **el polvo**.*   3. *Nosotros preparamos **los aderezos**.*

4. *Ellos limpian **los cubiertos**.*   5. *Ustedes necesitan **uniformes**.*

6. *Yo aspiro **el pasillo**.*   7. *El cocinero corta **las papas**.*   8. *La mesera sirve **el desayuno**.*   9. *Usted plancha **las sábanas**.*   10. *Ella dobla **las colchas**.*

C. Translate the following sentences using direct object and indirect object pronouns.

Example: I wash it (the floor). = **yo lo lavo.**

1. I see it (the hotel).   2. She cleans them (the rooms).

3. You cook them (the potatoes).   4. He dusts it (the chair).

5. We wash them (the glasses).   6. I wash it (the bathtub).

7. We prune them (the trees).   8. He waxes it (the wooden floor).

9. I see her (the room attendant).

10. He gives it (the rag) to her (the waitress).

11. She gives them (the cups) to us.

12. The supervisor gives them (the paychecks) to them (the waiters).

13. I give it (the broom) to you.

14. You give them (the daily work reports) to them (your supervisors).

15. He gives them (the plates) to her (the waitress).

D. Answer the following questions in Spanish using direct object pronouns instead of the nouns in bold.

Example: *¿Aspira usted **la alfombra**?-Sí la aspiro.*

1. *¿Tiene usted **la llave**?*   2. *¿Lavamos **las sábanas**?*   3. *¿Pone la mesera **la mesa**?*

4. *¿Sirven **las bebidas**?*   5. *¿Retira el mozo **la basura**?*   6. *¿Tenemos suficientes **sillas**?*

7. *¿Trapea la camarista **los muebles**?*   8. *¿Espera usted **la comanda**?*

9. *¿Habla usted **español**?*   10. *¿Le da usted **el cuchillo** al cocinero?*

E. Create commands from the following sentences using direct object pronouns instead of nouns.

Example: *Limpie el baño. = **Límpielo**.*

1. *Ponga la mesa.*   2. *Friegue el suelo.*   3. *Cambie las sábanas.*

4. *Aspire la alberca.*   5. *Encienda la luz.*   6. *Apague la calefacción.*

7. *Corte la hierba.*   8. *Deme la llave.*   9. *Lave los platos.*   10. *Sacuda las sillas.*

11. *Planche los uniformes.*   12. *Doble las sábanas.*   13. *Traiga los condimentos.*

14. *Lleve los helados.*   15. *Traigan los carros de servicio.*

Verb Exercises

A. For each of the following regular verbs, give the corresponding form of the present indicative.

Example: *Pedro (trabajar) aquí.= **Pedro trabaja aquí.***

1. *¿(Hablar) usted español?*   2. *Sí (hablar) español un poco.*

3. *Yo (preparar) el comedor.*   4. *Las camaristas (trabajar) en el hotel.*

5. *El jardinero (podar) los árboles.*   6. *El plomero (arreglar) el grifo.*

7. *Los mozos (tirar) la basura.*   8. *Los huéspedes (comer) en el comedor.*

9. *¿(Trabajar) usted en este hotel?*   10. *El ama de llaves (inspeccionar) los cuartos.*

11. *Los empleados (cobrar) todos los viernes.*

B. For each of the following irregular verbs, give the corresponding form of the present indicative.

Example: *Yo (saber) manejar. = **Yo sé manejar.***

1. *El cajero (dar) el dinero al cliente.*   2. *Yo no (decir) nada.*

3. *Los empleados (ir) a la junta de departamento.*   4. *Yo (poner) los cubiertos en el cajón.*

5. *Yo (saber) hablar español.*   6. *Nosotros (venir) al hotel en carro.*

7. *Pedro (ver) la bicicleta de Antonio.*   8. *Pedro y Antonio (ir) a la cocina.*

9. *Nosotros (salir) a las cinco.*   10. *Yo (hacer) la cama de los huéspedes.*

C. Translate the following sentences into Spanish, using ser or estar.

Examples: I am from Mexico. = ***Soy de México.***
I am in the kitchen. = ***Estoy en la cocina***

1. How are you? I am very well, thank you!   2. The houseman is in room 210

3. The houseman is very tall.   4. We are tired.   5. Who is the supervisor?

6. It is two o'clock.   7. Where is the laundry room?   8. How is your daughter?

9. What is this?   10. Are you a plumber?   11. I am eating now.

12. Pedro is waxing the floor in the lobby.   13. Antonio is a very good worker.

14. The employee cafeteria is in the basement.   15. Where is the security guard?

D. Answer the following questions in Spanish using the correct form of each stem-changing verb.

1. *¿Almuerzan los empleados en el hotel?*   2. *¿Cierra la cafetería a las cinco o a las seis?*

3. *¿Comienza usted a trabajar el lunes?*   4. *¿Cuánto cuesta este uniforme?*

5. *¿Duerme usted en el hotel o en su casa?*

6. *¿Encienden las luces las camaristas o los mozos?*   7. *¿Entiende usted inglés?*

8. *¿Quién mueve los muebles, el mozo o la camarista?*

9. *¿Prefieren ustedes trabajar el turno de mañana o el turno de tarde?*

10. *¿Se sienten ustedes contentos en este empleo?*

E. Translate the following sentences into Spanish using the reflexive verbs indicated.

1. (*reunirse*) The employees meet in the cafeteria at five o'clock.

2. (*encenderse*) The lights are turned on in the evening.

3. (*regarse*) The trees are watered once a week.

4. (*pintarse*) The ceiling is painted before the walls.

5. (*podarse*) The trees are pruned in the fall.

6. (*enjuagarse*) The pots are rinsed in this sink.

7. (*limpiarse*) The tiles are cleaned with Ajax.

8. (*encontrarse*) The laundry room is located downstairs.

9. (*ducharse*) The employees should take a shower before work.

10. (*levantarse*) I get up at six in the morning.

F. Translate the following singular commands into Spanish.
Example: Turn on the lamp. = *Encienda la lámpara.*

1. Open the door.   2. Mop the floor.   3. Wash the pots.

4. Paint the walls in the kitchen.   5. Water the grass.   6. Mow the lawn.

7. Work faster, please.   8. Go to the laundry room now.

9. Come to the kitchen.   10. Bring a bucket of soapy water.

11. Dust the furniture.   12. Put the hangers in the closet.

13. Clean the bathroom first.   14. Work in the dining room tomorrow.

15. Knock at the door before entering the room.

G. Translate the following plural commands into Spanish.
Example: Dust the table. = *Sacudan la mesa.*

1. Turn on the lights.   2. Start serving the soup.   3. Clean the tables.

4. Count the sheets.   5. Dry these pillowcases.

6. Come to work at ten o'clock tomorrow.

7. Wash your hands after using the bathroom.   8. Sign here.

9. Come up to the second floor.   10. Peel these potatoes.

11. Cut the tomatoes in half.   12. Make an omelet with three eggs.

13. Put detergent in the dishwasher.   14. Open the refrigerator door.

15. Repeat it again.

H. Translate the following singular negative commands into Spanish.

1. Don't arrive late to work.   2. Don't speak on the phone while on duty.

3. Don't watch television while working in the guest rooms.

4. Don't put your fingers in the glasses.

5. Don't vacuum the hallways before ten o'clock.

6. Don't clean the floor with towels.   7. Don't overwater the trees.

8. Don't go in public areas without wearing your uniform.

9. Don't forget to lock the door.   10. Don't use strong perfume when on duty.

I. Form commands using pronouns instead of the nouns given.
Example: *Ponga la escoba aquí.* = ***Póngala aquí***

1. *Lave los vasos rapidamente.*   2. *Sirva el agua en la mesa cuatro.*

3. *Haga más panqueques.*   4. *Llame a su supervisora.*   5. *Limpie los cuartos.*

6. *No lave la ropa todavía.*   7. *No aspire la piscina.*   8. *Enjuague la cubertería.*

9. *No cierre la puerta con llave.*   10. *No pongan las toallas limpias en el suelo.*

11. *Traigan los carros de servicio después de terminar su turno.*

12. *No pelen las papas todavía.*   13. *Pongan los ganchos en los closets.*

14. *Limpien el suelo con polvo limpiador.*   15. *Rieguen las plantas con manguera.*

J. Answer the following questions in Spanish.

1. *¿Trabajo mañana?*   2. *¿Cúanto pagan por hora?*

3. *¿Lavo los platos o las cacerolas?*   4. *¿Sacudo las mesas?*

5. *¿Con qué limpio las ventanas?*   6. *¿Puedo fumar en la cafetería de empleados?*

7. *¿Pueden los empleados usar el bar del hotel?*   8. *¿Ofrecen seguro de enfermedad?*

9. *¿Es el empleo de tiempo completo o de tiempo parcial?*

10. *¿Tengo que trabajar los fines de semana?*

Adjective Exercises

A. Complete the following sentences.

1. *Las toallas están limpi—.*   2. *Las camas son grand—.*

3. *Las meseras son mexican—.*   4. *Este detergente es buen—.*

5. *Los mozos son buen— trabajadores.*   6. *El ama de llaves es amabl—.*

7. *Estos ejercicios son muy difícil—.*   8. *Las camaristas son muy rápid—.*

9. *El supervisor de pisos es mexican—.*   10. *El agua no está fría, está caliente—.*

B. Translate the following Spanish sentences into English.

1. *Las toallas blancas están aquí.*   2. *La cubertería limpia está en el comedor.*

3. *Las mesas redondas llevan cuatro sillas cada una.*

4. *La lavadora pequeña es para lavar los trapos de cocina.*

5. *La cafetería de empleados se abre a las seis.*   6. *Estos platos están sucios.*

7. *Esta habitación es de salida.*   8. *Estas esteras de goma se lavan los martes.*

9. *Este cocinero es de México.*   10. *Mis hermanos trabajan en Phoenix.*

11. *Sus uniformes están en la lavandería.*   12. *Nuestros carros de servicio no están listos.*

13. *Su turno comienza a las ocho de la mañana.*   14. *Mi aspiradora no funciona.*

15. *Estos mozos son buenos trabajadores.*

C. Answer the following questions in Spanish.

1. *¿Es éste mi carro de servicio?*   2. *¿Son éstos mis suministros?*

3. *¿Dónde está mi aspiradora?*   4. *¿Trabajo hoy en mi sección de cuartos?*

5. *¿Quién es mi supervisor?*   6. *¿Dónde está mi ropero?*

7. *¿Está reparada aquella lavadora?*   8. *¿Están aquellos cubiertos limpios?*

9. *¿Quién es mi ayudante de mesero?*   10. *¿Están listos nuestros uniformes?*

D. Supply the correct possessive adjective for each of the following sentences.

1. (My) *hermana trabaja en el restaurante Royal.*   2. (Her) *turno es por la tarde.*

3. (Our) *supervisora está libre hoy.*   4. (His) *uniforme está sucio.*

5. (Their) *cubos están en el almacén.*   6. (Your) *día de descanso es el martes.*

7. (Your) *bandejas no están limpias.*   8. (My) *guantes están rotos.*

9. (Their) *padre vive en México.*   10. (Our) *beneficios son buenos en esta empresa.*

Adverb Exercises

A. Form adverbs from the following adjectives, then translate them into English.

1. *excelente*   2. *estupendo*   3. *bueno*   4. *actual*   5. *necesario*   6. *especiales*

7. *malo*   8. *rápida*   9. *claro*   10. *natural*

B. Translate the following sentences into Spanish.

1. Pedro is taller than Antonio.   2. Breakfast must be served quickly.

3. You work tomorrow.   4. Wash the floor now.

5. See your supervisor immediately.   6. Pedro always arrives to work on time.

7. Park your car behind the restaurant.   8. Vacuum under the beds.

9. This hotel is rather busy.   10. He comes back from Arizona in June, perhaps.

11. I just want very little.   12. The eggs are here.   13. Come here, please.

14. I live very far from the restaurant.   15. I never smoke when I work.

C. Give the equivalents of the following Spanish adverbs.

1. *bien*   2. *mal*   3. *mejor*   4. *entonces*   5. *todavía*   6. *delante*

7. *ahí*   8. *dentro*   9. *despacio*   10. *bastante*   11. *casi*   12. *absolutamente*

13. *ciertamente*   14. *luego*   15. *menos.*

Preposition Exercises

A. Translate the following sentences into English.

1. *Juanita viene a trabajar el lunes.*   2. *Sacuda bajo el sofá.*

3. *Usted trabaja hoy con Pedro.*   4. *Ponga las sillas contra la pared.*

5. *Antonio es de México.*   6. *Ella no viene a trabajar desde el domingo.*

7. *El hotel cierra durante el invierno.*   8. *El horno está en la cocina.*

9. *La oficina está entre el comedor y el almacén.*

10. *La supervisora va hacia la lavandería.*   11. *Trabajo hasta las seis.*

12. *Estos suministros son para usted.*   13. *Por aquí, por favor.*

14. *Según mi supervisora, yo estoy libre mañana.*   15. *Lave la ropa sin poner almidón.*

B. Ask your employees to do the following.

1. Come to work tomorrow at eight o'clock A.M.

2. Put the clean pots under the sink.

3. Scrub the frying pans with scouring powder.

4. Set the tables against the wall.   5. Get these supplies from the storeroom.

6. Don't take a break during breakfast hours.   7. Use the lockers in this room.

8. Pick up your paycheck between ten o'clock and two o'clock on Friday.

9. Work until six o'clock.   10. Bring the soiled linen here.

Conjunction Exercises

A. Translate the following sentences into English.

1. *Pedro y Antonio enjuagan los vasos.*

2. *La mesera trabaja hoy pero no trabaja mañana.*

3. *Aunque gana poco dinero, el jardinero es buen trabajador.*

4. *El plomero que trabaja en el hotel es de México.*

5. *Esto no es una sábana, sino una funda de almohada.*

6. *Ni el ama de llaves ni el jefe de mantenimiento están en el hotel ahorita.*

7. *Soy de San Diego, sin embargo no hablo español muy bien.*

8. *Necesito guantes y un delantal.*

9. *Inspeccione el primer piso porque necesitamos habitaciones limpias.*

10. *Aunque Pedro a veces llega tarde, siempre completa su trabajo.*

B. Translate the following sentences into Spanish.

1. The general manager and the head housekeeper are very good friends.

2. Please, fry the onions but not the garlic.

3. Although your day off is tomorrow, please come to work in the morning.

4. The chair that is broken cannot be used.   5. Do not bring soap but bleach.

6. Neither you nor Pedro are scheduled to work on Thursday.

7. She doesn't know how to speak English; however, she understands it quite well.

8. Please plant these bushes and water them.

9. Turn on the heat because it is cold.

10. Although I am the boss, I want to be your friend.

Question Exercises

A. Form questions from the following statements.

1. *La oficina de personal está en el primer piso.*
2. *El jefe del departamento de alimentos y bebidas necesita un mesero.*
3. *La máquina lavaplatos no funciona.*
4. *Las bandejas de room service no están listas.*
5. *No hay suficientes manteles limpios.*   6. *El día libre de Pedro es el miércoles.*
7. *El electricista habla español.*   8. *Ponga una rodaja de limón en cada vaso de té frío.*
9. *Los menús están en el cajón del aparador.*
10. *El jefe de cocina está hablando con la gerente.*
11. *Prepare la carne para el almuerzo.*
12. *La parada del autobús queda cerca del hotel.*
13. *El plomero no trabaja hoy porque está enfermo.*
14. *Ayude al ayudante de mesero a recoger las mesas.*
15. *Este puesto paga cuatro dólares y cincuenta centavos por hora.*

B. Ask the folloving questions in Spanish

1. Why do you use the guest elevator instead of the service elevator?
2. How do you change this light bulb?   3. Where do you put the trash?
4. What do you want?
5. Do you have transportation to come to work early in the morning?
6. Do you have a green card?
7. How many uniforms do you have in your locker?
8. Can you work this weekend?   9. Do you know how to make pancakes?
10. Have you prepared the ice cream dishes?
11. How many rooms have you cleaned so far?   12. Is the bacon ready?
13. Do you have enough soap for your guestrooms?
14. Are you happy working in this department?
15. Why do you want to leave this company?

C. Answer the following questions in Spanish.

1. *¿Dónde está la oficina de personal?*   2. *¿Cuánto pagan por hora en este trabajo?*
3. *¿A qué hora empieza mi turno?*   4. *¿Dónde recojo mi carro de servicio?*
5. *¿Dónde llevo la ropa sucia?*   6. *¿Cuántos cubiertos pongo en esta mesa?*

7. *¿Cuándo echo el cloro en la alberca?*

8. *¿Por qué no se puede fumar en la cafetería?*

9. *¿Quién va al almacén por los suministros?*

10. *¿Cuál es el número de teléfono del departamento de mantenimiento?*

11. *¿Dónde está el líquido de limpiar alfombras?*

12. *¿Puedo hacer una llamada telefónica cuando estoy en mi descanso?*

13. *¿Cuál es el día de pago?*   14. *¿Tienen trabajo para ayudantes de mesero?*

15. *¿Por qué está usted enfadado conmigo?*

Negation Exercises

A. Answer the following questions negatively.

1. *¿Trabajo mañana?*   2. *¿Puede el restaurante darme diez dólares hasta el viernes?*

3. *¿Enciendo el horno?*   4. *¿Tiene usted la llave maestra?*

5. *¿Quiere usted que riegue los árboles del jardín?*   6. *¿Empiezo a pelar las papas?*

7. *¿Paso los manteles por el mangle?*   8. *¿Puedo tomarme un descanso ahora?*

9. *¿Habla español el jefe de recepción?*   10. *¿Subo las sábanas limpias a los pisos?*

B. Translate the following sentences into Spanish.

1. I don't have enough glasses to set the tables.   2. The cook hasn't arrived yet.

3. If you don't have a green card you cannot work here.

4. Don't use the napkins to clean the floor.

5. You cannot borrow money from your salary.

6. Pedro never arrives late to work.

7. You musn't clock in until you are in uniform and ready to start work.

8. Nobody speaks Spanish in this department.

9. Your friends cannot visit you at work.

10. Smoking is not allowed in the kitchen.

C. Translate the following sentences in English.

1. *No recoja las tumbonas hasta las seis de la tarde.*   2. *No use el baño de los clientes.*

3. *Este grifo no funciona.*   4. *No tengo teléfono en mi casa.*

5. *El ama de llaves no quiere que las supervisoras de cuartos usen el elevador de huéspedes.*

6. *Las fundas de almohada no están listas todavía.*

7. *No hay nadie en la lavandería.*

8. *Pedro no puede venir a trabajar hasta el próximo martes.*

9. *No lleve los cubiertos en la mano, use una servilleta.*

10. *Los ayudantes de mesero no reciben propinas.*

D. Make the following sentences negative.

1. *El ama de llaves habla español.*   2. *Las camaristas secan el suelo con toallas.*

3. *La máquina de refrescos se limpia antes del almuerzo.*

4. *Los empleados del hotel pueden ordenar comidas del room service.*

5. *El reporte de habitaciones se entrega a recepción a las ocho de la mañana.*

6. *El departamento de alimentos y bebidas solicita suministros del departamento de ventas.*

7. *Los meseros menores de dieciocho años pueden servir bebidas alcohólicas.*

8. *Los cocineros pueden llegar tarde al trabajo.*

9. *Los mozos de pisos utilizan el elevador de huéspedes.*

10. *Las camaristas sacuden los muebles antes de aspirar la alfombra.*

Greetings Exercises

A. Respond to the following greetings in Spanish.

1. *¡Hola, buenos días!*   2. *¿Cómo está usted?*   3. *¡Buenas tardes, señor Robinson!*

4. *¡Hóla!*   5. *¡Qué tal!*   6. *¡Hasta mañana!*

B. Translate the following sentences into Spanish.

1. Good evening!   2. Hi!   3. Good morning!   4. See you!

5. How are you!

Introduction Exercises

A. Respond to the following comments in Spanish.

1. *¿Cómo está usted?*   2. *¡Encantado de conocerle!*   3. *¡Tanto gusto!*

4. *¿Cómo se llama usted?*   5. *¡Me alegro de verle!*

B. Translate the following sentences into Spanish.

1. My name is Pedro.   2. Pleased to know you!   3. How are you?

4. What is your name?   5. Very well, thank you, and you?

Communication Exercises

A. Answer the following questions in Spanish.
1. *¿Me entiende?*   2. *¿Cómo se dice "servilleta" en inglés?*
3. *¿Puede hablar más despacio, por favor?*   4. *¿Sabe usted inglés?*
5. *¿Comprende inglés?*

B. Translate the following sentences into Spanish.
1. Thank you very much.   2. I'm sorry!
3. I don't understand what you are saying.   4. Repeat it, please!
5. Speak louder, please.   6. Do you know how to write?
7. How do you say "vinegar" in Spanish?   8. I don't understand English well.
9. Speak slowly, please!   10. Don't speak so quickly!

Leave-taking Exercises

A. Translate the following sentences into Spanish.
1. Have a good day!   2. I'll see you tomorrow!   3. Goodbye!
4. I'll see you!   5. Bye!

B. Translate the following sentences into English.
1. *¡Hasta la vista!*   2. *¡Que lo pase bien!*   3. *¡Adiós!*   4. *¡Hasta mañana!*
5. *¡Hasta luego!*

Numbers Exercises

A. Answer the following questions in Spanish.
1. How many days are there in one week?
2. How many hours are there in one day?
3. How many seconds are there in one minute?
4. How many days are there in one year?
5. How many fingers are there on one hand?   6. What is 20 plus 30?
7. What is forty-eight minus six?   8. How many weeks are there in one year?
9. What is four times nine?   10. What comes after third?

B. Translate the following sentences into Spanish.

1. Bring these glasses to the seventh floor.

2. Make 12 ham-and-cheese sandwiches.

3. Cut three lemons into eight slices each.   4. We need 43 slices of bacon.

5. Each box has 70 to 80 oranges.

6. The second and third floors are closed to the public.

7. Put seven melon balls in each cup.   8. There are 16 ounces in a pound.

9. Place four rolls in each basket.   10. Pick up the empty trays on the tenth floor.

Time Exercises

A. Answer the following questions in Spanish.

1. *¿A qué hora empieza mi turno?*   2. *¿Qué hora es?*   3. *¿A qué hora almorzamos?*

4. *¿Son las cinco ya?*   5. *¿Cerramos el restaurante a las nueve o a las diez?*

B. Translate the following sentences into Spanish.

1. It is five minutes to eleven o'clock.   2. The storeroom opens at 7:30.

2. Breakfast begins at six o'clock A.M.   3. The restaurant closes at midnight.

4. Turn off the ovens at ten o'clock P.M.

5. Come to work Monday at eight o'clock A.M.   6. What is the time?

7. You can take your morning break between ten o'clock and eleven o'clock.

8. Can you work till midnight twice a week?

9. At what time does the coffee shop open?

10. You can pick up your paycheck between one o'clock and five o'clock on Fridays.

Calendar Exercises

A. Translate the following sentences into English.

1. *Mi fecha de nacimiento es el nueve de mayo de mil novecientos sesenta y tres.*

2. *Marcho para México el seis de agosto.*

3. *Regresamos a los Estados Unidos el quince de septiembre.*

4. *Navidad es el veinticinco de diciembre.*   5. *Este año, febrero tiene veintiocho días.*

B. Translate the following sentences into Spanish.

1. My birthday is on October thirteenth.

2. My birthdate is January twenty-first, 1973.   3. Labor Day is September third.

4. You start work on July first.

5. Your last day is August twentieth.   6. What is today's date?

7. Do I work Sunday or Monday next week?   8. What is the date?

9. Next year is my fifth anniversary with this company.

10. My wife's birthday is November fourth.

C. Answer the following questions in Spanish

1. *¿Qué dias trabajo la semana próxima?*   2. *¿Cuál es su fecha de nacimiento?*

3. *¿Qué día de la semana tiene usted libre?*

4. *¿Cuándo marcha usted para Nuevo México?*

5. *¿Cuándo regresa usted de sus vacaciones?*

Color Exercises

A. Translate the following sentences into English.

1. *Pinte usted esta pared de color blanco.*   2. *Traiga las sábanas azules.*

3. *Las toallas rojas se usan en la zona de albercas.*

4. *Los cubos con la etiqueta verde son para los desperdicios.*

5. *En caso de fuego, apriete el botón rojo.*

B. Translate the following sentences into Spanish.

1. Bring five red peppers from the storeroom.

2. The yellow ice cream is vanilla, the white one is lemon.

3. Put the long blue chairs on the left and the black ones on the right of the swimming pool.

4. The brown chairs need to be varnished.

5. Put two spoonfuls of green food coloring in the dough.

Employee Handbook Exercises (Advanced)

A. Give the following statements in Spanish, as you would say them to a new employee.

1. Welcome to the Royal.

2. We are proud to count you as a new member of our team.

3. We hope that you will feel comfortable in your new job.

4. This manual details the rules to follow in your work.

5. Welcome aboard.   6. This is an equal-employment opportunity company.

7. If you have any problems or suggestions about your job, address yourself to your department head.

8. It is the mission of our company to serve our guests well.

9. Here is your employee handbook.

10. The handbook is written in English and Spanish.

B. Answer the following questions in Spanish

1. *¿Está este manual escrito en español?*

2. *¿Ofrece esta compañía igual oportunidad de empleo?*

3. *¿A quién me dirijo si tengo problemas en el trabajo?*

4. *¿Quién es mi supervisor inmediato?*   5. *¿Para qué es este manual de empleados?*

C. Translate the following sentences into Spanish, as if you were explaining them to a Spanish-speaking employee.

1. The first three months of employment are considered a period of review.

2. At the completion of the review period you are eligible for employee benefits.

3. You are considered a full-time employee because you work more than 30 hours.

4. You are not considered a full-time employee because you don't work a minimum of 30 hours.

5. You are a part-time employee because you work less than 30 hours per week.

6. You can participate in our health insurance program if you pay the premiums.

7. Payday is Friday.

8. Don't punch your time card until you are ready to start work.

9. Overtime must first be approved by your supervisor.

10. Never punch a time card for other employees.

D. Answer the following questions in Spanish.

1. ¿En qué consiste el período de prueba?

2. ¿Cuándo recibo los beneficios que ofrece la compañía?

3. ¿Es este empleo de tiempo completo?

4. ¿Qué beneficios recibo como empleado de tiempo parcial?

5. ¿Cuántas horas debo trabajar para ser empleado de tiempo completo?

6. Como empleado de tiempo parcial, ¿puedo tener seguro de enfermedad?

7. ¿Qué día pagan?   8. ¿A cómo pagan las horas extras?

9. ¿Se pueden trabajar horas extras en este empleo?   10. ¿Dónde está el reloj registrador?

E. Translate into Spanish the following information for employees.

1. You may have a free meal if you work a minimum of a four-and-one-half-hour shift.

2. All meals must be eaten in the employee cafeteria.

3. You can request a leave of absence for personal, medical, or military reasons.

4. A leave of absence should not last longer than 30 days.

5. The company will pay your total salary during the first 15 days of jury duty.

6. The company offers medical and hospitalization insurance.

7. If you are injured on the job, you must notify your supervisor within 48 hours of the accident.

8. You must park your car in the designated area for employee parking.

9. The personnel department will provide you with a locker for your personal belongings.

10. There is a suggestion box in the employee cafeteria; we give a $20 reward for the best suggestion each month.

11. All employees must obtain the permission of a supervisor to use the hotel restaurant.

12. Never order a meal or drink from room service.

13. If you have permission to use the restaurant or bar, you must be adequately dressed.

14. The restaurant may not be used between twelve o'clock and one o'clock P.M.

15. Do not chat with working hotel employees when you are off duty.

F. Answer the following questions in Spanish.

1. *¿Cuántas horas debo trabajar para recibir una comida gratis?*
2. *¿Dónde está la cafetería de empleados?*
3. *¿Qué debo hacer para obtener una ausencia con permiso?*
4. *¿Qué seguros ofrece la compañía?*   5. *¿Ofrece la compañía seguro de enfermedad?*
6. *¿A quién debo comunicar un accidente de trabajo?*
7. *¿Hay aparcamiento para empleados?*   8. *¿Dónde están los roperos de empleados?*
9. *¿Dónde puedo guardar mi uniforme?*
10. *¿Pueden los empleados utilizar el restaurante del hotel?*
11. *¿Se puede beber en el bar del hotel después del trabajo?*
12. *¿A qué hora es el almuerzo de empleados?*   13. *¿Cuánto tiempo dura cada descanso?*
14. *¿Puedo invitar a mi esposa a comer en la cafetería de empleados?*
15. *¿Quién limpia los uniformes de empleados?*

G. Translate the following policies into Spanish.

1. The company expects you to report to work on time.
2. Habitual tardiness will result in termination.
3. All employees must use the employee entrance to enter and exit the hotel.
4. You must wear your name tag at all times when on duty.
5. All items leaving the hotel must by shown on a parcel pass signed by your supervisor.
6. Personal telephone calls are not allowed.
7. If you need to make an emergency call, contact your supervisor.
8. When on break, you can use the public telephone located by the employee cafeteria.
9. The use of guest elevators is not allowed.
10. You must report to work well groomed and wearing a clean uniform.
11. Smoking is not allowed in public areas.
12. The third write-up within six months may result in termination.
13. If you have a problem, discuss it with your immediate supervisor.
14. Teamwork is important in the hospitality industry.
15. Please read and sign the company's conduct policy form.

H. Answer the following questions in Spanish.

1. ¿Qué pasa si llego diez minutos tarde al trabajo?
2. ¿Dónde está la puerta de servicio?   3. ¿Donde se recibe la placa con mi nombre?
4. ¿Puedo llamar por teléfono a casa durante mi descanso?
5. Dónde hay un teléfono público?   6. ¿Dónde está el elevador de servicio?
7. ¿Dónde se reciben los uniformes limpios?
8. ¿Se puede fumar en la cafetería de empleados?
9. ¿Dónde se puede fumar en los descansos?
10. ¿Quién puede asesorarme en este problema?
11. ¿Dónde puedo recibir una copia de las reglas de conducta de la compañía?
12. ¿Se pueden recibir mensajes telefónicos de emergencia?
13. ¿Qué quiere decir "teamwork" en español?
14. ¿Por qué debo firmar las reglas de comportamiento de la compañía?
15. ¿Cuánto cuesta reponer la placa con mi nombre?

I. Translate the following rules into Spanish.

1. Our guests return because of the quality of service this hotel provides.
2. Do not pass on any information regarding the company or the guests.
3. You must report any found items immediately.
4. After 90 days, found items are given to the employees who found them.
5. You receive a performance appraisal three months after your initial hiring.
6. Your wage is increased based on your job performance.
7. Departmental transfers may be considered after you work three months in the same job.
8. The first three months in a new position is considered a period of review.
9. Promotions are based on the employee's ability to take on added responsibility.
10. There is possibility for advancement for those employees who show initiative.

J. Answer the following questions in Spanish

1. ¿Dónde se reportan los objetos encontrados?
2. ¿A quién pertenecen los objetos encontrados?
3. ¿Cuándo se reciben los objetos encontrados que no son reclamados?
4. ¿Cada cuánto tiempo se reciben evaluaciones de rendimiento?
5. ¿Dan aumento de sueldo si el rendimiento es satisfactorio?

6. *¿Qué debo hacer si deseo cambiar de departamento?*

7. *¿Cuándo puedo pedir traslado de departamento?*

8. *¿Qué debo hacer si deseo ser promocionado?*

9. *¿Quién hace mi evaluación de rendimiento?*

10. *¿Debo rellenar una solicitud para cambiar de departamento?*

K. Translate the following sentences into Spanish.

1. Make it a habit to read the bulletin board located in your department.

2. You are required to attend your scheduled department meetings.

3. The company pays for the time you spend in departmental meetings.

4. Tipped employees are paid minimum wage for attending these meetings.

5. The company employs relatives, provided that they don't supervise each other.

6. Visiting of friends and relatives during work is not allowed.

7. The hotel doesn't cash payroll or personal checks.

8. If you change your address or telephone number, please notify your supervisor as soon as possible.

9. This company prohibits personal harassment, including harassment based on sex, race, or national origin.

10. Contact your supervisor, or the personnel department, immediately if you feel you are being harassed.

11. Solicitations during work time are not permitted.

12. If you must resign your position, please give at least two week notice.

13. You must return all company property before your final check is issued.

14. When resigning a position, the employee loses his (her) longevity with the company.

15. Please read carefully the following acts resulting in disciplinary action or termination.

L. Answer the following questions in Spanish.

1. *¿Debo asistir a las juntas de mi departamento?*

2. *¿Paga la compañía el tiempo empleado en las juntas de departamento en el día de descanso?*

3. *¿Permite el hotel el empleo de miembros de la familia de empleados?*

4. *¿Puede visitarme mi esposa durante las horas de trabajo?*

5. ¿*Puedo cambiar este cheque salarial en la caja del restaurante?*

6. ¿*A quién debo notificar mi cambio de dirección?*

7. ¿*A quién debo reportar cualquier acoso sexual?*

8. ¿*Puedo solicitar de los empleados donativos para mi iglesia?*

9. ¿*Cuántos días de notificación requiere la compañía si deseo dimitir de mi empleo?*

10. ¿*Quién puede darme una carta de recomendación por mis servicios prestados?*

11. ¿*Puedo volver a trabajar en el hotel en el futuro?*

12. ¿*Tienen trabajo para mi hermana?*

13. ¿*Cuánto pagan por hora para trabajo de camarista?*

14. ¿*Hay puestos vacantes para cocineros?*

15. ¿*Paga el hotel por asistir a clases de inglés?*